OPPOSITION & INTIMIDATION

OPPOSITION & INTIMIDATION

The Abortion Wars & Strategies of Political Harassment

Alesha E. Doan

The University of Michigan Press   Ann Arbor

2010   2009   2008   2007   4   3   2   1

A CIP catalog record for this book is available from the British Library.

Library of Congress Cataloging-in-Publication Data

Doan, Alesha E., 1972–
    Opposition and intimidation : the abortion wars and strategies of political harassment / Alesha E. Doan.
        p.   cm.
    Includes bibliographical references and index.
    ISBN-13: 978-0-472-09975-7 (cloth : alk. paper)
    ISBN-10: 0-472-09975-2 (cloth : alk. paper)
    ISBN-13: 978-0-472-06975-0 (pbk. : alk. paper)
    ISBN-10: 0-472-06975-6 (pbk. : alk. paper)
    1. Pro-life movement—United States.   2. Abortion—United States.
3. Harassment—United States.   4. Political violence—United
States.   I. Title.
    HQ767.5.U5D63   2007
    363.460973—dc22   2006021885

For Spencer Thomas
May you grow up in a world where life and choice
are valued together at every stage of your development.

CONTENTS

PREFACE

One of the distinguishing features of the abortion conflict compared to other social debates of our times is the level of protest, harassment, and violence generated over this issue. Journalists, physicians, and activists on both sides of the debate have talked about the spectacle occurring outside of clinics across the nation. Media frequently cover the confrontational aspects of the abortion debate at the expense of the "less dramatic" (but important) policy developments surrounding abortion politics. Media pundits and pro-choice politicians discuss these tactics in terms of personal acts of harassment, completely devoid of any political implications.

As I started studying in the PhD program at Texas A&M University, I became intrigued by the lack of scholarly attention (particularly the relative absence of political analysis) given to the activities taking place outside of clinics. As I completed my first year at the university, a rather fortuitous event occurred in a nearby town. The Planned Parenthood in Bryan, Texas, announced its plans to build a new clinic facility that would be equipped to provide abortion services for its clients. Prior to its announcement, Planned Parenthood had been running a family planning clinic in town for twenty-four years. During this time, the clinic did not generate any significant attention from religious organizations, interest groups, or the media. It operated in relative obscurity and provided services to men and women from the community and university.

Within days of Planned Parenthood's announcement, a group of local citizens went to the construction site and started to pray. Many pro-life supporters turned for direction to one particular woman, who had been involved with pro-

life groups since she was in high school. This woman ended up forming, direct-
ing, and leading the Brazos Valley Coalition for Life (BVCL) for several years.
Over the course of this project, Planned Parenthood in Bryan, Texas, has gained
notoriety; it quickly became the most heavily protested abortion clinic in the
country. The battle unfolding outside of the clinic's doors is simply one illustra-
tion of the dedication that activists on both sides of the conflict possess, the
intractability of the conflict, and the scope of the abortion "war" that continues
to play out across America.

Quickly after Planned Parenthood's announcement I approached Planned
Parenthood and the BVCL (as well as smaller local organizations involved with
the abortion conflict) and began conducting interviews with activists on both
sides of the issue. I also spent hours being an observer at the Coalition's events
as well as the clinic's events and daily operation of services. Over the years I
spent hundreds of hours conducting interviews with pro-choice and pro-life
leaders, physicians, nurses, community educators, activists, clients, and law
enforcement agents. Many participants in my research did not want their names
or organizational affiliations used, some only felt comfortable having their first
names used, and others were willing to have their whole names and affiliations
used (this is reflected in the interviews' notation).

I ended up conducting interviews from September 1998 to August 2000 and
then again from November 2003 to March 2004. Several of the activists I interviewed have gone on to gain national prominence in their respective movements. I was fortunate enough also to conduct interviews with leaders involved
at the national level of the conflict. Although the interviews used throughout
this book primarily represent one clinic in Texas, I believe (based on my interviews and research) there is much commonality between local direct action
groups and national direct action groups. The difference appears to be one of
magnitude (that is, differing levels of resources), but the goals remain the same:
dealing with the urgency of abortion by trying to eliminate the need for services
and to end the delivery of those services. I use the interviews to bring depth,
meaning, and understanding to aspects of the abortion conflict that cannot be
captured through a quantitative analysis. I believe interviewing those most intimately drawn into this conflict was imperative for understanding the strategies
(and their implications) used in this social-political conflict.

The interviews and observations provided a close-up view into the dynamic
and iterative relationship between protesters and the targets of their protest. I

witnessed how quickly the abortion conflict can be socialized and spread to other organizations that are forced to become involved in a battle they do not want to participate in, and finally, how quickly the dynamic between the opposing sides can intensify and escalate. This part of the research helped me reconceptualize unconventional political participation, particularly those activities that blur the lines between legal and illegal, appropriate and inappropriate activities, with the purpose of changing the behavior of nongovernmental actors. I wanted to examine the intent, goals, and outcomes of using politically harassing tactics that cannot easily be compartmentalized into behavior that is either legal and sanctioned, or illegal and rejected. Currently, there is a gap in our knowledge as to what political harassment is, why it is used, and what impact it has on its targets.

Throughout the book I weave in the words of activists to more clearly illustrate different nuances to the abortion conflict. The interviews bring the various dimensions of the debate to life and I want to give a special acknowledgment to the participants in my research who so generously and graciously shared their stories and time with me. During my interviews I was often moved by pro-choice and pro-life supporters' beliefs in their respective sides of the issue as well as their respective dedication to the cause. I also want to acknowledge the Alan Guttmacher Institute (AGI) and express my gratitude for allowing me to use the unique data gathered by the institution. Without the use of AGI's data, a systematic and empirical analysis of the outcomes of anti-abortion activities would not have been possible. Any errors should be attributed to the author.

I want to thank Jim Reische for his persistence and belief in this project. It has been a pleasure working with Jim and the University of Michigan Press. On a personal note, I want to thank Don Haider-Markel for all of his help and encouragement with this project over the years. He continues to be a great mentor and friend. I also want to thank my family. They have been unfailingly supportive of me and have always been my best friends. Finally, I want to thank Tom Farrell for being a warm, loving partner and father. I could not have finished this project without his support. And I cannot end without thanking Spencer for making us laugh and appreciate every day in a way we never knew was possible before he joined us.

Chapter 1

POLITICAL PROTEST OR POLITICAL HARASSMENT?

Social Movements, Morality Politics, and Abortion

> I made a particular point of wanting to be here because of all the challenges
> they had. I know this clinic has been under siege and I want to show my
> support. [We need to] stand up against the bullying and threatening
> tactics of anti-choice zealots.
>
> —Gloria Feldt, president of Planned Parenthood,
> addressing an audience in Bryan, College Station, February 29, 2004

Chris Danze, a construction industry executive and staunch pro-life supporter, was shocked to hear the news in 2003 that Planned Parenthood was going to open up a new clinic equipped to perform abortion services in Austin, Texas, so he decided to do something about it.[1] Danze began making phone calls to dissuade companies from working on the construction of the facility. Within a few short weeks, carpenters, plumbers, electricians, drywall installers, heating subcontractors, and cement layers all backed out of the project, delaying the construction of the facility.

In the pro-life movement community, forty-eight-year-old Chris Danze's effort to stop the construction of the abortion facility in Austin is being dubbed as the twenty-first-century biblical story of David and Goliath (Pro-Life Rally for Life 2003). Danze is simply one man who saw an injustice in his community, whereas Planned Parenthood is a multi-million dollar organization. Instead of using a stone to defeat Goliath, Danze used a phone to organize a boycott designed to prevent the construction of a privately funded Planned Parenthood. Danze believes that the boycott's success is evidence that God does not want an "abortion mill" built in Austin (Associated Press 2003).

Despite the initial success of the boycott, by January 2004, two months after the construction stopped in its tracks, Planned Parenthood hired a new contractor to pour the cement for the facility. Danze and his organization, Texas Contractors and Suppliers for Life Association, did not take the news lightly. They immediately contacted other pro-life organizations throughout Texas. Newsletters and e-mails containing the home address and phone number of the concrete contractor were sent out to members, who were instructed to "contact the concrete supplier to politely encourage him to continue resisting the mounting pressure to pour concrete for the Planned Parenthood abortion facility" (Brazos Valley Coalition for Life Annual Newsletter 2004).

Danze's boycott was the first of its kind to be successfully mounted against Planned Parenthood, even if only temporarily. While the pro-life movement has been ecstatic over the victory and emboldened by what it perceives as the community's disapproval of the abortion facility, Planned Parenthood as well as many of the contractors involved interpret the situation dramatically differently. Planned Parenthood contends the boycott is simply a campaign of intimidation and harassment.

Danze and his organization tracked down personal information about people involved with the construction project, making phone calls to individuals' local churches, pastors, and friends (Chris Danze's Speech at the Pro-Life Rally for Life, 2003). During the initial stages of the boycott, contractors were receiving up to 1,200 phone calls a day urging them to withdraw from the project and warning them that their names would appear on a list of "abortion mill supporters" that would be circulated throughout Austin (Associated Press 2003; Pro-Life Rally for Life 2003). Pro-choice supporters do not see the success of the boycott as being born out of pro-life sentiment in the community; rather it resulted from inundating contractors with harassing phone calls and making overt economic threats.

The Austin boycott is yet one more unconventional tactic used by the pro-life movement in the ongoing abortion debate. For decades, the media have been chronicling the drama unfolding outside of clinics around the nation ranging from routine protest to violence. Pro-choice activists, media pundits, and pro-choice politicians typically discuss these tactics in terms of personal acts of harassment, completely devoid of any political implications. When explaining the magnitude of anti-abortion activity at clinics, pro-choice activists contextualize the debate as a question of women's rights: the pro-life movement does not believe in a woman's right to choose. Conversely, pro-life activists see their unconventional activities at clinics as stemming from their belief that abortion is murder and they are simply trying to prevent the wholesale slaughter of innocent children. Both camps draw on simplistic explanatory frames to make sense of the saliency of the abortion issue and breadth of activities occurring at clinics. However, the abortion controversy is anything but simple.

The pro-life movement's use of unconventional tactics to gain leverage in its fight to end abortion is not a straightforward story of equating abortion to murder, nor is it plainly a question of choice, as characterized by the pro-choice side. Abortion continues to be a salient, divisive issue in society. This is most obviously evidenced by the longevity of anti-abortion protesting at clinics around the country as well as the different meaning assigned to the protests by each side of the abortion debate. Anti-abortion activists believe they are exercising their constitutional right to engage in political protest and free speech outside of clinics. Abortion supporters view the protesting as unwanted acts of harassment that interfere with their ability to deliver reproductive health services.

Over the past three decades, anti-abortion protesting has taken on a life of its own. In many aspects, the development and growth of the pro-life movement mirrors the trajectory of typical social movement development from origination to evolution to sustainability. Yet, the movement's continuous protesting at clinics signifies a departure from many other social movements primarily in terms of the targets of protest and the longevity of the protesting. Pro-life leaders engaging in direct action tactics overtly claim that clinic protesting is designed to "close an abortion facility [and] also to reduce the perceived need for abortion" (Interview with David Bereit, executive director of BVCL, December 2003).[2] Importantly, closing an abortion facility is achieved by circumventing government intervention and engaging in direct action at clinics.

Devoid of context, protesting at clinics is not inherently threatening; however, anti-abortion activity exists within a backdrop of inflammatory rhetoric, physical threats, and executed threats in the form of chemical attacks, arson, and murder, which have been carried out in the name of saving babies. Contextualizing anti-abortion protest and coupling it with its intended targets (clinic employees, women seeking abortion services, and potential women in need of abortion services) changes the scope and meaning of the protest altogether. Rather than benign political protest, much of the activity outside of clinics takes on a threatening element that transcends political protest and becomes harassment.

Currently, we have multiple theoretical models explaining political behavior, social movement behavior, and even political violence. When dealing with behavior that does not easily fit into one of these categories, our understanding of the behavior becomes murky. Discussing aggressive anti-abortion protests in terms of individual behavior misses the main point: the tactics are a coordinated attempt by the pro-life movement to achieve a political agenda. Until we understand political harassment, we will never fully appreciate the strength of the anti-abortion strategists or the influence they have had on the political culture in the United States.

In this chapter, I develop a framework for understanding political harassment, which builds on traditional paradigms of both social movement and morality politics literature. Social movement theories explore the development and maintenance of social movements (including the use of violence within a movement). Several factors contribute to the success of a social movement, ranging from a movement's ability to capitalize on political opportunities, to mobilizing participants, to providing a collective identity for members. The morality politics literature identifies and explains the unique parameters surrounding policy areas that involve legislating morals and values among society.

These theories provide a foundation for this study, but developing a framework for understanding political harassment requires a more nuanced analysis beyond social movement and morality politics theories. The anti-abortion movement is motivated by a desire to impose its moral code on society: it is a value-driven social movement. Similar to other organizations, the pro-life movement has evolved in a predictable pattern. However, ultimately, the use and acceptability of harassing tactics is intimately tied to the larger culture wars taking place in American society where cultural progressivism is in direct conflict with cultural traditionalism (Hunter 1991, 1994). Reproductive rights issues often occupy center stage between these dueling perspectives because they encompass larger questions of morality, competing definitions of personhood and rights, as well as questions regarding female sexuality and autonomy.

The intensity of the modern abortion debate is rooted in the larger cultural conflicts shaping up in society, but the debate is much more than a dispute over progressive versus traditional mores. Abortion is a political issue. Pro-choice and pro-life activists are vying to achieve political legitimation, leverage, and success. Within this political and cultural conflict, harassment is simply *one* strategy used by the pro-life movement to achieve a positive political outcome.

I argue that harassment needs to be understood as a purposeful, rational, political strategy that is used to reach their goal.

Throughout this chapter, I attempt to sketch the components needed to understand the origin, evolution, and success of the pro-life movement as a morality movement. I contextualize anti-abortion activity in terms of the movement's reliance on inflammatory and militaristic rhetoric, veiled physical threats, and successful perpetration of violence. I end by defining more concretely why much of what passes for anti-abortion protest is actually political harassment. Viewing the movement's unconventional political participation within this larger framework will ultimately allow us to move beyond an understanding of the behavior into an exploration of the actual outcomes and consequences of political harassment.

The Rise and Maintenance of Social Movements

The summer of 2003 was marked by the appearance of flash mobs in New York City, San Francisco, Minneapolis, and Seattle. Flash mobs are organized via e-mail; people are given instructions on where to meet and provided with a loosely written script to perform at the designated location. Hundreds of people gather, interact with others according to the prearranged script, and then the crowd dissipates as quickly as it formed (Delio 2003). By early fall, less prankish forms of collective action were making the headlines. That October, 70,000 United Food and Commercial Workers union members (ranging from cashiers, to pharmacists, to meat cutters) went on strike in Southern California contesting the reduction in their medical benefits (CNN News 2003). After four months of striking, a resolution between the union and grocery stores remained elusive.

Later in the same month, on October 25, 2003, thousands of protesters opposing America's occupation of Iraq lined the streets in Washington, DC, San Francisco, and dozens of other cities across the nation. Demonstrators called for withdrawing the military and ushering in a liberated Iraq, where Iraqis instead of the U.S. military govern their country (United for Peace and Justice 2004). Roughly a year later on August 29, 2004, around 400,000 anti-Iraq war protesters marched down the streets of Manhattan the night before the opening of the Republican national convention (McCool 2004). Demonstrators carried colorful banners espousing antiwar and anti–President Bush slogans. One group of protesters carried over one thousand coffins to pay tribute to the American soldiers killed in the war and symbolize the "true" cost of the war.

Technological advances in modern times such as global communication systems, computers, and transportation have diminished the costs of collective action leading to a rise in the frequency of their occurrences regardless of the intent of the action—a prank, a temporary demonstration of anarchy, or an organized protest surrounding a political agenda. In its most rudimentary form, collective action, whether directed at the government, elites, or other authorities, stems from citizens rallying around a common cause. Unlike collective action, contentious collective action results from ordinary people being either completely or effectively shut out of the political process with little to no access to political institutions (Tarrow 1998). The duration of the action may be a moment in time or it can last decades, resulting in temporary political changes or permanent alterations in the political landscape.

The presence of a collective action event such as a flash mob does not necessarily indicate the existence of a social movement. Underlying most social movements is the presence of contentious politics. Even when a social movement's mission is apolitical, it will often encounter authorities (who are charged with maintaining law and order) in contentious ways (Calhoun 1994). Social movements' causes, methods of organizing, tactical approaches to authorities, and desired outcomes vary dramatically, from the extremism fostered by the French Revolution to the more subdued tactical approach of centrist environmental groups such as the Nature Conservancy.[3] Given the vast range of organizations, distinguishing a social movement from other groups is important.

While definitions of *social movement* vary, they generally include two points: participants share similar belief systems and act in a collective manner to change existing arrangements. Paul Wilkinson's definition illustrates the multiple forms that social movements can take.

[A social movement is] a deliberate collective endeavor to promote change in any direction and by any means, not excluding violence, illegality, revolution or withdrawal into "utopian" community . . . A social movement must evince a minimal degree of organization, though this may range from a loose, informal, or partial level of organization to the highly institutionalized and bureaucratized movement and the corporate group . . . A social movement's commitment to change and the *raison d'être* of its organization are founded upon the conscious volition, normative commitment to the movement's aims or beliefs, and active participation on the part of the followers or members. (1971, 27)

Sidney Tarrow provides a more concise definition of a social movement as "collective challenges, based on common purposes and social solidarities, in sustained interaction with elites, opponents, and authorities" (1998, 4). This definition contains four main properties: collective challenge, common purpose, social solidarity, and sustained interaction. Even though all movements are to some degree distinctive, the definition of a social movement (even in various iterations) implies that movements often share comparable patterns of development and characteristics because they are generated from a similar political process. A social movement typically arises and either flourishes or falters from three cumulating factors: political opportunities, mobilizing structures, and cultural framing (Tilly 1978; McAdam 1982; Tarrow 1994; McAdam et al. 1996; Aminzade et al. 2001).

The Role of Political Opportunities

Political discontent exists in every society, but discontent does not necessarily translate into political action. For example, in the postbellum South, Blacks faced tremendous discrimination preventing them from fully (or even marginally) participating in political life. Despite their widespread discontent, African Americans were not able to parlay their grievances into significant political action until the civil rights movement of the 1960s. The environmental constraints facing Black Americans stifled their ability to effectively mount any type of massive political action campaign. African Americans were isolated both geographically and politically. They lived under Jim Crow laws, in a segregated educational and economic system, and were subjected to daily discriminatory acts, often in the form of physical threats and violence. Over time, as environmental conditions changed and political opportunities opened up, African Americans were able to launch the civil rights movement (McAdam 1982).

While collective discontent is a necessary condition of social movement formation, the origination of a social movement is shaped by the political opportunities and constraints within the environment rather than emerging from a spontaneous, unstructured context (McAdam et al. 1996). Political opportunity refers to "consistent—but not necessarily formal, permanent, or national—dimensions of the political environment which either encourage or discourage people from using collective action" (Tarrow 1996, 18). Both weak and strong challengers can arise because the key is identifying external resources. In other words, political arrangements may open, close, or change, encouraging collective action by lowering the cost of organizing. Alternatively, those changing political arrangements may serve to undercut a social movement: the welfare rights movement quickly lost steam following the election of the Nixon administration, which was very hostile toward welfare rights (Piven and Cloward 1977).

Political opportunities may also result from an external crisis. A crisis can stimulate collective action, serve to mobilize existing organizations, or aid in maintaining mobilization within a movement (Jenkins 1987). The Three Mile Island nuclear accident resulted in major concerns and grievances being articulated about the safety of power plants, thus mobilizing the antinuclear power movement (Walsh 1981, 1986).

Changes in political opportunities come from many sources. "The most salient changes . . . result from the opening up of access to power, from shifts in ruling alignments, from the availability of influential allies and from cleavages within and among elites" (Tarrow 1996, 18). Public policy and political realignments provide new political opportunities by widening or creating new political space in which to discuss issues (Meyer 1993). For example, in 1961 President John F. Kennedy authorized the creation of the President's Commission on the Status of Women. The commission published a report in 1963, *American Woman*, documenting the extent of discrimination facing women. Following the report, Congress added "sex" to Title VII of the 1964 Civil Rights Act (enforced by the Equal Employment Opportunity Commission), prohibiting gender-based discrimination in the workforce. These political opportunities benefited the women's movement by stimulating a more centralized organization for women. The National Organization for Women (NOW) developed from these political opportunities, and Title VII provided women with legal recourse for gender discrimination (Freeman 1999). In 1967, a year after its inception, NOW included reproductive rights in its bill of rights enabling the abortion movement to capitalize on and expand the initial political opportunity stemming from the President's Commission (Risen and Thomas 1998; Rubin 1994).

Once challengers collectively recognize and exploit political opportunities, they can then go on to create new ones. New political opportunities, however, also enable challengers to exploit the vulnerabilities of existing elites, identify allies, and create opportunities for opposing movements (Tilly 1978; McAdam 1982). Through this process, a social movement can generate opposition for itself by becoming the vehicle for a countermovement to develop (Zald and Useem 1987). A countermovement holds opposing beliefs to the social movement and vies for political and societal attention for its views. Ultimately movements and countermovements alter the political landscape in which they both operate by directly challenging each other as well as creating or stifling future political opportunities available to each movement (Meyer and Staggenborg 1996). Meyer and Staggenborg (1996) have specified three conditions that spur the development of a countermovement: the countermovement experiences success, the oppositional movement's agenda threatens some constituency, and political allies are available for the countermovement.

Roe v. Wade (410 U.S. 113, 1973) represented one victory for the women's movement and simultaneously contributed to the creation of the pro-life movement (Mansbridge 1986). Anti-abortion sentiment existed in society prior to the Supreme Court's decision, but as long as abortion was illegal there was no motivation for an anti-abortion movement to form (Jacoby 1998). The legalization of abortion became the catalyst for the pro-life movement, which has continued to gain momentum over the past three decades largely resulting from its policy and public opinion victories. The anti-abortion movement has experienced policy victories on a national level (e.g., The Hyde Amendment, *Webster v. Reproductive Health Services* [492 U.S. 490, 1989]), a state level (e.g., legislating elaborate consent requirements, the ban on "partial-birth abortion") and on a local level (e.g., including exaggerated claims about "the harm of abortion," in most abstinence-only curricula used in roughly one-third of public schools) (Edwards 1997). The pro-life movement has cultivated much support from political elites and continues to pose a threat to the pro-choice movement. In response to the pro-life movement, the pro-choice movement has changed its agenda and tactics, and it remains mobilized because of the continual threat posed by the anti-abortion countermovement (Staggenborg 1988; Meyer and Staggenborg 1996). The interaction between the two movements has created and closed political opportunities for each other and altered the political environment in which they both operate. Abortion politics are shrouded in intense conflict because the parameters of the debate have been defined around questions of morality: right versus wrong.

Morality Movements

At its core, the pro-life movement is motivated by a moral opposition to abortion. Its mandate is a value driven one rather than an economic based mandate that often drives "politics as usual" (Meier 1994; Mooney and Lee 1995). Even though morality movements are governed by similar political environmental constraints and opportunities encountered by nonmorality social movements, they also contain distinguishing characteristics (Meier 1999; Mooney and Lee 1995, 2000; Haider-Markel and Meier 1996; Sharp 1999, 2002; Hunter 1991, 1994). The most important difference is the tractability of the issue. Deep-seated values are at the core of culture wars, which pit culturally progressive and secularist beliefs against culturally traditional and religiously fundamentalist beliefs. Morality movements seek to change the behavior and activity of people through "social regulatory policy" and moral persuasion (Tatalovich and Daynes 1988). The ultimate prize involves gaining the legal authority to redistribute values in society, "to modify or replace community values, moral practices, and norms of interpersonal conduct with new standards of behavior" (Tatalovich and Daynes 1988, 1).

Morality politics leave little room for political compromise, negotiation, or coalition building because ultimately the issues at hand are ones that pose a moral affront to people (Meier 1999; Mooney and Lee 1995). The scope of conflict surrounding culture wars is very intense and lends itself more easily to escalation and even violence compared to nonmorality politics where economic interests typically underlie the conflict (Hunter 1994; Meier 1994). Morality politics generate widespread responses from the general public because the conflicts are rooted in belief systems. Everyone has a belief system, which means that people feel qualified to make political evaluations regarding morality issues (Meier 1994; Mooney 2001; Tatalovich and Daynes 1988; Hunter 1991).

Morality movements use simplistic explanatory frames to define their issues, and they discuss them in nontechnical language that is accessible to the general public to help generate a lot of attention to the issue. Even if an issue is complicated, morality movements portray it in basic terms. This encourages people to participate based on their sense of right versus wrong rather than their grasp of a technically sophisticated policy issue. Stem cell research illustrates this phenomenon well. Stem cell research is a scientifically and socially complex issue, yet as long as it is linked to the immorality of abortion it can be discussed as a question of good or evil rather than a question of medical science (Sharp 1994; Karnein 2005).

The accessibility of participating in morality politics, coupled with the salience generated by morality issues, makes politicians more responsive to them (Haider-Markel and Meier 1996; Meier 1994; Mooney and Lee 1995). Responsiveness, however, is mediated by the level of public consensus surrounding a morality issue and whether or not there is a material stake in the particular issue (Meier 1999; Mooney 1999; Smith 1999; Mooney and Lee 2000; Sharp 2005). Pure morality issues (those that do not have economic stakeholders vested in the outcome of the conflict) elicit a more direct response from politicians to public opinion, whereas material morality issues are more elite dominated (Sharp 2005).

Morality issues can be divided between contentious morality issues, such as abortion or gay and lesbian rights, and consensus morality issues, such as prostitution or recreational drug use (Meier 1999; Mooney and Lee 2000; Sharp 1999, 2002). Consensus morality issues are issues that only have one legitimate side; they are "sin" issues (Meier 1999). Drinking and driving is an example of a sin issue, no group is willing to advocate for an increase in the legal blood-alcohol limit while operating a vehicle. Contentious issues, on the other hand, generate a flurry of conflict because opposing sides exist in the debate, and both sides ground their opposition in their respective sense of moral supremacy on the issue. These types of morality politics generate an incredible amount of conflict and can involve multiple political actors, elites, and general participants because the intensity and scope of these conflicts are easy to expand and socialize across various political venues (Meier 1999; Haider-Markel and Meier 1996). In reality, morality issues are better conceptualized along a continuum between contentious and consensus politics rather than in discrete categories (Mooney and Lee 2000).

Abortion politics has moved along the morality politics continuum; it has been defined as a nonissue, a consensus morality issue, and for the past four decades as a contentious morality issue. Public opinion toward abortion has been divided along three main lines: supporters, opponents, and people who believe abortion should be legal but regulated in varying degrees by the government. Over the years public opinion regarding abortion has ebbed and flowed. There has been an increasing polarization in attitudes toward abortion along religious lines and, importantly, within religious denominations (Evans 2002). On the other hand, public sentiment regarding the use of recreational drugs or support for prostitution forms much more of a consensus—most people oppose both. Politicians follow the nuances of public opinion more closely when opinion is divided around a morality issue. The more contentious the issue the more responsive politicians will be to their constituents' opinions on the issue.

Culture wars have unique parameters that differentiate them from non-morality politics. The nonnegotiable, uncompromising, salient characteristics associated with culture wars have implications for morality movements, particularly in terms of tactical strategy implementation and desired political outcomes. Even though morality movements are unique, they are governed by similar environmental constraints as well as opportunities found in nonmorality movements.

Movement formation efforts interact in complex ways with opportunities and constraints. Simply having new political opportunities does not lead to the development of a social movement; conversely, when political opportunities diminish, it does not necessarily result in the end of a social movement (Staggenborg 1989). Similarly, when political opportunities arise giving way to social movement formation, it can also create a countermovement. Although institutionalized political systems can either foster or retard collective action via the provision of political opportunities, they cannot create a movement. Social movements, including both morality and nonmorality movements, do not spontaneously arise from the masses even when political opportunities are available. Mobilization structures need to be in place prior to movement formation.

Mobilizing Structures and Tactical Repertoires

On December 1, 1955, a longtime civil rights activist named Rosa Parks refused to sit in the back of the bus in Montgomery, Alabama.

> Our mistreatment was just not right, and I was tired of it. . . . The only tired I was, was tired of giving in. . . . I didn't want to pay my fare and then go

around the back door. . . . It was not pre-arranged. It just happened that the driver made a demand and I just didn't feel like obeying his demand. . . . I was quite tired after spending a full day working. (Quotations Page 2006)

Parks's example led to a 381-day bus boycott in Montgomery and is often viewed as the catalyst for the civil rights movement. This event certainly played a focusing role in highlighting racial discrimination in society; however, structures already existed within African American communities that could be used for mobilizing people. Black churches and colleges provided two resources necessary for movement development: social networks and leadership (McAdam 1982).

Churches and colleges are formal organizations, representing only one type of mobilizing structure. Many other forms exist. More specifically, mobilizing structures are "those collective vehicles, informal as well as formal, through which people mobilize and engage in collective action" (McAdam et al. 1996, 3). This encompasses a diversity of organizations. To simplify, John McCarthy has proposed a two-dimensional typology: nonmovement/movement and informal/formal. Friendship networks, neighborhoods, and work networks are considered nonmovement, informal mobilizing structures whereas churches, unions, and professional associations are examples of nonmovement, formal structures. Movement-informal structures include activist networks, affinity groups, and memory communities. Finally, movement-formal structures contain social movement organizations, protest committees, and movement schools (McCarthy 1997, 145).

Pro-life activists were able to quickly launch a countermovement following the *Roe* decision because they had access to organizational structures already operating in society. The Catholic Church, which has an extensive organizational history, access to tangible resources (e.g., money, membership), and intangible resources (e.g., leadership skills, communication skills, a committed constituency) has long opposed abortion (Freeman 1979). Church leadership provided immediate direction and was able to tap into established resources including hundreds of local Catholic Churches throughout the nation. Catholic Church leaders were able to galvanize pro-life supporters into political participation through their preexisting mobilization structures. Essentially overnight, the Church mobilized a countermovement (Blanchard 1994; McCarthy 1987).

Initially, the Catholic Church encouraged its members to engage in civil disobedience to protest the legalization of abortion. Civil disobedience is only one type of participatory activity. Organizations develop different types of collective action strategies to suit their particular needs. An organization may borrow participatory strategies from other movements or it may innovate within its own organization.

> Based on past periods of conflict with a particular group(s) or the government, individuals construct a prototype of a protest or riot that describes what to do in particular circumstances as well as explaining a rationale for these actions. (Hill and Rothchild 1992, 192)

Borrowing from other groups provides a baseline for new groups, enabling them to innovate while relying on tactics that have been successful in the past. Charles Tilly refers to this as the "repertoire of contention." Tilly argues that a movement constantly experiments with new tactics to produce an advantage over its opponents. But he is quick to point out that new tactics rarely endure beyond a single event, unless the new tactic aids multiple actors (1992).

The pro-life movement (in theory) has modeled its repertoire of contention after the civil rights movement's nonviolent tactics. Activists participate in peaceful protests, sit-ins, vigils, and prayers. They have recently borrowed the strategy of economic boycotting implemented by the civil rights movement. After having some success in preventing the construction of a Planned Parenthood facility in Austin (by dissuading subcontractors from participating in the construction) pro-life groups have turned their attention to starting boycotts in other states (Crary 2004). Over the Christmas season of 2005, pro-life supporters were asked to boycott the doll maker American Girl. The company contributes money to Girls Inc., a youth group that runs educational and empowerment programs for young girls. Pro-life organizations view Girls Inc. as a "pro-abortion, pro-lesbian advocacy group" because of the organization's comprehensive approach to issues of sexuality and female empowerment (Fredrix 2005).

Protesting at abortion clinics and more recently organizing boycotts are two forms of collective action the pro-life movement uses because they have proven successful in the past. In conjunction with this old strategy, pro-life groups continue to innovate. Experimenting with new tactics led one pro-life protester to tie black dolls around his waist and walk up and down the sidewalk in front of a clinic yelling out "How many little black babies are going to be dragged to their death today?" The theatrics were lost on other protesters and spectators who did not understand the sophisticated symbolic reference the protester was trying to make to the link between the eugenics movement and abortion rights. Dragging dolls on the sidewalk did not catch on with other pro-life protesters; at the next protest, the activist resorted to the usual tactics—holding posters, singing, photographing people, and "counseling" (Interview with pro-life protesters and pro-choice employees, 1999).

Aside from innovation, repertoires can significantly change when organizational structures are altered. The level of institutionalization within a movement typically shapes the type of collective action tactics used by a group. Initially, a movement relies on direct action tactics because it is a loose, informal collection of groups, lacking the resources to engage in more legitimated, formalized, and professionalized political activity (Staggenborg 1988). Disruptive tactics are a valuable macro- and microlevel resource for new movements. Confrontational tactics function as a macrolevel resource by providing a movement with unpredictability, uncertainty, and media attention, all of which gain the attention of political elites and potential participants (Tarrow 1996; Offe 1990).

Unconventional participation also operates as a microlevel resource by recruiting individuals into a movement. The motivation to engage in protest politics, which runs the gamut from signing petitions, to boycotts, to lawful demonstration, to violence, is not the same as the motivation to participate in orthodox political activities (Bean 1991; Brady 1999). Support for the political system tends to foster traditional, electoral participation, whereas participation in protest politics is often motivated by the desire to voice dissent over specific political issues and values (Bean 1991). Dissent may occur because an individual feels alienated from the system or deprived by the system, or it may be a rational political strategy to bring about change (Gurr 1970; Muller 1979; Oberschall 1973). A self-interested, rational individual may refrain from engaging in traditional forms of political participation and group activity because the rewards of participation do not offset the costs of participation (Finkel, Muller, and Opp 1989; Muller and Opp 1986; Muller et al. 1991; Finkel and Muller 1998). But the desire to voice dissent or change the current system may be enough to inspire participation in collective action because the potential rewards are enough to offset the costs of participation to the individual.

People engage in collective action because the issue at hand is salient and the rewards—such as feelings of solidarity, networking, activism, friendship—are valued by them (Bean 1991; Chong 1991; Inglehart 1977; Opp 1986). As a movement matures, these participation incentives are difficult to maintain. Movement survival depends on the creation of formal organizations, which tends to pull a movement in a more bureaucratic and conservative direction, mitigating the utility of direct action tactics (Freeman 1975; Staggenborg 1988). Consequently, movement evolution and the resulting tactical repertoire changes can cause fragmentation and loss of membership for the movement.

The evolution from a loose, casual movement into an institutionalized one includes building financial and legal resources, formalizing participants' roles within the organization, formalizing communication networks via meetings and conferences, and even attempting to build organizations such as political action committees, interest groups, or political parties (Tarrow 1996; Offe 1990). Institutionalization provides stability, legitimacy, and the capacity for a movement to continue after its members' initial enthusiasm wanes. For example, the professionalization of the pro-choice movement helped it survive in the "lean" years during the 1970s when many activists (believing the legalization of abortion was secure) became involved in other political issues (Staggenborg 1988). Once a movement begins to institutionalize, then disruptive, direct action tactics cease to be appropriate. Confrontational tactics tend to delegitimate a movement as a permanent and serious political actor (Offe 1990; Tarrow 1996).

Conflict within a movement is generated from the differing opinions of participants as to what strategies, tactics, and goals are more appropriate. Even though movement leaders share the same core values, they may vehemently disagree about what the movement should look like. Factionalism can undermine a movement's efficacy because the more radical groups directly compete with the larger movement for resources. Movement supporters are asked to pick between the vying factions, often resulting in confusion, divided loyalties, and, most important, a division in resources (Frey, Dietz, and Kalof 1992; Gamson 1968). The resulting tension can create further movement fragmentation and participant alienation, especially as old allies begin to view each other as obstacles to their respective groups. Eventually, militant factions of a movement splinter off and create their own groups, ultimately contributing to a movement's demise (Tarrow 1996; Gamson 1968). This pattern occurred in the civil rights movement when the Black Power faction continued to support the use of confrontational tactics, while the bulk of the movement was becoming more formalized (Chong 1991).

Group Identity: The Role of Cultural Framing

A movement attempts to minimize tension, fragmentation, and the possibility of total collapse through a cultural framing process where symbols and ideology are used by the movement to shape, stimulate, and aid in its origination and continuation. A large part of group survival requires members to view themselves as collectively sharing meanings and definitions of their situation (Berbrier 2002; Cerulo 1997). Newer (post–civil rights) social movements blend both political and cultural goals, often seeking either to preserve old identities or to gain recognition for new ones (Pizzorno 1978; Jasper 1997; Tilly 1998; Berbrier 2002). David Snow coined the phrase "framing processes" to refer to the complex social-psychological dynamics that give meaning to ideas and sentiments (Snow et al. 1986; Snow and Benford 1988, 1992). Snow defines the framing process as a deliberate attempt made by groups of people to craft a common worldview and a common understanding of themselves, which leads to their participation in collective action.

Social networks play a crucial role in group identity (Gould 1995, 1998; Mische 1996; Polletta 1999; Whittier 1995, 1997; Reger and Taylor 2002). Member recruitment can originate from these preexisting social networks where people already have strong feelings toward the specific group (Goodwin, Jasper, and Polletta 2000). David Bereit (the executive director of the BVCL) and his wife were recruited through their church.

> We were asked to serve on the board of the Coalition for Life. That was when we said that this is what we were supposed to do. So Margaret and I both served together as one seat on the board, and as I began to learn more about it, that is when I went from being what I call a passive pro-lifer to being a passionate, active pro-lifer. And that is when I realized that to do nothing is to, in a sense, passively allow this injustice to continue. (Interview with David Bereit, December 2003)

The prior bond David and Margaret had with their church spurred them to participate in solidarity behavior, even though it was initially uncomfortable for them.

> I didn't go out and pray out in front of the abortion facility for a long time because I was nervous. I was worried what will people think? What will happen? What would it be like? Ultimately, I went there with a group of

friends who were doing a procession down to the facility so I was with others that I felt comfortable with and I remember when I went out there that
day, the first time I'd ever looked at the facility from out in front of it, in
the public right of way and again it was another one of those moments
where I just developed a really strong conviction that I was suppose to do
everything that I could to try and bring an end to what I recognize to be a
terrible evil that had come to our community. (Interview with David Bereit,
December 2003)

As a participant becomes involved, his reputation begins to build within the
social network, and expectations of continued support and participation are
placed on the new recruit by the social network (Fireman and Gamson 1979;
Polletta and Jasper 2001; Chong 1991).

Other scholars have acknowledged the seminal role that ideas, emotions, and
collective identities can play by either breathing new life into an existing movement or helping to spur a new one (Gamson 1992; Tarrow 1996; Tilly 1978; Pizzorno 1978; Oliver and Strawn 2003). Zald (1997) discusses the framing process
in terms of six categories: cultural construction, cultural contradictions and historical events, framing as a strategic action, competitive process, mass media,
and outcomes.

Cultural construction refers to the larger societal context that movements
take place in. For example, within the women's movement the phrase "a
woman's body is her own" only makes sense in a society that values individual
autonomy and equality. This phrase would not make sense in other cultural settings (Zald 1997). Zald points out that even within the same society, not all
movements have access to or draw from the same cultural context. This is particularly true for morality movements. "A violent tactic such as bombing a clinic
feels right to antiabortion advocates who equate a fetus with a person; it is
extremist behavior to those who deny that equivalence" (Zald 1997, 267).

Cultural contradictions and historical events are similar to what policy
scholars refer to as "focusing events" (Kingdon 1995) and "punctuated equilib-
rium" (Baumgartner and Jones 1993). Dormant issues may exist in society for
long periods of time until some event occurs that redirects attention to the
issue. For example, the Anita Hill–Clarence Thomas hearing had such an effect
on sexual harassment (Wood and Doan 2003), and the Three Mile Island inci-
dent focused attention on nuclear power (Zald 1997). Movements can also cap-

italize on cultural contradictions. The civil rights movement successfully exploited the irony of a racist and segregated society being housed in a democratic nation that promises equality to its citizens.

Strategic framing requires leaders and core participants to actively define ideology, symbols, and iconic events; assign blame; and suggest alternatives (Snow and Benford 1988, 1992; Snow et al. 1986). Strategic framing can have substantial consequences in terms of movement success or failure. Banaszak (1996) traces the development of the beliefs and values in both the American and Swiss suffrage movement, demonstrating how the framing process handicapped the movement in Switzerland as evidenced by the delay of Swiss women's suffrage until 1990.

Strategic framing is an active process that takes place in multiple venues, with the goal of winning the support of authorities and individuals. Framing is a competitive process because movements must vie with countermovements, unrelated movements, and other newsworthy stories for media attention. Pro-choice supporters frame abortion as the pinnacle of women's rights, whereas pro-life supporters frame abortion as state-sanctioned murder. These frames change depending on where the discourse is taking place and the desired outcomes for the movement. Anti-abortion groups successfully framed abortion as a funding issue within Congress, arguing that public monies should not be spent on abortion services. Framing abortion as an appropriations issue led to the passing of the Hyde Amendment, which eliminated federal funding of abortion for indigent women.

Within this competitive framing process, the role of the media cannot be discounted. In that very competitive profession, success is measured by ratings. The media constantly report personalized, overly dramatized, and fragmented news stories to accommodate the short attention span of the public (Bennett 2004). Activists learn to respond to this by crafting five-second sound bites to convey their message and by developing new strategies aimed at gaining the media's attention (Zald 1997; Bennett 2004).

Finally, the framing process results in cultural outcomes. Movements that are successful contribute new "cultural stock" to society—their slogans and symbols become absorbed into the larger society, and their demands are addressed through public policy (Morris 1984; Baierle 1998; Fine 1985; Scott 1990; Rubin 1998). For example, the idea of "pride," articulated by the gay and lesbian movement, has become incorporated into mainstream culture, shifting society's focus from deviant homosexuality to one of an acceptance of alternative lifestyles (Munt 1998). This cultural change is most obviously reflected in popular prime-time television programs that have openly (and unapologetically) homosexual characters (e.g., *Will and Grace* and the reality television program *Queer Eye for the Straight Guy*). Unsuccessful movements eventually fade away completely or lay dormant until some future event reactivates the cause (Zald 1997). Together, these six components make up the framing process that provides the "ideological cement" for a movement.

Movements interact with society, creating the potential for transformation in terms of political or cultural changes. Social movements are complex, varying in organizational form, movement tactics, ideology, and outcome. In this range of activities, militant groups engaging in violence represent the extreme side of movements. Violence can play an instrumental role by conveying a political message to authorities and the public. Violence can be a form of political collateral for a movement when it is used in a political context.

Violence as a Political Resource

The early literature on political violence established the difference between random acts of violence and group-affiliated actions that are destructive and have a political intent (Gurr 1989; Nieburg 1969; Gamson 1968, 1990; Tilly 2002). Nieburg (1969) argued that focusing on the pathological and erratic aspects of violence obscured the role of societal factors, specifically the values and institutions that may have contributed to the violence. Nieburg distinguishes between random violence and political violence by defining the latter in terms of a continuum of behavior that has a purposive goal:

> Acts of disruption, destruction, injury whose purpose, choice of targets or victims, surrounding circumstances, implementation, and/or effects have political significance, that is, tend to modify the behavior of others in a bargaining situation that has consequences for the social system. (1969, 13)

Random violence differs from political violence in two significant ways: the message and the connection to a larger social group. Social meaning is attached to acts of political violence and supported by other individuals with similar beliefs. An advocate of political violence is connected to a larger solidarity group that provides an ideological foundation for political action (Gamson 1968, 1990;

Mason 2002a, 2002b; Gould 1999; McAdam, Tarrow, and Tilly 2001). These social networks glue people together, reinforcing their commonality, which may be based on ethnic, religious, ideological, or other associations (Lichbach 1994a, 1994b, 1995; Coleman 1990; Gould 1999). Networks act as "policing" squads by monitoring the behavior of members; enforcing sanctions against those individuals who do not participate and rewarding those who do (Francisco 2004a; Moore 1995). Viewed within this societal context, the use of violence is a rational action even though it appears to be counter to an individual's self-interest.

Most groups pursue traditional strategies of action; but once a group begins to lose confidence in its ability to alter the behavior of its antagonists, other avenues of action may be explored. Diminishing levels of trust and confidence in authorities may initially stimulate a group to become more politically mobilized (Gamson 1968, 1990; McAdam, Tarrow, and Tilly 2001). An organization may use its slack resources (e.g., time, money, nonviolent protest) in an attempt to influence authorities. Once a group experiences failure and frustration because its efforts to influence the relevant actors have not materialized into favorable policy outcomes or societal behavioral changes, it may view violence as the only strategy available.

After a group believes that legitimate political options are no longer viable because political authorities are biased against the group, or the system is not responsive, it may push for more drastic measures. Violent protests and actions are essentially a group's way of increasing the political system's costs for maintaining current policy. Groups can use violence as an instrumental act, either offensively (meaning prior to assimilation into the polity), defensively (after assimilation into the polity), or both (Gamson 1975, 1990; Wallace 1991; Tilly 2002).

Defensive violence tends to grow out of cleavages between militants and moderates in a social movement. As a movement institutionalizes, it begins to adopt more insider tactics—lobbying, litigation, or advertising. This causes tension among those participants that value outsider tactics, such as protests and boycotts. As a movement assimilates into the polity, militants may resist this move by using even more radical tactics, resulting in defensive violence. Within the Vietnam antiwar movement, for example, a violent faction named the Weatherman Underground emerged as the movement became assimilated into the political system. The Weatherman Underground was dedicated to committing terrorist acts against the system (Tarrow 1996). More recently, in the midst of institutionalization, radical activists in the environmentalist movement have resorted to tree spiking (hammering steel spikes into trees), which can cause considerable damage to both loggers and their equipment (Earth First 1990).

Offensive violence is generally used when a movement is essentially shut out from the political system. Relative deprivation models hypothesize that varying degrees of inequality drive political violence. Discontent results from inequality, which in turn leads to collective political violence (Davies 1962; Feierabend and Feierabend 1966; Gurr 1968, 1970). Empirically, the evidence for this relationship is mixed. Some studies have found weak to moderate evidence of this relationship depending on the measure used to capture inequality (Midlarsky 1988; Muller 1985; Dudley and Miller 1998), while other research has turned up no relationship (Lichbach 1990; Brush 1996). Despite the mixed findings, scholars continue to support the idea that inequality factors into political violence (Brush 1996).

Resource mobilization models posit that a group's organizational capacity to extract and control resources, rather than inequality, is the key link to understanding political violence[4] (Jenkins and Perrow 1977; Snyder and Tilly 1972; Tilly 1975, 1978). When a dissident group has few resources relative to the state, it is expected that violence is more likely to occur (Dudley and Miller 1998). A disparity in resources does not, however, mean political violence will be the outcome to a dispute. Even when the state possesses far greater resources compared to rebelling groups, it can mitigate violence by curbing the use of its authority. In low-repressive regimes alternative channels are available for groups to voice their discontent, thereby reducing the use of violence (Benson and Kugler 1998; Dudley and Miller 1998; Muller 1985; Geller 1987).

The state can adjust its level of repression in response to the dissident group's tactics (Francisco 2004a, 2004b; Hoover and Kowalewski 1992). The state, like rebelling groups, changes tactics and strategies. Resource mobilization models conceptualize the dissident-regime relationship as interplay between movement and countermovement activity, where the state acts as a countermovement to the dissident group. Violence results from the capacity (or sometimes incapacity) of one group to use resources effectively to rectify its grievances with the other group.

Violence can surface in a variety of settings, ranging from radical factions of a social movement to groups that use violence as their primary resource to states that employ violence to maintain or reestablish power (Williams 2003; Francisco 2004a, 2004b). Violence works by introducing high costs to the system—uncertainty, terrorism, property damage, or death. In terms of political participation, violence clearly represents the extreme side.

Pro-life groups have relied on violence even though they have not been shut out of the political process, face minimal repressive sanctions from the government, and have received many favorable policy decisions. For example, the Supreme Court reaffirmed its willingness to allow restrictions against abortion services in two cases: *Ohio v. Akron Center for Reproductive Health* (497 U.S. 502, 1990) and *Planned Parenthood of Southeastern Pennsylvania v. Casey* (505 U.S. 833, 1992). The Court's decisions fueled the pro-life movement's efforts to criminalize abortion services through mainstream political institutions. In 1990, 465 abortion-related bills were introduced in state legislatures, and the vast majority were anti-abortion bills (NARAL 2006). This number continued to climb; by 2001, there were 620 anti-abortion measures introduced in to the state legislatures (NARAL 2006).

Despite the pro-life movement's policy successes and assimilation into political institutions, it continues to wage extreme acts of violence toward abortion clinics. Beginning in the 1970s, the National Abortion Federation has recorded 40 bombings (at both abortion and family planning facilities), over 160 arsons, and thousands of acts of vandalism (National Abortion Federation 2006). During the 1990s, over the course of nine years, anti-abortion extremists murdered 7 clinic employees and wounded another 13 people. Moreover, the number of clinic workers receiving death threats continued to climb: 77 death threats were made between 1977 and 1990; that number grew to 250 threats spanning 1991 to 1999. Chemical attacks have also grown in popularity among pro-life extremists; abortion clinics received a record high 500 anthrax threats in 2001 (Alan Guttmacher Institute 2001).

Violence represents one form of political tactics used by the pro-life movement. The movement's political gains have not offset its reliance on protest tactics nor curbed the use of extreme violence. Over time, the frequency and prevalence of the movement's confrontational tactics have not waned. In 1985, 85 percent of abortion providers were experiencing some form of anti-abortion contentious activities (including picketing, clinic blockades, and invasion of the facility). By the 1990s, 86 percent of abortion providers continued to be the targets of various forms of harassment (Forrest and Henshaw 1987; Johnson 1999, 248; Cozzarelli and Major 1998; Henshaw 1995a).

Harassment is not a tactic typically associated with participation, yet, like violence, harassment can be used to convey a political message and increase the costs of maintaining current policies. Under these conditions, harassment can be used as an instrumental resource by a group, making it politically motivated harassment. Abortion is an issue that is infused with competing sets of moral beliefs that structure very different ideas about gender roles, sexuality, religion, and notions of "choice." Cultural traditionalists and cultural progressivists have differing worldviews that shape the societal context in which political harassment has emerged as a form of political protest.

Political Harassment and the Pro-Life Movement

Political protest is typically a benign (albeit unconventional) activity; however, in the context of abortion politics it represents much more than unconventional political activity. While the motivation for and outcome of using disruptive tactics and even violence are understood, the use of political harassment is not. Politically motivated harassment introduces costs into the political environment that are largely ignored by governmental authorities and absorbed by the targets of the harassment. A definition of political harassment has to take into account the unique circumstances that contextualize the activity as well as who bears the cost of the activity. I define political harassment as persistent verbal or physical collective challenges intended to change the behavior of others, to have political significance, to create a reasonable fear, and to be directed at nongovernmental actors because of their beliefs.

There are theoretical consequences to conceptualizing political harassment as part of a continuum of activities that are designed to achieve a movement's goals. It changes the calculation of costs and benefits of protest activity. Typically, costs and benefits are discussed in terms of the rewards and expenditures of the behavior to the individual and her group engaging in the activity. The largest cost often comes from the state's response to the dissident's activity, in the form of repression. The state possesses the resources to control, curb, minimize, or eliminate challenges. Unlike the state, nongovernmental targets do not have similar resources, which can put them in a more vulnerable position relative to the dissident group.

Targeting nongovernmental organizations is not a practice unique to the pro-life movement. In the mid-1960s, consumer, environmental, and civil rights groups began to confront corporations directly for practices these groups found offensive (Vogel 1974, 1975, 1978, 1981). Groups used a range of unconventional tactics: consumer boycotts, picketing, disruptions at business meetings, invasions of business headquarters, class-action lawsuits, and even harassing corporate recruiters on college campuses (Vogel 1974, 1975, 1981). Corporations had to shoulder the costs of this protest. In a survey of corporate America conducted in 1965, businesses reported that 74 percent of the demands and pressures on them stemmed from government and only 9 percent from the public. By 1971 there was a marked shift: 48 percent of the demands originated from government, whereas 26 percent were generated from the public (Vogel 1974).

Singling out corporations led to some significant changes in both management and company decisions. Dow Chemical ceased producing napalm, AT&T upgraded the position of its female employees, Kodak agreed to employ African Americans, and many companies implemented environmentally friendly practices and policies (Vogel 1974). Targeting nongovernmental actors proved to be successful but limited, because corporations have the resources to insulate themselves from the protest activities. Approximately thirty years later global corporations such as McDonalds, Starbucks, and Nike have come under attack by activists. Relying on disruptive tactics, antiglobalization protesters successfully disrupted the five-day World Trade Organization Ministerial Conference in Seattle at the end of 1999 (Canadian Security Intelligence Service 2000). Corporate and governmental actors quickly countermobilized. By time the G-8 summit was held in Genoa, Italy, the state retaliated, arresting over 280 protesters and curtailing the antiglobalization movement's ability to disrupt the July 2001 meetings.

Technically, corporations are not governmental actors, but because of their pivotal role in the economy, corporations enjoy much support from the government. Public interest groups simply have a weak power and resource base relative to capitalist interests. No amount of unconventional collective challenges will halt economic production (Vogel 1974, 1975, 1978). Moreover, consumer groups did not create a "reasonable" fear for corporations (other than the risk of profit loss); therefore it does not fall within the purview of political harassment.

Persistent, collective challenges waged at nongovernmental actors, which also evoke a reasonable fear in individuals, have operated in society. The Ku Klux Klan (KKK) garnered power from its reliance on political harassment as well as more extreme violence. Following the Civil War, the KKK formed in reaction to a changing political environment where former slaves were accorded the rights of citizenship. The KKK sought to reverse these political and societal changes. It engaged in several unconventional tactics ranging from night rides, to home visits of local Blacks, to economic threats, to burning crosses, to extreme violence and death (Southern Poverty Law Center 2004). Klan members, donning face masks and dressed in robes, participated in dramatic demonstrations. These events were orchestrated as a display of power, intended to cast fear over communities of color as well as ward off any potential sympathizers to the plight of Blacks (Southern Poverty Law Center 2004).

The KKK wanted to reestablish the political and social order in place prior to the Civil War. Klan members targeted Blacks who outwardly appeared to believe in equality and possessed some type of resource. African Americans who were literate, employed, owned a small business, or were politically active were frequently targets of Klan harassment. Although the KKK's membership remained low, the group enjoyed the tacit support and sympathy of Southern whites who did not want to see a change in the political or social order in society. Klan tactics proved very effective at reestablishing the racial social order in the South: by the mid-1870s white Southerners had taken back sole control of state governments and successfully implemented a system of segregation (Southern Poverty Law Center 2004). Blacks, who were the most vulnerable people in society, were forced to pay the costs for the political harassment. They lived in a system of segregation, where they were continuously confronted with the possibility of harassment, violence, or death.

Relatedly, in the anti-abortion movement, the government has placed few costs on the dissident group. The real costs are transferred to the individuals working at or receiving services from women's health care clinics.[5] This abortion provider details a few of the costs he has had to contend with resulting from pro-life groups' activities that are directed at him:

For the longest time they thought I was wearing a disguise—you know, the long beard . . . they went on the radio and said a lot of outrageous things. And then it began to get more personalized. And they called my house, wrote letters, things like that. There were occasions when they tried to follow us after leaving the clinic but they always gave up. [Now] they are actually using my physical image and broadcasting it around. (Interview with a doctor who works for several abortion clinics, 1999)

Physicians are not the only nongovernmental targets of pro-life activity. The costs of harassment are also transferred to clinic employees and volunteers. The director of a clinic explains the precautions and associated costs she has undertaken due to the escalation and corollary harassment occurring at the clinic.

It's uglier now; the tone [of the protest] is uglier. I had to tint my [car] windows because I pick up the doctor, and install a security system in my house because I know they were coming within two blocks of my house. I have a young son at home. So these were the steps we had to take. (Interview with the director of a women's health clinic, 1999)

Barbara Anderson, an escort volunteer at a Planned Parenthood facility, explains her brushes with protesters and harassment.

Right away they were drawn to me because I'm an older woman and they thought they were going to scare me off. So they lit right into me and started with the postcards after they got my license plate number. And they sent postcards to my neighbors where I live and it said "this is Barbara Anderson and she is happy. She wants you to know that she is very pleased to be killing babies at the Planned Parenthood Clinic." One time I returned home to find a plastic bag of rose heads hanging on my gate . . . with a letter saying we hope you like roses and it went on to say that they wished I wouldn't do this terrible thing. (Interview with Barbara Anderson, Planned Parenthood volunteer escort, November 2003)

Many of the tactics used by pro-life groups are not physically harmful to their targets—picketing clinics, picketing in front of the homes of clinic employees, shouting at and photographing employees and clinic clients, jamming clinic phone lines, mailing literature to staff and clients, tracing license plate numbers of clients and employees, and infiltrating clinics. All of these activities share common characteristics; they are directed at nongovernmental actors and grounded in a common language that encourages the use of militaristic rhetoric. At a pro-life training seminar, Brian Clowes explained to participants why he embraced this rhetorical method. "I use military terms and concepts because we need to recognize that we are in a war and we need to arrive at a state of mind where we want to win the war—we need to develop a battle mentality" (Brian Clowes, director of Human Life International, speaking at a training seminar, 1999). Carol Mason (2002a, 2002b) has documented the explicit links between anti-abortion rhetoric and the rise in paramilitary rhetoric and culture; activists constantly evoke guerrilla warfare language as well as engage in guerrilla-style political tactics.

Pro-life "apocalyptic narrative" and unconventional tactics are further embedded in a reality where extreme violence and death have occurred. Over several decades, dozens of reproductive health care professionals have been murdered or severely injured. Thousands more have been the objects of extreme threats of violence ranging from arson to bombing to chemical attacks. The actual number of victims of pro-life violence compared to the number of people involved in reproductive health services is minimal, but much like Klan harassment and violence, it creates a larger culture of fear in these communities. The inflammatory rhetoric and harassing tactics serve to reinforce the sense of fear within women's health clinics. Several pro-life tactics are borrowed from the KKK. For example, anti-abortion activists frequently display crosses in lawns, nooses, distribute wanted posters targeting specific individuals as deserving of lynch law, and show pictures of dismemberment (displaying fetal parts) during demonstrations (Mason 2002a).

Contextualizing pro-life protest activities forces us to conceptualize these tactics as more than unconventional political tactics. The inflammatory rhetoric and extreme forms of violence (occurring at the national level) create an atmosphere of reasonable fear among individuals affiliated with clinics (at the local level), even if their objective probability of being a victim of extreme pro-life violence is minimal. The link between the larger national abortion political scene and how it interacts with local abortion politics was noted by one police officer who is a regular participant in the abortion conflict occurring in his community:

We initially thought that we were going to deal with the clinic like any other business. But then we noticed that tensions were heightened on one side or the other in response to what's going on in the national scene. So at that point we decided that we'd better start watching what's going on in the bigger stage when dealing with the issue here locally. (Interview with a police officer, November 2003)

Several police officers involved with mediating abortion conflicts between clinic employees and protesters have commented on the "siege mentality" that developed in the employees. As protests have increased in frequency and duration at the clinic, employees' sense of threat and fear has intensified particularly as more severe forms of violence randomly occur across the nation. The culture of fear and anxiety surrounding clinics can color employees' assessment of protest activities or, as this police officer explains, their assessment of the protesters.

We would get calls where someone would call up and say, "There's a gentleman standing outside of the fence. He's not clean shaven, we haven't seen him before. And he's staring at the people that are entering the clinic." Staring is not something that we can do anything about. But we would still respond to the call because they would call it in to the 911 dispatch center—there was a suspicious person. We'd get out there and find out the guy just woke up early in the morning, didn't shave, but wanted to come out and pray, or do something at the clinic. (Interview with a police officer, December 2003)

Another police officer, who was frequently called to manage conflict between pro-life groups and clinic employees, explained why his department's approach toward the abortion conflict taking place at the clinic has changed over time.

We are more cautious, I mean we just have to be . . . I don't know if it's a direct effect because of our local protesters [or] because we're hearing the news that fringe groups are bombing or sending anthrax through the mail. . . . We have to go down there [to the clinic] occasionally just to talk to them and diffuse their level of anxiety. It comes in cycles where they have a lot of anxiety. (Interview with a police officer, December 2003)

The point of the confrontational tactics taking place at clinics is not one of executed threat, but rather shaping an environment of continuous, implied threat and fear. Many of the tactics the pro-life movement relies on foster a sense of fear that has come to epitomize the culture surrounding abortion clinics. Consequently, the anti-abortion movement's persistent verbal and physical collective challenges are a strategy of political harassment—designed to change the behavior of nongovernmental actors who hold differing beliefs.

The Payoff of Political Harassment

Once contextualized, much of what passes for unconventional protest is better defined and understood as political harassment. Yet the larger question remains: why would a social movement engage in political harassment? Simply stated, it serves two important goals: movement cohesion and outcome success.

Social movements typically stem from a set of social grievances that people believe need to be fixed. Within these movements, large agendas develop, making compromise between the movement and the movement's adversaries possible. For example, the defeat of the Equal Rights Amendment was a large setback for the women's movement but did not end it, because the movement was addressing and making progress on other issues. Even the pro-choice movement functions as a multi-issue movement. Pro-choice groups are involved in population and fertility issues and are strongly linked to the women's movement and professional associations representing the concerns of health care practitioners (McCarthy 1987).

The pro-life movement is a large counter–social movement that developed around a single issue, rejecting the legality of abortion on moral grounds. Over time, the anti-abortion movement has expanded its litany of grievances to include related morality issues such as family planning and sex education issues; however, compared to the pro-choice movement, the pro-life movement primarily consists of single-issue groups dominated by opposition to abortion. Equally as important, the pro-life movement's dedication to the issue is unmatched by pro-choice groups (McCarthy 1987; Mason 2002a; Young 2002). For example, the Brazos Valley Coalition for Life has at least one protester at the Planned Parenthood clinic in Bryan, Texas, every hour and every day the clinic is open for business.

Social networks play a crucial role in all social movements—stronger interrelationships translate into stronger dedication to the cause. The pool of potential pro-life activists primarily comes from Catholic, Pentecostal, and evangelical Protestant churches (Green 1999; Johnson 1999; McCarthy 1987; Jelen and Wilcox 2003). Potential activists share a common grievance. They believe the activities of the 1960s and 1970s contributed to the moral decay of American society, and the legalization of abortion represents one of the more obvious offenses (Green 1999). Legalized abortion is perceived as a moral wrong, not a political issue that can be compromised.

The pro-life movement initially grew from the encouragement of elites who were institutionally well connected. The Catholic Church played a pivotal role, encouraging the development of the movement and lending resources to early anti-abortion activists. Business and political professionals helped create political action committees, organized mass mailing campaigns, and partnered up with other preexisting organizations (Johnson 1999; McKeegan 1992).

From the beginning, the pro-life movement was institutionalized. The movement has several organizations based in Washington, DC, lobbying groups, political action committees, and legal experts (McCarthy 1987). Institutionalization provides a movement with important linkages to formal and legitimate political arenas, but it simultaneously forces a movement to negotiate and cooperate. Instead of using confrontational tactics, these groups must rely on compromise in order to achieve any measurable political success. While the pro-life movement made institutional inroads, its membership started to expand in the 1980s to most notably include fundamentalists. These newer members were disappointed and impatient with the movement's strategy of pursuing incremental institutional changes and started calling for more radical approaches, such as implementing confrontational tactics, to aid the movement in its fight against abortion.

As a movement becomes increasingly institutionalized and adopts conventional tactics, it frequently creates what Michels (1962) terms "goal displacement" (Tarrow 1996). Essentially, long-term goals are sacrificed for short-term gains. Many movement participants may become disillusioned as they watch their leaders compromise and lose sight of the "true" goals. Goal displacement is particularly salient for morality movements. The rank-and-file members of the pro-life movement do not believe abortion is a negotiable issue or that there is room for middle ground, particularly among the more radical participants. Abortion is viewed in absolute and simplistic terms. Activists belonging to anti-abortion groups that use confrontational strategies commonly discuss the "wrongness" of abortion in black-and-white terms as evidenced by this pro-life movement member. "All life is precious and we can not choose or have the right to control when and where it is created or destroyed" (Interview with a pro-life activist, September 1999). Members that articulate and view abortion in these terms are more vulnerable to goal displacement. Tension arises when the absolutist members witness the institutionalized branch of the movement making political compromises on abortion issues in various political venues.

The larger movement cannot afford to sacrifice the support of its most dedicated members who are instrumental in keeping the issue visible and salient in society. One solution to this dilemma is organizational diversification, which allows a social movement to incorporate multiple strategies and tactics, ultimately creating a much more viable movement (Zald and Ash 1966; Freeman 1999). This was exactly the case for the anti-abortion movement. Grassroots organizations, with local leadership, started to develop across the country and push for direct action (Johnson 1999; McCarthy 1987). The growth of local direct action groups helped mitigate the tension developing between the different branches of the pro-life movement.

Operating at the grassroots level enables the movement to circumvent political compromise by avoiding political authorities and instead focusing on a different opponent. Social movements generally view the government simultaneously as the target of their grievances and as the solution. For many grassroots organizations within the pro-life movement, the government is not the primary target of their grievances because, barring the outright elimination of abortion services, government cannot satisfactorily respond to the movement's demand. Unless *Roe v. Wade* is overturned, the pro-life movement is essentially shut out from ultimate formal political success, so it has turned to other avenues for success. Direct action groups in the movement have pursued the eradication of abortion through personal transformation and confronting the urgency of the issue at the perceived source: abortion clinics.

Other movements have used "personal transformation" as an awareness tactic. Within the women's movement, self-transformation and actualization were tools used to raise women's consciousness and form a shared identity. The pro-life movement incorporates self-transformation into its tactical repertoire, but the transformation process is external to the movement (as opposed to internal). Many of the protest tactics used by the anti-abortion movement are aimed at proselytizing employees of abortion clinics and women seeking abortion services, with the intent of converting them to a pro-life stance and preventing abortions. "The main goal [of protesting at a clinic] is to save a life, save two lives really—the child and the mother—through love and the grace of God" (Interview with a pro-life activist, 1999). Conversion to pro-life ideology represents one victory activists are willing to accept.

The director of a pro-life organization described the goals of their protests.

To see the elimination of abortion and not just to get rid of the abortion facility. But even if the abortion mill is still there and no woman desires to get an abortion then that would be a success to us. Our primary goal is prayer, which we believe in the power of prayer. Probably another goal is the visibility so that people can see that people care and that this is an issue that people are not just going to go sit at home and watch TV. And that there are people that are willing to give up part of their day and stand in the sun or rain and hold a sign and pray. And also for the women that go inside as well as the employees of [the women's health facility] to see that we care about them and we care about this issue and that we are serious about it. (Interview with the director of a pro-life organization, January 1999)

In several interviews, leaders of different pro-life, grassroots organizations expressed the common, collective goal of evangelizing people through prayer and one-to-one contact. "What is our real mission? We realized it's simply to end abortion in the Brazos Valley in a peaceful, prayerful fashion but it's to end abortion . . . And we're going to work until that ultimately is accomplished, however long it takes" (Interview with David Bereit, executive director of BVCL, December 2003).

Personal transformation is not inherently threatening, but it exists within a continuum of activities grounded in a larger environment of fear and intimidation. An educational outreach intern at Planned Parenthood explained the two pro-life tactics that have been used on her: sidewalk counseling at the clinic and confrontation with pro-life activists at public events where the intern is working.

Before they knew who I was, if I walked in [to the clinic] they'd say, "Mom you don't have to go in there." And I'm not a mother. . . . One time one of the other opposition groups waited until I was by myself at the table [at an educational outreach event] and then came up and started asking me questions. (Interview with Planned Parenthood intern, December 2003)

Along this continuum, the dynamic between pro-life protesters and the objects of protest can quickly change, as activities progress toward the more aggressive end of the continuum. Two clinic employees explained why the changes in recent anti-abortion protesting felt harassing and intimidating compared to the pro-life group's earlier protesting.

> They just lay on the fence screaming at people, and the clients. They always address us by name. And they say stuff like we see blood dripping off your fingers and calling us murderers. And they bring little babies and call our names and say look "Beth," this is what you are killing and they started yelling at the clients and calling them murderers. (Interview with an employee at a women's health clinic, March 1999)

The move toward more aggressive and individualized protesting that had a personalized tenor was also noted by another clinic employee.

> When they [the protesters] call you by your first name, call you by your husband's name, call out your address, and know different, little things about you that are personal—it is very, very, threatening. It is the closest thing to stalking that I have ever seen. (Interview with an employee at a women's health clinic, August 1999)

Targeting clients and employees as recipients of pro-life protest provides movement cohesion. Rank-and-file pro-lifers avoid political compromise and focus on individual victory—stopping one abortion at a time. According to the Coalition for Life's 2003 Annual Review Newsletter, "Local pregnancy centers have shared numerous stories of women who have been spared from regrets by choosing life instead of abortion as a result of the efforts of the *Coalition for Life*." At a grassroots organizational level, members engage in activities that are more directly carrying out "God's work" by dealing with the immediacy of attempting to end abortion, which in turn serves to strengthen their commitment to the issue: "Galatians tells us, let us not become weary in doing good, for at the proper time we will reap a harvest if we do not give up. The *Coalition for Life* is committed to press on until abortion ends" (Brazos Valley Coalition for Life Annual Newsletter 2004).

Political harassment also serves the larger pro-life movement by keeping opposition to abortion salient, visible, and providing political currency to politicians willing to endorse a pro-life agenda. The Coalition for Life has been featured in local, state, and national newspapers and televisions shows; on the thirtieth anniversary of *Roe,* the coalition was featured on ABC's *Nightline.* National pro-life organizations highlight the achievements of grassroots organizations to encourage new local groups to form. In the past twelve months, the coalition's organization (including structure, tactics, and purpose) has been duplicated in five more communities across Texas (Brazos Valley Coalition for Life Annual Newsletter 2004).

For politicians, affiliating with local pro-life groups is an asset, providing media attention and name recognition among a constituency that will vote solely based on the abortion issue. Texas state senator Steve Ogden is very supportive of the coalition and frequently gives the keynote address at larger coalition events. In turn, he earns the loyal support of coalition members who regularly feature his name in their newsletters. The visibility of the protesters aids the entire movement in garnering legislative victories. In conjunction with movement cohesion, engaging in political harassment achieves movement goals. Anecdotally, the sheer visibility of the movement provides politicians with an incentive to endorse anti-abortion legislation, particularly at the state level where pro-choice groups are generally weaker compared to pro-life groups. Strategically, protest is much more cost effective than lobbying, crafting legislation, filing lawsuits, or engaging in electoral campaigns. Although financial costs are incurred via protest, these costs pale in comparison to the costs associated with operating in formalized political arenas. Anti-abortion protest is also largely unrestricted (the 1994 Freedom of Access to Clinic Entrances [FACE] Act being a notable exception) by the government; activists experience minimal restrictions during their protest.

Political harassment creates costs for clinic clients, employees, and even supporters of abortion rights. Many of these costs—added security expenses, higher insurance premiums, closing clinic facilities—have anecdotally been documented. Political harassment also introduces emotional costs to clinic employees and clients. Physicians not only worry about their own safety, but they also worry about the safety and emotional well-being of their families. Clinic workers contend with protesters appearing at their home, having their children approached by pro-life members in public places, and having their professional reputations muddied by pro-life protest campaigns. The possibility of these activities occurring functions as a deterrent to physicians who believe in abortion rights but find the associated burdens too costly (Interview with an ob-gyn abortion provider, December 2003). Physicians who specialize in other fields but are supportive of abortion rights are also vulnerable to pro-life harassment. Internist "Dr. Barry" supports the local Planned Parenthood in her community. She has been the target of anti-abortion harassment. Dr. Barry has been called "Dr. Death," she has received anonymous, harassing e-mails, and her colleagues have received letters informing them that she helps "kill babies in the Brazos Valley" (Interview with a physician, December 2003).

The distress it causes clients has also been noted by clinic employees as well as clients themselves. "I think that they have a harassing presence out there because they are intimidating to our clients that have never seen them before. Our clients are not just from Bryan/College Station, they come from all over" (Interview with a Planned Parenthood intern, December 2003).

The pro-life movement relies on politically harassing tactics because they are an effective strategy that can easily coexist with an institutionalized strategy to end abortion. Harassment is relatively cheap to implement, generates publicity, and introduces costs to clinic employees and clients. Intimidation is a more immediate way to deter clinic employees from providing abortion services relative to working on long-term legislation aimed at incrementally restricting services. Moreover, neither patients nor employees possess the necessary resources to curb the activities—they are politically weak nongovernmental actors. Clinic employees are also more vulnerable to political harassment because they must contend with it on a regular basis compared to patients who typically face limited exposure to protest activities.

Conclusion

This chapter has weaved together and built upon theories from the social movement, morality politics, and political violence traditions. These respective literatures theoretically aid in explaining the origin, maintenance, and longevity of the pro-life movement. Yet to fully appreciate the scope of the movement's political reach, our framework needs to include a more thorough examination of the movement's reliance on gray-area activities. Pro-life activists have blurred the boundaries between unconventional protest and harassment.

Abortion politics continue to play out in an environment that has witnessed extreme forms of anti-abortion violence. The pro-life movement's unconventional activities must be viewed in a multidimensional context that includes political harassment. Similar to other protest tactics, political harassment is a rational, instrumental resource used to achieve a movement's goals and engender movement cohesion. Only by understanding the nuances of movement tactics can we begin to systematically examine the impact of the pro-life movement in American politics and begin to learn about other social movements that are primarily concerned with morality issues.

Chapter 2

SHIFTING CONTEXTS
The History of Abortion in America

Since my last little girl was born, I can safely say I have been pregnant fifteen times, most of the time doing things myself to get out of it and no one knows how I have suffered from the effect of it, but I would rather die than bring as many children into the world as my mother did and have nothing to offer them.
—Anonymous letter written to Margaret Sanger in 1923

The decision whether to have children is one of the most life-altering decisions faced by women. Child-rearing responsibilities disproportionately fall on women, so it is not surprising that the desire to regulate fertility has long been a concern for women. Abortion has historically been used by women as a form of birth control and as a means to terminate an unwanted pregnancy. Women have routinely taken advantage of abortion practices, although its legality and permissibility have been inconsistent throughout history. Women's ability to make these decisions freely and to have significant control over reproduction has been repeatedly challenged, with varying degrees of zealousness and efficacy, by institutions ranging from the state, to the medical community, to religious organizations.

Roe v. Wade is thought of as the catalyst to the modern abortion debate, but the current struggle over reproductive rights has roots in the nineteenth century. Today's abortion debate is ensconced in morality politics and framed as a straightforward question of "life" versus "choice" by adversaries and supporters of abortion rights. Questions of morality have underscored the discussion of abortion practices, but unlike today's simplistic approach, ancient debates provoked thoughtful analysis where theologically difficult questions regarding ensoulment, the value of life, and the human costs of unwanted pregnancy were debated (McFarlane and Meier 2000). Morality concerns were only one aspect of abortion practices. Population control, fertility regulation, maternal health, and cultural norms also factored into abortion discourse. Sentiment toward American abortion practices has also been shaped by much more than moral support or opposition toward the practice. Table 1 presents a timeline of significant events related to abortion, events that span hundreds of years. Throughout the history of abortion practices in America, the issue has been tied to greater societal concerns over economics, reproductive health, and the changing status of women, all of which have repeatedly transformed this private issue into a political issue.

"Accidents" and Abortion in Colonial America

Moral rhetoric has always accompanied the abortion debate, but the historical record indicates that abortion, or the circumstances leading up to one, are complex, more than a question of morality. Unwanted pregnancies present society with multiple dilemmas ranging from economic problems to a confrontation with sexuality, in particular women's sexuality (Morone 2003; Schnucker 1975; Brodie 1994). These modern dilemmas can be traced back to colonial America.

Puritan culture disapproved of sexual activity outside of marriage for both moral and economic reasons. The church viewed premarital fornication as a sin and believed sex was a privilege reserved for married couples. Puritans spent a lot of energy monitoring young people's behavior and steering them away from committing sexual transgressions outside of marriage (Morone 2003; Schnucker 1975; Dayton 1997). Despite their best efforts, much like today, Puritans were competing with the passions of youth. Many unmarried Puritans engaged in premarital sex, which was most obviously evidenced by pregnancy.

An out-of-wedlock birth posed a real problem in Puritan society. An unmarried pregnant woman was visible proof that the sin of sexual activity outside of marriage had occurred. Equally problematic, her offspring presented an economic hardship for society (Schnucker 1975). Colonial America was agrarian, composed of small, rural communities that frequently faced economic adversity. Although children were a valuable labor asset on the farm, orphaned children, whose parents suffered untimely deaths, posed an economic burden on the communities that became responsible for their welfare (Schnucker 1975). Children who were conceived outside of marriage presented yet another finan-

TABLE 1. Timeline of Abortion History in America

1712	Benjamin Wadsworth, future president of Harvard, writes one of the first documents about the immorality of abortion.
1742	Early documented abortion case in Pomfret, Connecticut.
1800s	Average 7.04 children per woman.
1809	Massachusetts Supreme Court dismisses an abortion case on the grounds of insufficient evidence. The Court rules that the prosecution failed to prove that an abortion occurred prior to quickening.
1821	Connecticut enacts the first abortion regulation in country. The new law prohibits the use of dangerous poisons to induce an abortion after quickening.
1831	Dr. Charles Knowlton publishes *The Private Companion of Young Married People*, which contains information about birth control and discusses the importance of practicing family planning.
1835	Advertisements for abortion services regularly appear in newspapers.
1847	The American Medical Association is formed.
1855	Abortion services are available in New York, New Orleans, Cincinnati, Louisville, Cleveland, Chicago, and Indianapolis.
1859	AMA passes anti-abortion resolution.
Late 1800s	Formal "Birth Control" and "Feminist" movements are formed. "Social Purity" movement forms.
1871	Two hundred full-time abortion providers are practicing in New York City.
1873	Federal law, the Act for the Suppression of Trade and Circulation of Obscene Literature and Articles of Immoral Use (commonly called the Comstock Act) is passed. The Comstock Act prohibits the trading, possession, sale, or mailing of contraception.
1900s	Average 3.56 children per woman.
1909	Fine for violating the Comstock Act increases to $5,000 and/or up to five years imprisonment.
1920 and 1921	The League of Women Voters refuses to include birth control reform on its agenda.
1921	Margaret Sanger forms American Birth Control League, begins to solicit support from doctors, social workers, and left-wing faction of eugenics movement.
1936	In the *U.S. v. One Package* case, the U.S. Court of Appeals rules that prescribing contraception to save a person's life or to promote a person's well being is not a violation of the Comstock Act.
1937	The American Medical Association Committee on Contraception reverses its position and gives tentative support for using contraception practices.
1938	374 birth control clinics operating in the United States.
1942	U.S. Surgeon General authorizes federal funding for birth control. Alan Guttmacher emerges as vocal supporter of abortion reform.
1950s	Media begin to sympathize with lack of abortion access for poor women.
1961	California begins proposing revisions to existing abortion laws.
1962	Sherri Finkbine receives public attention for abortion.
1963	The Society for Human Abortions forms.
1965	In *Griswold v. Connecticut*, the Supreme Court invalidates Connecticut's anti-contraception statute, establishing a constitutional right to privacy for married couples.
1967	The National Organization for Women adds reproductive rights to its bill of rights.
1969	NARAL (the National Association for the Repeal of Abortion Laws) is formed.
1970	Hawaii becomes the first state to legalize abortion for state residents only. New York follows, does not include residency requirement.
1971	The Supreme Court overturns a Massachusetts' law that prohibited unmarried people from using contraception in *Eisenstadt v. Baird*.
1973	The Supreme Court legalizes abortion in its *Roe v. Wade* decision.

cial drain on society and, importantly, a burden that Puritans believed could have been prevented by abstaining from premarital sex.

Communities implemented harsh penalties intended to curtail out-of-wedlock childbirth and deter the economic hardship posed by "illegitimate" children. Several states used a combination of fines and physical punishment, which legally applied to both men and women who violated the law (Schnucker 1975; Dayton 1997). In practice, men were seldom convicted or punished because it was difficult to prove whether they had a role in the pregnancy. Paternity could not be scientifically established based on the technology available in colonial times. In the unlikely case they were convicted, men had access to capital, such as property, that they could use to pay the fines. Women did not fare as well in Puritan society. They were more easily convicted for the crime because of the obvious physical relationship between a woman and her child. Women also lacked the means to pay the fines because it was illegal for them to inherit or own property.

Women were typically punished with public lashings. For example, in Maryland a court sentenced Agnes Taylor to twelve public lashings for having a child outside of marriage, a fairly lenient punishment considering the maximum penalty for an illegitimate birth was thirty-nine lashes (Schnucker 1975). Connecticut punished premarital pregnancy with up to ten lashes and a five-pound fine; the maximum penalty in Massachusetts was a public whipping or a ten-pound fine. Attempting to prevent illegitimacy, Maryland also enacted penalties specifically intended to punish men. Any man convicted of fathering a child outside of marriage was stripped of his right to hold office or testify in court (Schnucker 1975).

Other women escaped public lashings by entering into a speedily arranged marriage to the father of the child—a solution that has been very common throughout history (Solinger 2000). Approximately one in ten women was pregnant at the time of her marriage in colonial Massachusetts, as were as many as one in three in the Chesapeake Bay (Schnucker 1975). Although marriage provided a solution, it did not absolve people of their sexual lawlessness. Puritans fined couples that had a child too quickly after marriage.

Despite the legal penalties and cultural humiliation associated with out-of-wedlock pregnancies, it was fairly common in colonial America (Brodie 1994; Schnucker 1975). Fearing legal and societal sanctions, many women eliminated an unwanted out-of-wedlock pregnancy by obtaining an abortion. Abortion was a regular practice in early America; however, it was not a very hygienic or safe practice, particularly when surgery was involved.

One of the earliest legally documented court cases pertaining to abortion highlights the medical risks involved with the procedure. In 1742, in the village of Pomfret, Connecticut, seventeen-year-old Sarah Grosvenor became sexually involved with twenty-seven-year-old Amasa Sessions and became pregnant (Dayton 1997). Sarah and Amasa were typical colonial American citizens who shared similar familial backgrounds. Both came from established, prominent families in Pomfret. Amasa was not interested in marrying Sarah; he wanted her to abort the pregnancy, and he arranged for Sarah to take abortifacients. Though Sarah took the abortifacients for several months, they did not cause her to miscarry. Fearing that the pregnancy would soon become visible, Amasa found a doctor willing to perform an abortion. The surgery ultimately led to Sarah's miscarriage and death from an infection several days later (Dayton 1997).

Three years later, officials investigated Sarah's death, uncovering the premarital liaison that resulted in her pregnancy, abortion, and death. Amasa's role in Sarah's death was overlooked, and all charges against him were dropped. The community forgave Amasa for his youthful mistakes, and he went on to live his life as a respected town citizen (Dayton 1997). The case of Amasa and Sarah illustrates the stark disparity in punishment and outcomes resulting from an unwanted pregnancy for women and men in colonial America. Men were often absolved of taking any responsibility for an unwanted pregnancy, whereas women disproportionately paid in many ways, most dramatically with their lives. Variations of this gendered pattern of blame and punishment continue in modern American society.

Abortion in Nineteenth-Century America

As the nineteenth century approached, America started to transition from an agrarian society into an urban and industrialized society. The need for many children during colonial times was disappearing, subsequently causing major demographic changes in America. Fertility rates dove from an average of 7.04 children per woman in 1800 to an average of 3.56 per woman in 1900 (Blanchard 1994; Reed 1978). The declining fertility rates were a clear indication that women were increasingly taking advantage of some form of fertility regulation. Women continued to rely on abortion for birth control as well as termination of an unwanted pregnancy.

Midwives had knowledge of herbal abortifacients, and select women had access to cookbooks and diaries containing recipes for herbal compounds intended to control fertility (Tone 1997, 2001; Rubin 1994). In 1831, two influential books were published that disseminated contraception information to a larger audience. Dr. Charles Knowlton wrote *The Private Companion of Young Married People,* which contained medical information about birth control and a discussion on the importance of practicing family planning. The same year Robert Dale Owens wrote *Moral Physiology* (Tone 2001).

Although an organized birth control movement did not exist in nineteenth-century America, the societal taboo against publicly discussing family planning was beginning to diminish (Brodie 1994; Burnham 1973). Advertisements for contraceptive services and disguised advertisements for abortion services regularly appeared in newspapers. By the mid-eighteen hundreds contraception information was widely available in books and pamphlets that could be bought from bookstores, newsstands, peddlers, or stationers, or by mail order. Condoms were sold in barbershops, and they were readily accessible in establishments where men frequently congregated. Several other birth control techniques were also available ranging from vaginal sponges to cervical caps to douche powders (Bullough and Bullough 1994; Finch and Green 1963; Gordon 1976). Abortion continued to be relied on for family planning purposes.

Changing conceptions about family, quality of life, and motherhood corresponded with the declining fertility rates and family planning publications. In particular the norms structuring marriages were being challenged. Marriage primarily served an economic function in society, providing women with economic stability and men with domestic labor. Under this arrangement, women were viewed as property and often suffered from their husbands' emotional, physical, or sexual cruelty (Griswold 1986; Freedman 1982). Women had limited legal rights (for example, they could not vote, own property, or sue another person in court), therefore there was little refuge from their situations. Women's advocates began lobbying to elevate the status of women in the domestic sphere, hoping to inspire a new recognition and appreciation for the important role women played in the household (Freedman 1982; Griswold 1986).

Women were demanding better treatment in their marriages, and their efforts started to materialize into an improved status, at least for upper-class women, within the household (Griswold 1986; Freedman 1982). For bourgeois women, their role within the household started to expand beyond their traditional roles of domestic servant and mother. Upper-class women were increasingly called upon to symbolize their husbands' affluence by being visible in society and devoting more of their free time to charitable events (Tone 1997, 12; Blanchard 1994, 14–15). These new socialite expectations were much easier to achieve with fewer child-rearing responsibilities.

In the working class, reducing family size was born out of economic necessity. Limiting the number of children in a family was the most obvious means of economic survival in newly industrializing America. Yet, while the desire to reduce family size was felt by many, it was not an attainable goal for all women. The nineteenth-century downward fertility trend masks an important relationship between wealth and access to birth control (Reed 1978; Brodie 1994). Declining fertility levels primarily occurred among those who were more affluent in society. Fertility rates for poorer women and immigrants remained high (Langer 1963). The disparity in fertility rates between the upper and lower classes alarmed many prominent people in society who began to question the desirability of this situation.

Certain enclaves of elitist society noticed that immigrants and poor women continued to have large families, leading them to voice their fears that there would be a shortage of "valuable" citizens in the future[1] (Meehan 1998; Roberts 1999; Weisbord 1973). They saw the declining fertility rates as an indication of an impending "race suicide," prompting many elites, including Theodore Roosevelt, the twenty-sixth president of the United States, to publicly condemn the practice of having smaller families (Blanchard 1994; Gordon 2002). The call for larger families was ignored by the middle-class population. Their fertility rates remained low and stable, while fertility rates remained high for the poor.

Urbanization and industrialization contributed to new social problems that were particularly acute among the poor. Social observers began to recognize that poor people did not have the financial capacity to meet their children's needs adequately (Reed 1978; Tone 2001). Lack of access to birth control, large family size, and poverty were identified as key contributors to the miserable living conditions experienced by immigrants and the poor[2] (Tone 2001; Reed 1978; Brodie 1994).

Throughout the late 1800s and early 1900s Margaret Sanger—one of the most important birth control advocates and founder of Planned Parenthood—was vocal about the inherent unfairness of the situation (Sanger 1970).

The woman of the upper middle class has all available knowledge and implements to prevent conception. The woman of the lower middle class is struggling for this knowledge. She tries various methods of prevention and after a few years of experience plus medical advice succeeds in discovering some method suitable to her individual self. The woman of the people is the only one left in ignorance of this information. . . . As is well known, a law exists forbidding the imparting of information on this subject, the penalty being several years' imprisonment. Is it not time to defy law? . . . What right has any government to inflict such tyranny on women as to keep this knowledge from them by law? (1923, 181–82)

Sanger ushered in a formal birth control movement at the end of the nineteenth century (Kennedy 1970; Sanger 1970; Douglas 1970).

Throughout the nineteenth century, America was not only changing demographically and economically but also culturally. Urbanization and industrialization brought new opportunities for people and simultaneously exacerbated existing societal ills. As America grappled with these changes, different groups emerged with competing ideas of how to solve social problems. Toward the end of the nineteenth century, the first feminist movement was emerging. Women were demanding "voluntary motherhood" and, among the more radical women, voluntary sex[3] (Tone 1997; Gordon 1976).

At the other end of the spectrum, the "social purity" movement surfaced and gained political support in the late 1800s (Morone 2003). Members of the social purity movement were involved in numerous issues such as reestablishing traditional morals and values, promoting temperance, Sunday closing laws, and reining in prostitution (Tone 2001; Reed 1978). They also had an active committee, mainly composed of ministers and physicians, dedicated to the suppression of vice. The committee lobbied the government to take an active role in limiting individual behavior it perceived as obscene, including restricting access to birth control and abortion services (Brodie 1994; Freedman 1982). All of these factors form the background in which abortion initially surfaced as a public issue.

Early Nineteenth-Century Abortion Laws and Practice

One of the earliest documents referring to abortion practices in America can be traced to a declaration written by Benjamin Wadsworth—future president of Harvard College—in 1712. He wrote that those responsible for contributing to an abortion, either directly or indirectly, were guilty of murder in God's eyes (Olasky 1988). Around this time, midwives practicing in New York City were required to take an oath swearing that they would abide by a regulatory law. The oath included a provision mandating midwives to abstain from administering any medicine, potion, or poison that would cause a woman to have a spontaneous abortion (Olasky 1988).

Historical evidence indicates that the midwives' oath and the Hippocratic oath were not closely followed.[4] Abortion was not only a common practice, it was a visible one (Rubin 1994). As America moved into the nineteenth century there was very little regulation of abortion services (Smith 1997; Tone 1997; Luker 1984). Guidelines pertaining to abortion were inherited from the English common law tradition,[5] which generally held that an abortion prior to quickening[6] was at most a misdemeanor (Reagan 1997; Rubin 1994; Luker 1984). Violations of this law were difficult to prosecute and generally received little support from authorities because a woman was the only reliable person who could testify as to when quickening occurred. For example, in 1809, the Massachusetts Supreme Court dismissed an abortion case because the prosecution failed to reliably establish if the woman had experienced quickening in her pregnancy (Cook, Jelen, and Wilcox 1992; Luker 1984).

The Massachusetts Supreme Court was reiterating the common law regulating abortion at the time. The first statutory abortion regulation did not surface until 1821 in the state of Connecticut. The intent of the statute was to protect women's health rather than eliminate elective abortions (Tribe 1992; Blanchard 1994). In the 1800s abortion methods were dangerous; poison was frequently administered to pregnant women to induce an abortion. Connecticut's statute only prohibited the use of dangerous poisons to induce abortion after quickening occurred (Tribe 1992).

Aside from the reliance on English common law and minor regulations in a couple of states, abortion practices were unmonitored. Society was fairly tolerant of elective abortion services. During the 1830s disguised advertisements for abortion services regularly appeared in newspapers (Olasky 1988; Tone 1997). Many of the ads claimed to help women with "obstinate cases" of "menstrual blockage," a condition resulting from pregnancy (Olasky 1988, 53). The following represents a typical advertisement for abortion services:

Dr. J.E. and Dr. Mary Grant GRADUATE PHYSICIANS FEMALE SPECIALISTS FOR 15 YEARS GUARANTEE to cure the longest and most obstinate female cases in 24 hours by STRICTLY up to date, ANTISEPTIC, SAFE and painless METHODS without delay from home or work. TRAV-ELERS can be treated and return home the same day. We never have a failure. Confinements and adoption arranged. PATIENTS unsuccessfully treated elsewhere will obtain relief at once. HONORABLE, RELIABLE, SCIENTIFIC TREATMENT GUARANTEED. Consult us freely and confidentially; it will save you time and money. (Olasky 1988, 53; emphasis in original)

Advertisements frequently stated that abortions were justifiable for economic purposes and to prevent both mental and physical health problems. Throughout the 1850s and 1860s, abortion services were readily available in New York, New Orleans, Cincinnati, Louisville, Cleveland, Chicago, and Indianapolis (Olasky 1988). Some estimates place the abortion rate at one induced abortion for every four live births during this time period (Tribe 1992).

The permissibility and availability of abortion services began to wane in the late 1800s. The impetus for change came from the medical community, which was undergoing a transition of its own. Abortion services were available, and frequently used, in the 1800s, but they were not very safe. Statistics from New York estimate a 30 percent death rate from infections following abortion surgery, regardless of whether the surgery was performed in a hospital (Tribe 1992). While there was a genuine and legitimate health concern related to abortion services, evidence suggests that the medical community's crusade against abortion was primarily based on economic and elitist concerns (Rubin 1994; Tribe 1992; Luker 1984). The medical community successfully framed abortion in a new light and moved the provision and regulation of abortion services into the exclusive domain of doctors.

The Nineteenth-Century Anti-Abortion Crusade

The nineteenth-century medical profession was not regulated. Medical professionals who received some formal training found themselves in direct competition with midwives, herbalists, alternative healers, and quacks (Reagan 1997; Luker 1984). Essentially anyone could claim to be a physician and advertise under the auspices of being a medical expert. For example, Madame Costello, a successful abortion provider, called herself a female physician and claimed the following about her abortifacient pills.

Their certainty of action has long been acknowledged by the medical profession, and hundreds that have uselessly tried various boasted remedies;
indeed so sure are these pills in their effects, that care is sometimes necessary in their use though they contain no medicine detrimental to the constitution. (Olasky 1988, 15)

Being an abortion provider was a lucrative business. In 1840, one abortion
provider based in New York City spent $650 a year on abortion advertisements,
when the price of a decent apartment was between $5 and $6 a month. Within
five years, this abortion provider opened offices in Boston, Philadelphia,
Newark, and Providence, as well as five different offices in New York (Olasky
1988). By 1871, New York City had two hundred full-time abortion providers,
even though the city's population was less than one million (Rubin 1994, 12).
Abortions were in high demand, and being a provider was profitable.

Medical schools were similar to modern vocational schools; entrance standards were minimal, and so anyone who could afford the tuition was accepted
into medical school (Luker 1984). Administrators were reluctant to fail any students that were paying their fees because it was the only income source for the
schools (Rubin 1994; Luker 1984). Incidentally, there was a desire on the part of
"real" doctors to regulate and license the profession. The real doctors were generally from the upper classes of society, had more expensive training—frequently including an overseas tour—and primarily served an upper-class clientele, in comparison to their sectarian competitors (Reagan 1997; Tone 1997).

Limiting the availability of abortion services, and making it a procedure that
only formally trained doctors could provide, created an opportunity for the
more affluent medical community to distinguish itself from its competitors and
monopolize the market for abortion services (Blanchard 1994, 12–13). In 1847 the
American Medical Association (AMA) was formed to improve the standards of
medicine and upgrade the profession as a whole. After establishing a formal
institution, physicians began to attack the legitimacy of practicing abortion
providers.

The AMA formally launched its crusade against abortion in 1859 by passing
an anti-abortion resolution as well as encouraging political actors to get
involved in the fight (Reagan 1997; Garrow 1994; Tribe 1992). Wanting to legitimate the medical field, the AMA developed a repertoire of action designed to
reflect a professional image. Formal tactics were employed by the AMA such as
lobbying judges, lawyers, and state legislatures (Rubin 1994; Olasky 1988). Over

the next several years the AMA stepped up its efforts and recruited leaders from the AMA national annual meetings (Reagan 1997, 82). For example, in his 1860 speech, AMA president-elect Henry Miller devoted the majority of his presentation to denouncing the prevalence of abortion practices in society.

Growing increasingly frustrated with its floundering political efforts to criminalize abortion—namely, trying to restrict abortion advertising and prosecuting abortion providers who were not members of the formally trained medical profession—the AMA started a public crusade against abortion. In 1864 the AMA held a contest challenging doctors to write anti-abortion books designed for the general public to understand (Tone 1997, 2001; Luker 1984). Trained physicians were beginning to frame the abortion issue, which they would come to dominate for nearly a century.

Framing the Abortion Issue in the Nineteenth Century

Responding to the AMA's contest, doctors increased their efforts to publish books and editorials pointing out the medical and moral reasons abortion should be illegal. As the campaign against abortion progressed, the rhetoric used by the AMA became more dramatic (Rubin 1994; Tone 1997). The AMA circulated a report "denouncing the perverted views of morality underlying abortion" (Olasky 1988, 29). The report also contained the following warning for doctors performing abortions: "We shall discover an enemy in the camp. . . . It is false brethren we have to fear; men who are false to their profession, false to principle, false to honor, false to humanity, false to God" (Olasky 1988, 29).

Many of the writings claimed that the popular and legal acceptance of abortion practices was based on the faulty belief that pregnancy was not a continuous process (Rubin 1994). Physicians argued that women, by virtue of their ignorance on the subject, were inadvertently committing a sin because they relied on the English common law tradition where having an abortion prior to quickening was acceptable (Reagan 1997). Medical doctors, on the other hand, claimed to possess expert knowledge on the subject.

Medicalizing the abortion issue and framing it as an educational and ethical issue provided physicians with leverage over their competitors. Claiming scientific expertise and a stronger morality, doctors were able to readily distinguish themselves from other practitioners (Reagan 1997; Rubin 1994). The provision of abortion services moved away from midwives, who had been providing reproductive health care to women for centuries, into the purview of physicians, who were establishing their reputations for possessing exclusive expertise about reproductive health.

The medicalization of reproductive health services in turn absolved women of taking responsibility for their decision to abort. Women receiving abortions were from affluent segments of society. Rather than denouncing upper-class women, who made up a significant portion of their clientele, doctors argued that women simply lacked the scientific expertise possessed by medical professionals to make "correct" decisions about reproduction. This change in rhetoric implied that a woman's decision to abort a pregnancy no longer reflected her immorality; instead, it reflected her ignorance. Ironically, evidence suggests that most people were aware of the scientific fact that pregnancy was a continuous process (Luker 1984). Casting abortion in this frame ignored the reality that women had been making reproductive choices and decisions, based on their life circumstances and individual sense of morality, for centuries and started to set the stage for medical intervention into women's choices governing reproduction. This pattern marked a significant departure in reproductive decision making and continues to be the norm in modern society.

As the AMA's anti-abortion campaign continued to grow, activists outside the medical community became involved. Physicians teamed up with the faction of the social purity movement dedicated to the suppression of vice in society (Tone 2001; Morone 2003). These reformers lobbied the government to implement stricter laws regulating abortion practices. By 1870, Louis Jennings, a conservative Christian, began a more intensive crusade against abortion. His tactics, which are frequently used in the modern anti-abortion movement, included using graphic rhetoric, protesting at providers' homes, and going undercover to infiltrate abortion clinics (Rubin 1994, 19–21; Olasky 1988). By and large, religious organizations were absent in the quest to criminalize abortion. Toward the end of the century, religious opposition to abortion began to grow; however, the medical community had initially influenced and stimulated the clergy's involvement (Tribe 1992; Reagan 1997).

Exploiting and Creating Political Opportunities for the Anti-Abortion Movement

Political support began to follow the organized campaigns against abortion. The mobilization and subsequent collective action of "legitimate" doctors resulted in legal changes that provided physicians with a monopoly over abortion services (Tone 1997, 2001). In March 1873, the U.S. Congress passed the Act for the Suppression of Trade in and Circulation of Obscene Literature and Articles of Immoral Use, commonly called the Comstock Act. The Comstock Act included a provision banning any advertisements for abortions, representing the first federal involvement in abortion-related policies. By 1909, the fine for violating this provision was increased to $5,000 and/or imprisonment for up to five years (Olasky 1988; Tone 2001).

Within two decades the medical community's campaign against abortion was successful. Several more laws, referred to as the "little Comstock laws," followed the original. Some states passed more restrictive laws than found in the original Comstock Act. Over the next decade and a half, forty anti-abortion statutes were passed in the United States; by 1910 nearly every state had anti-abortion laws (Graber 1996; Rubin 1994; Tribe 1992; Tone 2001). Most of the laws contained a clause authorizing licensed physicians to perform therapeutic abortions, which finally provided the medical community with a monopoly over the issue.[7]

Following the passage of these laws, abortion faded from the public and political front, becoming a nonissue from the early 1900s to the 1950s. Media coverage of abortion was rare. The few stories that appeared across the country mainly focused on the arrest of physicians who performed illegal abortions, not the women who sought out abortions. Maternal death and other grave side effects of illegal abortions were neglected in media stories (Olasky 1988). The absence of public discourse about abortion did not stop the practice.

Women who had access to necessary resources like money, transportation, and time continued to have abortions at approximately the same rate as they did before abortion was criminalized (Tribe 1992). The availability of abortion services depended on the social status of a woman, whom she knew, and the attitude and practice of her physician or hospital. Many government officials and agencies did not actively enforce the anti-abortion laws. The barriers for women wanting abortion services were frequently demographic, not legal.[8] Posner (1992) has estimated that 70 percent of the abortions occurring today would have occurred prior to the legalization of abortion (Solinger 1998; Graber 1996, 41). The hypocrisy of abortion being illegal yet widely used by wealthier women continued until the 1950s.

Abortion from the 1950s to *Roe v. Wade*

As the twentieth century progressed, abortion issues were eventually reintroduced to the public, largely paved by the efforts of Margaret Sanger's birth control movement. Margaret Sanger founded the American Birth Control League
(ABCL) in 1921 and published a monthly journal, the *Birth Control Review*
(*BCR*). The ABCL called for changes in the laws prohibiting the distribution
and use of contraception (Douglas 1970; Sanger 1970). Sanger exploited loop-
holes in the law allowing her to legally operate a physician-run birth control
clinic.

Despite the growing success of Sanger's reform efforts, public and political
opposition was still prevalent. Many in society were not ready to embrace
Sanger's radical ideas such as supporting individual rights and eliminating governmental influence over women's private lives (Tone 2001; Brodie 1994; Douglas 1970). The rhetoric in the *Birth Control Review* was off-putting to many; it
frequently criticized the government and likened the members of the judicial
system to lifeless, antiquated relics of the past who were fifty years behind in
their beliefs. The majority of society was also resistant to Sanger's tactics. She
was a proponent of using civil disobedience and challenged reformers to break
the Comstock laws. In the end, most Americans were resistant to publicly
embracing family planning because it necessitated discussing sex and sexuality,
two topics that were not openly discussed in early twentieth-century American
society (Freedman 1982; Griswold 1986).

Sanger ran into several political obstacles. The public was uncomfortable
with the topic of birth control, and many politicians and political organizations
were similarly uneasy (Sanger 1970). In 1919 the Supreme Court refused to hear
an appeal to Sanger's 1917 conviction, meaning that the Comstock laws could
not be legally challenged or overturned (Douglas 1970; McCann 1994). Shortly
thereafter, two women's political organizations rejected Sanger's plea for birth
control reform.[9] The League of Women Voters would not include birth control
reform on its 1920 agenda, and at the 1921 National Woman's Party convention,
organizers prevented the issue from even being introduced on the convention
floor (McCann 1994; Kennedy 1970).

Sanger also encountered difficulty gaining public support from doctors. In 1920,
she sponsored the first American Birth Control Conference in New York. For
the conference, several rooms were rented to run a birth control clinic, but it

ended up being canceled because the physician hired to run the clinic backed out (McCann 1994; Kennedy 1970; Douglas 1970). Several years later, Sanger approached the League of Women Voters and the National Woman's Party and was met with the same resistance from both organizations she had experienced in 1920 and 1921.

Growing frustrated with the slow progress of reform, Sanger turned her efforts to public education and outreach (Sanger 1970; Kennedy 1970). She believed that the only way to make progress was to gain widespread public support for birth control reform. Sanger began to solicit support from doctors, social workers, and the left-wing faction of the eugenics movement.[10] Despite the public and political resistance to reform, the birth control movement continued to make progress.

The first significant victory came in 1936 from the ruling in *U.S. v. One Package.* In the *One Package* ruling, the U.S. Court of Appeals determined that medically prescribing contraception to save a person's life or to promote a person's well-being was not illegal under the Comstock Act (McCann 1994; Tone 2001; Reed 1978). The Court argued that if the creators of the Comstock Act had known (sixty years earlier) the dangers associated with pregnancy and the benefits of contraception they would not have considered all forms of birth control as obscene. The Court effectively allowed physicians to import, sell, and distribute contraception to their married clients. Following this ruling, the American Medical Association Committee on Contraception revoked its 1936 statement condemning birth control and organizations that sponsored it, and tentatively endorsed birth control practices (Reed 1978).

Public opinion had dramatically shifted. National surveys conducted in 1937 demonstrated that 71 percent of the adult population supported the use of contraception, and 70 percent believed that legal reform was necessary (Tone 2001). By 1938, there were 374 birth control clinics operating in America even though it was illegal to advertise their services (Sanger 1970; Tone 2001). Contraception for married women, particularly diaphragms and cervical caps, were in short supply (Reed 1978; Tone 2001). Those women who were able to purchase a diaphragm either through a physician or pharmacy often ended up with the wrong size. Other problems arose with diaphragm usage: after one year of use it is only 80 percent effective, it requires planning, it is difficult to clean in a house that does not have running water, and women who are uncomfortable with their bodies have difficulty inserting it (Tone 2001).

Poor women continued to have limited access to birth control education and contraceptive devices (Tone 2001; McCann 1994; Gordon 1976). Even though the diaphragm had some limitations, it was the most effective technique available at the time, but a woman had to obtain a medical prescription for one. Poor women were less likely to have a private physician who could prescribe a diaphragm. The U.S. surgeon general responded to this situation in 1942 by authorizing federal funding for birth control through the maternal and child health funds. First lady Eleanor Roosevelt was also publicly supportive of birth control reform and very influential in many of the family planning decisions of the time (Tone 2001; McCann 1994; Brodie 1994).

The open political support led to some important changes, particularly for poor women (Petchesky 1997). In 1958, the municipal hospitals in New York City changed their birth control policy, allowing their doctors to prescribe birth control. Several other municipalities looked to the New York Board of Hospitals to set medical standards and shortly adopted similar policies (Brodie 1994; Tone 2001). This change expanded poor women's access to contraception because they were much more likely to seek treatment at a public hospital rather than through a private physician.

The liberalization of laws and attitudes toward birth control helped lessen the stigma governing discussions of abortion practices (McFarlane and Meier 2000; Brodie 1994). Physicians were increasingly confronted with medical contradictions and ethical dilemmas over the regulation of abortion services. Over time, medical knowledge became more sophisticated, improving both gynecological and obstetrical care. Technological advances reduced the need to perform an abortion to save a woman's life, making it more difficult for doctors to validate therapeutic abortions (Blanchard 1994; Rubin 1994). Thus two definitions of "protecting a woman's life" began to develop. One definition was a narrow interpretation of life where abortion was justifiable only when a woman's death would result from the continuation of the pregnancy. The second definition was much broader, considering concepts such as "quality of life" issues and the emotional or mental consequences of pregnancy for a woman.

The total discretion that doctors had over permitting abortion for medical purposes created obvious inequalities. For example, two women with identical situations and reasons for wanting an abortion could easily receive two different outcomes in their quest for a therapeutic abortion (Roberts 1999; Solinger 1998, 2000). Women who had more financial and educational resources were advantaged by this system (Solinger 1998, 2000; Roberts 1999; Luker 1984).

In the 1950s, media stories began to surface that focused on the plight of poor women in need of abortion services. Stories appeared in local newspapers around the country detailing the thousands of maternal deaths resulting from abortions, the unsafe conditions, and unnecessary risks women had to take because abortion services were illegal (Olasky 1988). Complications resulting from illegal abortion were so prevalent that many hospitals had wards specifically set aside for women injured from abortions. In the mid-1950s, Los Angeles County Hospital admitted over 2,000 women a year suffering from septic abortions; ten years later, Chicago Cook County Hospital was admitting over 5,000 women a year for the same illness (Graber 1996, 42–43).

In the 1955 Los Angeles County Hospital annual report, physicians stated that "the only significant causes of maternal death are complications of induced abortion, which has a death rate seven times greater than all other obstetrical conditions combined" (Graber 1996, 43). Seeing wards filled with women dying from botched abortions had a powerful impact on many doctors. The inherent unfairness of this gatekeeping system was questioned within the medical community, eventually leading many doctors, lawyers, and theologians to reevaluate their stance on abortion laws (Solinger 1998; Rubin 1994; Luker 1984). Ironically, the medical community, which was firmly entrenched in society as a professional discipline, possessed the organizational capacity to pursue collective action in reforming abortion laws even though it was primarily responsible for criminalizing abortion in the nineteenth century.

The Quest to Legalize Abortion

Private decisions that had been made solely by a physician were increasingly susceptible to scrutiny from other medical professionals. As the need to perform "medically necessary" abortions waned, doctors, fearing lawsuits, started to push for clarification of abortion policy. One quasi solution to the problem was the establishment of review boards that typically consisted of several doctors who decided which abortions were permissible. This solution caused further grief because it highlighted and exacerbated the arbitrary and unequal nature of the decision-making process (Solinger 1998, 21–23; Tribe 1992).

Abortion reform was initially instigated by professional elites in medical, public health, legal, and political fields. The medical community took a lead role in the call for reform. As early as 1942, Alan Guttmacher, chief of obstetrics at Sinai Hospital in Baltimore, emerged as a vocal supporter of abortion reform[11]

(Risen and Thomas 1998, 10). In conjunction with the birth control movement and the development of the population movement in the 1950s, other organizations began participating in abortion-related discourse. The efforts of these early reformers started to materialize. A couple of states began to entertain ideas of reforming abortion laws, and by 1961 state legislators in California were proposing revisions to existing abortion laws. Public discussion of abortion was still taboo and largely absent (Risen and Thomas 1998, 11).

Although professionals were the forerunners in the abortion reform movement, two highly publicized events occurred that catapulted abortion back into the public spotlight. In 1962, Sherri Finkbine, a popular television personality and a mother of four, discovered early in her fifth month of pregnancy that she had taken the drug thalidomide. The horrific side effects of thalidomide on a fetus were well documented; Finkbine and her doctor agreed that an immediate abortion was necessary. Wanting to warn other pregnant women about the dangers of the drug, Finkbine called a friend that worked at a local television station. The story ended up receiving a lot of attention, and the hospital where Finkbine was scheduled to have an abortion denied her one. Unable to abort in the United States, Finkbine flew to Sweden to obtain a legal abortion (Blanchard 1994, 23). Finkbine later wrote about her experience.

> I am not a doctor who can give you medical insights into the dangers of illegal abortion, nor a lawyer who can speak on the absurdities of our archaic laws. I am not a religious person with dogma decrying the murderous aspects of the subject. I am a person who is much more deeply involved than any of those people could ever be. I am a mother who desperately needed a pregnancy terminated. I can truthfully say to you that an abortion was to me a very sad, ugly experience, but definitely the lesser of two evils. (1967, 15)

Around the same time (1962–65), there was an outbreak of the German measles, which causes serious birth defects in embryos. Approximately 15,000 babies were born with grave defects resulting from the outbreak (Rubin 1994; Tribe 1992). Physicians were moved to reevaluate the restrictive abortion laws that allowed this tragedy to occur, and by 1967 the AMA issued a statement favoring the liberalization of abortion laws. Public outrage followed both the Finkbine and measles cases and started moving the parameters of the abortion debate beyond the scope of the medical field. Public opinion was beginning to lean toward abortion law reform, especially for hard cases. The National Opinion Research Center conducted a poll in 1965 that showed support for abortion services when a woman's life is at risk (73 percent), the fetus is suffering from severe birth defects (57 percent), or when the pregnancy resulted from sexual assault (59 percent) (Nossiff 2001, 37). Other interested parties—specifically women—began to get involved in the movement to legalize abortion. As the abortion debate expanded to include nonmedical activists, the framing of the abortion debate began to change from one based on medical arguments to one grounded in rights arguments.

The New Framing of Abortion

The absence of women from the early abortion reform efforts reflected the societal taboo prohibiting public discussions of sexuality and abortion. Abortion was perceived as a tool that would lead to promiscuity and a breakdown of traditional gender roles (Reagan 1997; Luker 1984). By the 1960s the improved status of women, which had been changing throughout the 1900s, was visible. Women were breaking with tradition by delaying marriage, attending college, and entering the labor force in unprecedented rates (Conover and Gray 1983, 51–53).

Coinciding with institutional changes, the public was experiencing a fundamental attitudinal change that had been largely absent in the nineteenth-century abortion debate. Two radically different views of individuals and family were developing throughout the 1900s and beginning to emerge in public discourse. The traditional perspective views the family as the central, divine societal institution. An individual's self-value comes from fulfilling her traditional gender role within the family. Adhering to specified male and female roles preserves the integrity of the family and, in turn, society (Falik 1983; Watson 1997).

The emerging conception of individualism represented a radical shift from believing in the centrality of the familial unit to believing in the importance of an individual's rights and freedom. Societal constraints including laws and adherence to traditional roles served to delimit individualism (Falik 1983; Watson 1997; Viguerie 1981). People were beginning to publicly challenge the legitimacy of traditional institutional arrangements, values, and morals. For example, in 1969, 70 percent of Americans disapproved of premarital sex, and a larger percentage objected to nudity in magazines and in Broadway shows. Four years later the proportion of Americans objecting to premarital sex and nudity had remarkably dropped by approximately 20 percent (Luker 1996, 87).

Within the context of enhancing individual rights and removing structural barriers to freedom, abortion discourse surfaced. As the abortion issue gained visibility, women began to get involved in the debate. In 1963 the Society for Human Abortions (SHA) was one of the first abortion rights organizations to form. SHA's involvement resulted in a new perspective on abortion, linking abortion rights to individual rights.[12] The SHA was one of the first organizations to frame abortion explicitly in this light. An early activist stated:

> When we talk about women's rights, we can get all the rights in the world—the right to vote, the right to go to school—and none of them means a dog-gone thing if we don't own the flesh we stand in, if we can't control what happens to us, if the whole course of our lives can be changed by somebody else that can get us pregnant by accident, or deceit, or by force. So I consider the right to elective abortion, whether you dream of doing it or not, is the cornerstone of the women's movement. (Luker 1984, 97)

The SHA set out to change public opinion, and, soon after, other women's organizations began to champion abortion rights. Modeling themselves after the civil rights and student movements' tactics, SHA activists declared civil disobedience against abortion laws. They set up networks that provided women with information on how to perform abortions or where to go to obtain one. Another women's organization, Jane, participated in civil disobedience. Jane trained its members to perform abortions for women in need of service, regardless of their financial circumstances (Kaplan 1998, 35). These early organizations launched a public education campaign including public lectures, speak-outs, and television and radio talk show appearances. All of these tactics were intended to raise people's consciousness and demonstrate how reproductive rights were crucial for women's equality (Kaplan 1998; Petchesky 1997; Luker 1984).

Reframing abortion as a rights issue significantly reduced the criminal and immoral representations of abortion. Articulating abortion as a rights issue had a profound effect on mobilizing women and moving abortion discourse into the public domain. Abortion was changing into an issue that women could be a part of rather than spectators to (Petchesky 1997). As more individuals came forward during speak-outs and started talking about the horrors, humiliation, and tragedy of illegal abortion, women increasingly recognized that abortion was not a personal problem, it was an issue that collectively affected women. By 1967, a year after its inception, the National Organization for Women added reproductive rights to its bill of rights (Risen and Thomas 1998; Rubin 1994).

The women's movement crystallized the framing of abortion by defining abortion rights as a fundamental aspect of equality and individual autonomy (Petchesky 1984, 662). By destigmatizing the issue, activists transformed abortion from a taboo subject to a political issue. New abortion rights groups formed, including the National Association for the Repeal of Abortion Laws (NARAL) in 1969.[13] NARAL and other national abortion rights groups established chapters throughout the country making coordinated action across states more feasible (Staggenborg 1999).

Discussing abortion rights in terms of women's equality was extremely successful in cultivating support from various enclaves of society. Pro-abortion advocates emerged from the medical community, women's groups, politicians, and even members of the clergy (Blanchard 1994; Petchesky 1997). In 1967, twenty-one members of the clergy announced in the *New York Times* that they would help women in need of abortion services locate safe providers (Tribe 1992).

New Political Opportunities within the States

The coalition of abortion rights supporters continued to grow throughout the 1960s. Activists cultivated bipartisan political support within state legislatures and Congress.[14] The reform movement was designed to liberalize abortion laws, but after some initial success the results of reform were mixed, sometimes resulting in greater access and other times not (Staggenborg 1999; Tribe 1992; Mooney and Lee 1995). Reform was limited to those states that had a demand for it (because of a large female labor force population and a large medical doctor population), public support for abortion law liberalization, interest group support, and little electoral competition within districts (Mooney and Lee 1995).

Many of the state-initiated reforms still contained stipulations preventing women from making their reproductive decisions without medical or legal involvement (Petchesky 1997, 172–74). Unhappy with the haphazard legislative reform effort, activists started to push for outright repeal of existing abortion laws because abortion reform was making the laws more complicated, which made it cumbersome for women to petition for an abortion (Garrow 1994; Epstein and Kobylka 1992). Their efforts led Hawaii to become the first state in 1970 to legalize abortion; however, fearing that women would flock to the state, the new law included a residency requirement. Following Hawaii's lead, other states began to liberalize their policies. New York was the next state to reform in July 1970. A mere fifteen months later, New York, which did not have a residency requirement stipulation, recorded 195,520 abortions of which 127,129 were obtained by nonresidents (Risen and Thomas 1998, 15). On the other side of the country, California became the West Coast mecca for nonresident women. By 1972, Californian physicians were performing approximately 100,000 legal abortions a year (Risen and Thomas 1998, 15–16). Alaska and Washington also repealed their abortion laws (Tribe 1992).

The efforts of the abortion rights movement had provided significant but limited dividends. Although fourteen states allowed abortions under certain conditions, by 1971 abortion rights advocates soon came to an impasse (Risen and Thomas 1998). Other states were ignoring the demand for abortion reform. The political opportunities created at the state level appeared to be evaporating. Thirty-four states considered repealing their abortion laws, but none of them adopted any type of reform (Epstein and Kobylka 1992). Two years later, states' resistance to abortion reform came to a halt with the Supreme Court's 1973 intervention in the abortion debate.

New Political Opportunities at the National Level

Norma McCorvey was a twenty-one-year-old divorced mother of two, who did not graduate from high school.[15] Norma had given her two children up for adoption. She did not belong to any women's organizations, nor was she politically active. In the summer of 1969, Norma was pregnant for the third time and had little money. She turned to Dr. Bradley for help, but he was "absolutely appalled" when he realized that Norma wanted an abortion (Garrow 1994, 403). A woman in the doctor's waiting room overheard Norma's story and advised her to try again but mention that the pregnancy was a result of sexual assault, which might make a doctor more sympathetic to her quest to obtain an abortion. Norma concocted an elaborate and complex tale of being sexually assaulted after work and conveyed the story to Dr. Lane. Like Dr. Bradley, Dr. Lane was unwilling to provide an abortion for Norma or direct her to an illegal abortionist. He suggested she try to raise money and go to California or New York where she would have a better chance at receiving an abortion (Garrow 1994). Norma did not have the money to travel from Texas to either California or New York, and she certainly did not have the money to cover the $500 fee for abortion services.

Out of options, Norma moved in with her father and returned to Dr. Lane's office; he gave her the name of an adoption attorney. Norma met with the attorney recommended by Dr. Lane; she immediately disliked the lawyer and felt uncomfortable seeking counsel from him. She returned to Dr. Lane's office and he gave her the name of another adoption attorney, Henry McCluskey. Norma asked McCluskey if he could assist her with obtaining an abortion, to which he promptly said no. Norma carried the pregnancy to term and gave the baby up for adoption, with the aid of McCluskey.

McCluskey had a friend, Linda Coffee, who had advised him in *Buchanan v. Batchelor*, a lawsuit brought forth by McCluskey that challenged the constitutionality of the nineteenth-century sodomy statute in Texas.[16] Sarah Weddington and Linda Coffee were two young, recently graduated and inexperienced lawyers who were involved in the women's movement and witnessed the significant social changes occurring in the 1960s and early 1970s. During their tenure at law school, the young women were exposed to the substantial changes taking place under Justice Warren—changes that affected constitutional law (Craig and O'Brien 1993).

Coffee was interested in challenging Texas's anti-abortion statute. She was working with Weddington who wanted to file a federal constitutional test case. Initially Weddington thought they could bring a suit forward on behalf of an Austin, Texas, women's group. For strategic purposes, Coffee and Weddington decided to bring suit in the Northern District of Texas rather than the Western District, which is where an Austin area plaintiff would place the lawsuit. The lawyers thought that a pregnant woman who was experiencing an unwanted pregnancy but by law was being forced to carry the pregnancy to term would make a good plaintiff. But neither Coffee nor Weddington had any idea where they were going to find this woman, until they received a call from McCluskey who arranged for them to meet with his client, Norma McCorvey (Garrow 1994; Craig and O'Brien 1993; Epstein and Kobylka 1992).

Weddington and Coffee needed legal standing to sue. They had to prove that someone was injured as a consequence of the law. Norma initially appeared to be the victim they needed for bringing forth a test case to the courts; she was pregnant, clearly did not want the pregnancy, and was unable to get an abortion so she was carrying the pregnancy to term. Weddington and Coffee met with Norma several times to assess her willingness and dedication to seeing the case through (Craig and O'Brien 1993). The young lawyers quickly recognized that Norma was unsettled, had a transient lifestyle, and was emotionally unpredictable (Garrow 1994). Even though Norma was *Roe*, they decided she was not the most dependable or credible witness and sought to supplement their case with other plaintiffs. David and Marsha King, a married couple, volunteered to become anonymous plaintiffs and challenge the legality of denying abortion services to married couples. They became John and Jane Doe in the second complaint, *Doe v. Wade*. *Roe* and *Doe* were filed against Dallas County district attorney Henry Wade as the defendant.

Both petitions charged that the law infringed on the plaintiffs' ability to have access to abortion services. The complaint stated that the plaintiffs could not afford to travel to other jurisdictions where abortion services were available (Garrow 1994). *Roe* challenged the legality of Texas's 1854 abortion statute. Coffee and Weddington alleged that the Texan law impeded "Roe's" "right to safe and adequate medical advice pertaining to the decision of whether to carry a given pregnancy to term" and "upon the fundamental right of all women to choose whether to bear children." The complaint also claimed that "Roe's" right to "privacy in a physician-patient relationship" and her "right to life" as protected by the Fourteenth Amendment was being violated (Garrow 1994, 405–7).

To establish standing, the lawyers used the Court's ruling in *Griswold v. Connecticut* (381 U.S. 479, 1965), which struck down Connecticut's law prohibiting the dissemination of contraception information. In 1965 the Court overturned Connecticut's law largely based on a constitutional "right to privacy"[17] (Craig and O'Brien 1993; Garrow 1994). Justice William O. Douglas argued that Connecticut's statute violated marital privacy, a right that could be extracted from the penumbras in the various parts of the Bill of Rights (Balkin 2005; Nossiff 2001). *Griswold* was extraordinarily significant on many legal fronts. It established the idea of a "zone of privacy" around marital relationships, meaning that the intimate decisions, including the use of birth control, made within the confines of marriage should be free from governmental interference. *Griswold* also linked the "right to privacy" to the constitutional guarantees of the Bill of Rights and the Fourteenth Amendment, tying the decision to traditional political theory and establishing precedent for future civil rights litigation (Nossiff 2001).

The Supreme Court extended the right to privacy in 1971 in *Eisenstadt v. Baird* (405 U.S. 438, 1972) to include single people. Justice Brennan wrote the plurality opinion in *Eisenstadt* where he asserted the importance of privacy in matters of reproduction. Brennan wrote, "If the right of privacy means anything it is the right of the individual, married or single, to be free from unwarranted governmental intrusion into matters so fundamentally affecting a person as the decision whether to bear or beget a child" (Balkin 2005, 8). Brennan underscored the importance of privacy not only to married people but also single individuals. He also extended the scope of privacy beyond contraception use to include the decision of parenthood. These judicial writings paved the way for the consideration of abortion reform. Weddington and Coffee wanted to extend the "right to privacy" rationale to the Texas abortion law. Shortly into the legal process, the lawyers changed their lawsuit to a class action suit, brought forth on behalf of all women who faced the same obstacles when making decisions concerning their reproduction (Epstein and Kobylka 1992). Another complaint was filed by Margie Pitts Hames, *Doe v. Bolton* (410 U.S. 179, 1973), challenging the legality of a 1968 Georgia abortion reform law that was based on the American Law Institute's Model Penal Code (Balkin 2005). *Doe v. Bolton* ended up being argued as a companion case to *Roe* in front of the Supreme Court.

Unlike today's pro-life movement, in 1973 there was little organized opposition to abortion rights. The Texas attorney general's office did not take the impending *Roe* case very seriously. During this time, the office was overwhelmed with civil rights suits and believed that the state had a strong legal interest in protecting life, leaving the *Roe* case without merit (Epstein and Kobylka 1992). The state's lack of preparation and Weddington's inexperience became apparent on December 13, 1971, when the Court first heard their respective oral arguments in *Roe v. Wade* (410 U.S. 113, 1973). Many judicial observers noted that neither party provided the justices with a clear legal path to follow (Garrow 1994; Epstein and Kobylka 1992). After deliberating throughout the spring of 1972, the Court decided to rehear *Roe* and the *Doe* companion case.

At *Roe*'s initial debut, the Court only had seven active members because Justices Hugo Black and John Marshall Harlan had recently retired. These justices were replaced with Lewis Powell and William Rehnquist, who participated in the rehearing of *Roe* (Balkin 2005; Garrow 1994). Given the controversial issue, the rehearing of the cases, and the Court's long deliberation, no one had a clear idea how the Court was going to rule (Epstein and Kobylka 1992).

The Court ruled, by a seven to two majority, that a woman's right to an abortion was a fundamental right, and therefore the government lacked the authority to interfere with her decision to abort in the first trimester of pregnancy[18] (Garrow 1994; Tribe 1992). Justice Harry A. Blackmun composed the majority opinion in both *Roe* and *Doe*, building on the right to privacy found in the *Griswold* and *Eisenstadt* rulings. Blackmun wrote the right to privacy "is broad enough to encompass a woman's decision whether or not to terminate her pregnancy," and denying women access to abortion caused a "detriment . . . on the pregnant woman" in terms of her physical and psychological well-being. Blackmun went on to lament the social toll unwanted pregnancy caused women and families, "the distress, for all concerned, associated with the unwanted child, and . . . the problem of bringing a child into a family already unable, psychologically and otherwise, to care for it, the additional difficulties and continuing stigma of unwed motherhood" (Balkin 2005, 8–9).

Justice Blackmun acknowledged the moral implications of abortion in terms of ending fetal life. He argued that the constitutional recognition of rights and duties did not make sense in the context of a fetus nor should it apply to fetal life. And while abortion ends fetal life (and therefore potential human life) Blackmun argued that moral questions attached to ending fetal life were best decided outside of the courts. Blackmun stated, "We need not resolve the difficult question of when life begins. When those trained in the respective disciplines of medicine, philosophy, and theology are unable to arrive at any consensus, the judiciary, at this point in the development of man's knowledge, is not in a position to speculate as to the answer" (Balkin 2005, 9).

None of the justices supported legalizing abortion practices up until the moment of childbirth, believing that at a certain point in the pregnancy the state had a compelling interest in protecting fetal life. To reconcile abortion rights with fetal protection, Justice Blackmun adopted the trimester framework as a compromise between the Justices' contradictory opinions on when fetal viability becomes an issue of interest to the state. Blackmun wanted to address and deal with the different developmental stages of pregnancy, so he proposed the trimester framework. He based the trimester framework on the historical practice of tolerating abortion until quickening and the medical understanding of pregnancy in 1973. The first trimester of pregnancy was left nearly unregulated; "the abortion decision and its effectuation must be left to the medical judgment of the pregnant woman's attending physician," whereas the state may "regulate the abortion procedure in ways that are reasonably related to maternal health" in the second trimester. After fetal viability, which happens in the third trimester of pregnancy around the twenty-fourth to twenty-eighth week of pregnancy, the state has the authority to "regulate, and even proscribe, abortion except where it is necessary, in appropriate medical judgment, for the preservation of the life or health of the mother" (Balkin 2005, 10).

Justices White and Rehnquist dissented in the ruling. Justice Rehnquist argued that the judgment in *Roe* was a misinterpretation of the Fourteenth Amendment. Justice White stated that the Court "apparently values the convenience of the pregnant mother more than the continued existence and development of the life or potential life that she carries" (Balkin 2005, 11). Justice White's characterization of women viewing pregnancy as an inconvenience that can easily be eliminated through the use of abortion is an idea that is still very prevalent in the pro-life movement.

Doe v. Bolton, the companion case to *Roe,* was also decided by a seven to two margin. The Court invalidated a Georgia reform statute permitting abortion only in cases where the continuation of the pregnancy would endanger a woman's life or physical and mental health, when the fetus would likely be born with birth defects, or when the pregnancy resulted from rape or incest. The Court also struck down a state residency requirement as well as mandating that abortions be performed in a hospital. *Doe* helped establish a broader definition of maternal "health," and its definition is frequently cited in other cases. The justices defined maternal health in terms of medical judgment: "the medical judgment may be exercised in the light of all factors—physical, emotional, psychological, familial, and the woman's age—relevant to the well being of the patient. All these factors may relate to health" (*Doe v. Bolton,* 410 U.S. 179 (1973), 192).

Abortion after *Roe v. Wade*

The Supreme Court's decision in *Roe* legalized abortion in all states and marked the beginning of what has become one of the most salient legal, political, and personal issues of the twentieth and twenty-first centuries. *Roe v. Wade* dramatically changed the abortion debate. Almost immediately following the Court's decision, anti-abortion supporters were galvanized into action. Although there was pro-life support in society prior to *Roe*, it was neither well organized nor visible. Pro-life advocates naively believed that "the wrongness of abortion is as obvious and as certain as the wetness of water—and as much a part of the natural order of things" (Jacoby 1998, 66). The Court's ruling took most pro-life supporters by surprise because they believed the majority of society was pro-life, and the government would never sanction—according to their belief system— murder (Jacoby 1998; Luker 1984). Even as states were beginning to reform and in some cases repeal their abortion laws, pro-life advocates did not believe legalized abortion would ever become a reality. After the Court's decision, one pro-life activist stated:

> Well, I think just about like everyone else in the league, we felt as though the bottom had been pulled out from under us. It was an incredible thing, I couldn't believe it. In fact, I didn't. For a couple of months I kept thinking, it can't be right, I'm not hearing what I'm hearing. . . . I think we all sort of took a lot of things for granted and one of them was that our government would follow itself, wouldn't start deviating from its original purpose, and this was such a strong deviation that it was kind of appalling to me. And it was sort of the beginning of a lot of deviations in various areas. (Luker 1984, 141)

Roe v. Wade essentially forced pro-life supporters to acknowledge that alternative belief systems and values, which they adamantly oppose, exist in society (Blanchard 1994, 41; McKeegan 1992; Watson 1997).

Mobilizing Structures in the Wake of *Roe*

Within a month following the Supreme Court's decision, the Catholic Church hierarchy called for civil disobedience against the ruling (Tribe 1992, 143; Risen and Thomas 1998, 4–6). Given the Church's long-standing operation in society, it provided immediate leadership, organizational capacity, community organization, and resources needed to launch an anti-abortion movement (Blanchard 1994: McCarthy 1987). Essentially overnight, the pro-life movement emerged as a widespread, predominantly single-issue social movement.[19]

The Catholic Church was the primary player in the anti-abortion movement throughout the 1970s. As the 1980s approached, new actors joined—most notably, the religious right, which was composed of neo-evangelical, fundamentalist, and Pentecostal churches[20] (Blanchard 1994; Johnson 1999). To date, the pro-life movement remains largely grassroots, with a single-issue focus on abortion.[21] Although pro-life groups engage in routine tactics such as lobbying Congress and making legal challenges against abortion, they also rely heavily on disruptive tactics (Blanchard 1994, chapter 6; Johnson 1999).

In contrast, following *Roe,* abortion rights groups moved away from grassroots mobilization. Abortion rights groups generally believed that *Roe* settled the abortion question and moved on to address other issues. This error in political judgment proved to be a handicap for abortion rights advocates in the ensuing decades (Epstein and Kobylka 1992; McCarthy 1987). Organizations increasingly began to professionalize, institutionalize, hire professional staff, and cultivate relationships with other groups focusing on issues expanding beyond abortion (McCarthy 1987).

Pro-choice organizations moved away from direct action tactics, preferring instead to work within governmental institutions. The abortion rights movement became institutionalized, enabling it to recruit members through professional campaigns and increase their budgets by soliciting foundation money even as public interest in protecting or expanding legalized abortion declined. These efforts helped sustain existing abortion rights groups through the "lean" period of most of the 1970s (Staggenborg 1999).

Framing Abortion after *Roe v. Wade*

The medical community continues to play a large role in the abortion conflict. Medical expertise dominates much of the discourse on abortion within certain political institutions, namely, state legislatures and Congress. Some pro-choice advocates, while pleased with the *Roe* decision, were also apprehensive. They feared that the medical community still functioned as a gatekeeper to women's autonomy. During the abortion reform movement, women's groups actively educated women about their bodies and how to take control of their sexuality and lives (Kaplan 1998). Advocates were concerned that abortion services would only encompass a limited medical procedure—abortion—rather than empowering women and comprehensively educating women about sexuality and reproductive choices.

To mitigate medical control, pro-abortion advocates adamantly frame abortion access as a rights issue, arguing that it is a fundamental aspect of women's autonomy, privacy, and control over their bodies (Kaplan 1998). Conversely, abortion opponents fundamentally view it as a morality issue, equating abortion with murder.[22] The simplistic frames used by both pro-choice and pro-life advocates to characterize the abortion debate—the rights of women versus the rights of the unborn—overlook the larger context of the debate (Watson 1997; Viguerie 1981; Luker 1984). Support for and opposition to abortion represent a deeper clash over belief systems and worldviews (Luker 1984; Falik 1983; Watson 1997).

Abortion rights advocates believe that women have an inalienable right to control their bodies and lives, which to the pro-life movement represents a direct assault on the traditional conception of family and gender roles (Conover and Gray 1983; Luker 1984). Pro-choice activists view abortion as more than a symbol of women's equality. Abortion rights cannot be divorced from women's equality—without it, women are relegated to exclusively being "a mother first, last, and always" (Falik 1983, 33). In essence the relationship between women's autonomy and abortion

> asserts the complete sovereignty of woman over her body. It is the supreme assertion of individualism, since the claims of the woman are judged to be superior to those of the man, whose contribution to conception, at least, is precisely equal, genetically, to that of the woman. (Degler 1980, 246)

For pro-life advocates, abortion represents the most obvious proof that the family is being threatened and society is evolving away from a "Christian" society toward a culturally permissive, secular society. Abortion epitomizes the "fallenness of humankind and the relentlessness of human cruelty" (Jacoby 1998, 2). Abortion is more than a struggle for the unborn's rights; it is the unraveling of traditional society (Watson 1997; Viguerie 1981). For example, the following was written in a fund-raising letter for the pro-life organization Focus on the Family.[23]

> Many signs point to the unraveling of a value system that has served us so well since the Pilgrims landed at Plymouth Rock in 1620. These developments . . . are being orchestrated with great care by those who hate the Christian system of values and are passionately dedicated to its destruction. A formidable army has been assembled . . . including the gay and lesbian

movement; the National Organization for Women and its minions; the American Civil Liberties Union; People for the American Way . . . the medical personnel who are slaughtering our unborn babies; the euthanasia organizations that are urging us to kill the old, the sick, the handicapped . . . These are the shock troops arrayed in full battle gear before us. (Letter written by James C. Dodson, May 1988)

The anti-abortion campaign is part of a strategy to return America to a culturally traditional society that respects the family and, importantly, adheres to traditional gender roles (Jacoby 1998; Luker 1984; Conover and Gray 1983; Watson 1997; Viguerie 1981).

Conclusion

Abortion services have been used in American society with varying levels of acceptance. Since 1973, abortion has been cast as a rights issue versus a morality issue. The simplistic rights and morality frame obscures the more complex, underlying cultural wars at play in society. The modern abortion conflict represents a fundamental rift over two radically different belief systems, thus contributing to the intractability of the issue.

Throughout the twentieth century, changing views of women, family, and society have been vying for public acceptance with traditional beliefs. The deep clash of worldviews differentiates the modern abortion conflict from past conflicts, adding to the rise, longevity, intensity, and saliency of the modern pro-life movement. To date, abortion remains legal; however it continues to be challenged by pro-life groups at the local, state, and federal levels.

In chapter 3, I investigate the political and rhetorical evolution of the pro-life movement following *Roe,* tracing periods of growth and stagnation in the movement. Specifically, the link between abortion and women's rights fueled the conception of abortion as a morality issue for the pro-life movement. Conceptualizing abortion as a morality issue has led to a different political structure and strategy for the pro-life movement compared to its pro-choice counterpart. This strategy has provided tacit support for those members who routinely engage in disruptive, politically harassing tactics, which are primarily directed at women seeking abortion services and the physicians who provide those services.

Chapter 3

THE RISE OF THE PRO-LIFE MOVEMENT POST *ROE v. WADE*

One can hardly imagine a single Supreme Court decision that has done more damage to our society. In this one decision, the court set the stage for the growth of moral relativism and hedonism in this once great Christian nation. Due to the moral decay that began with *Griswold,* self-gratification is of the utmost importance to a large portion of our society.
—Jim Sedlak, executive director of STOPP International, commenting on the fortieth anniversary of *Griswold v. Connecticut,* June 7, 2005

Pre-*Roe* Anti-abortion Activism

Pro-life support existed within society long before the 1960s move to liberalize abortion laws, but there was no reason to organize formally because the law and public sentiment appeared to reflect anti-abortion beliefs. In reality, although abortion was illegal, the absence of public discourse surrounding abortion was a product of society's general discomfort and shame about openly talking about sexuality rather than majoritarian support of pro-life beliefs (Luker 1984). As abortion rights gains were being made, pro-life supporters had to begin to acknowledge that differing views regarding abortion existed in society, particularly in the states where abortion reform was successful.

Initial reform efforts were concentrated at the state level, where lawmakers were willing to liberalize abortion statutes. On April 25, 1967, Colorado was the first state to pass a reform measure liberalizing its abortion law, and it was quickly followed by North Carolina on May 8. As abortion reform momentum built, more states introduced liberalized abortion measures, however, the majority of states continued to enforce strict anti-abortion laws, and even in the states that had reformed abortion laws, elective abortion practices were not widely available (Tribe 1992; Luker 1984).

Women, particularly middle-class educated women, were flocking to the states where safe and legal abortion services were available. By 1972, the Center for Disease Control reported that 586,800 abortions were being performed nationwide (Risen and Thomas 1998). For those who were supportive of abortion rights, tangible progress was being made; yet for those who adamantly opposed abortion, the turn of events was alarming.

Early opposition to abortion originated in states where abortion rights advocates had made minor, but legislatively formal, inroads. For example, in California, an anti-abortion group formed after the passage of the 1967 Beilenson bill. Anthony C. Beilenson was a thirty-year-old freshman representative from Beverly Hills who decided to promote an abortion reform measure when other state representatives decided against reintroducing the measure in 1963 (Garrow 1994). Beilenson reintroduced the reform measure in a new legislative session, but the opposition voiced by the Catholic Church hierarchy tempered the likelihood of successfully moving the bill forward. After several years of lobbying and using his interpersonal skills to build relationships within the assembly and senate, Beilenson was able to get his bill passed. The Beilenson bill was sold to legislators as "a means to alleviate the tragic results of rape and incest" and "to provide relief for women in situations of hardship" (Garrow 1994, 332). The bill decriminalized abortion services for three conditions: when continuance of a pregnancy would "gravely impair the physical or mental health of the mother," the child would be born with "grave physical or mental defect," or the pregnancy resulted from sexual assault or incest (Beilenson Senate Bill 1967). In reality, the passage of the bill was only going to help about 5 percent of women seeking abortions, but for abortion opponents, the bill symbolically and legislatively established the path for more significant abortion reform (Garrow 1994; Nossiff 2001).

Following the passage of the Beilenson bill in 1967, an anti-abortion group formed, consisting of nine male Catholic professionals, one housewife, and one non-Catholic male (Luker 1984). In the same year, the Virginia Society for Human Life was established after abortion reform efforts were making some headway in that state during 1966 (Risen and Thomas 1998). These early anti-abortion reform groups primarily consisted of Catholics.

The Catholic Church played a crucial leading role in the anti-abortion movement. The main policy-making branch of the Catholic Church, the National Conference of Catholic Bishops (NCCB), spearheaded early opposition. The

NCCB became a conduit for collective political action and was the sole anti-abortion lobbying group prior to *Roe* (Byrnes 1993; Risen and Thomas 1998). Church leaders were called upon to recruit Catholics into local anti-abortion organizations. Eventually, the NCCB established the National Right to Life Committee in 1966, which served as a national umbrella for many of the local organizations (Risen and Thomas 1998; Baird-Windle and Bader 2001). By 1967, the NCCB budgeted $50,000 to fight abortion reform efforts occurring in various states (Ginsburg 1989).

The Catholic Church did not initially receive much support from other religious denominations. Quite the opposite: Protestant clergy and Jewish rabbis were actually vocal in their support of abortion reform. Shocking many, in May 1967, twenty-one religious leaders announced on the front page of the *New York Times* that they would direct women in need of abortion services to doctors who were legitimate and safe (Tribe 1992). Abortion supporters capitalized on the Church's participation, characterizing its opposition to abortion as religiously motivated and touted it as a "Catholic issue," particularly in states that did not have a large Catholic population such as North Carolina, which in 1967 became the second state to reform its abortion statute (Nossiff 2001).

During this time, sporadic and relatively isolated anti-abortion protesters started to surface around the country; they were not officially supported by the Catholic Church. Church leaders frowned on unconventional protest tactics and instead encouraged abortion opponents to participate in conventional groups. Most pre-*Roe* anti-abortion efforts occurred among small Catholic groups that were mainly formed by professionals. These early activists had community ties, typically belonged to professional organizations, and engaged in protest activities like outreach that were designed to show the irrationality, immorality, and injustice of abortion (Blanchard 1994; Luker 1984). Participants saw themselves as public educators with a twofold mission: they were going to demonstrate to the public that support of abortion reform was not universal and simultaneously awaken pro-life activism (Blanchard 1994).

These pioneering activists never thought abortion would be nationally decriminalized. They were comforted by the political reality that abortion reform efforts at the state level were tapering off by 1972. Between 1967 and 1973, nineteen states liberalized their abortion laws; however, many of these legislative victories were won by a small margin (Tribe 1992). Much like the Beilenson bill, the reformed laws often did not lead to tangible changes; access to abortion remained problematic especially for poor women. Only four states assured women the right to terminate an unwanted pregnancy, and two of those states were geographically remote—Hawaii and Alaska (Tribe 1992). Pro-life advocates had good reason to believe that the legalization of elective abortions on a national scale would remain elusive, which is why January 22, 1973, was a devastating day for activists.

Early Fallout from Roe v. Wade

The Supreme Court's decision to legalize abortion came as an absolute shock to pro-life activists who truly believed that the majority of Americans held similar beliefs regarding the sanctity of human life. Pro-life supporters saw the Court's ruling as a complete and radical departure from traditional mores held by many of them (Luker 1984; Petchesky 1984; Blanchard 1994). Immediately following *Roe*, the anti-abortion movement was launched on a much wider scale than previously existed. The Catholic Church took the lead role in expanding anti-abortion opposition from small, scattered anti-abortion groups into a nationally formidable social movement.

The emergence of the Catholic Church in the anti-abortion movement was not coincidental; it reflected demographic patterns that had been occurring among the Church's membership for several decades (Tribe 1992; Byrnes 1993). As Catholics became more educated and prosperous, they began to assimilate into American culture, greatly reducing anti-Catholic sentiment in society. Many Catholics no longer needed the local direction, leadership, and protection of the clergy (Byrnes 1993). As local political opportunities started to wane and decrease the influence of the Catholic hierarchy in shaping policy, national politics provided endless opportunities for them, where they could apply Catholic social teachings to a whole range of public policy issues.

By the 1960s the Catholic hierarchy began to take advantage of these new opportunities. The Catholic Church clergy direct the largest single religious denomination in the United States; over one-fourth of the national electorate has membership in the Catholic Church (Byrnes 1993). And while Church leaders cannot force their members to vote in particular ways, they have a sizable captive audience every week. Many political candidates continue to believe that the Catholic hierarchy is well positioned to shape opinions. Politicians often stress the commonalities between their issue positions and the Church leadership's positions.

The legalization of abortion provided a national political issue for the

Catholic Church. Even though they were vocal opponents to abortion reform for several years predating *Roe,* their activism after *Roe* was unmatched by any other religious organization. The Church used the Supreme Court's decision to reaffirm its stance that abortion is "an unspeakable crime." Bishops publicly denounced the Court's decision, characterizing it as "an unspeakable tragedy for the nation" and calling for "every legal possibility [to] be explored to challenge the opinion of the United States Supreme Court" (Byrnes 1993, 502).

The Catholic Church not only publicly condemned the legalization of abortion, it also put up resources. Catholic leaders have unparalleled resources at their disposal. Beyond a large membership, the Church wields an arsenal of institutional supplies (space, organizational capacity, leadership, communication networks, ideology, and experience in activism) as well as money (Ginsburg 1989; Byrnes 1993). The Church quickly became involved in national politics, calling for "well planned and coordinated political action" in electoral campaigns to promote pro-life political candidates (Byrnes 1993, 503).

The Church's centralized role in the anti-abortion movement started to make several local activists uncomfortable. By the summer of 1973, during an annual pro-life conference, leaders voted to sever official ties with the Catholic Church and establish the National Right to Life Committee (NRLC) as an independent organization. The NRLC continued to work closely with Catholic leaders, but it also wanted a broader, more inclusive constituency. It sought members who were united by opposition to abortion regardless of their religious or political affiliation (Ginsburg 1989). Many other anti-abortion groups started to form in the early 1970s. An outgrowth of the anti-nuclear pacifist movement, Pro-Lifers for Survival, formed in 1971 and was quickly followed by the formation of Feminists for Life (Ginsburg 1989).

The anti-abortion movement began to diversify its organizational structure by including single-issue groups, multiple-issue groups, and many groups that were linked to larger political ideologies and agendas (Blanchard 1994; Petchesky 1984). For example, many activists (outside of the Catholic Church leadership) had previously been involved in the peace movement and saw little distinction between war and abortion violence (Risen and Thomas 1998). Opposition to abortion was also tied to other "pro-life" issues such as opposing euthanasia, capital punishment, and the use of nuclear and chemical arms. Several leaders such as John O'Keefe believed in nonviolent civil disobedience and borrowed the sit-in strategy from the civil rights movement to peacefully highlight the wrongness of abortion (Mason 2002a). In short, the pro-life movement was no longer a monolithic group, and it has retained its diversity into the twenty-first century.

Early Protest Rhetoric and Strategies

For many early pro-life activists, anti-abortion support was primarily articulated via liberal principles of natural or human rights, which grew out of a larger belief in an ideal egalitarian democracy. From this vein, every individual has the right to life and the right to be protected by the government (Blanchard 1994; Petchesky 1984). "For those who take the right-to-life stance, granting an individual fetus the liberal 'right' to live, to grow, and to be born presupposes many things, not the least of which is that particular rights should be granted equally among all citizens of the United States" (Mason 2002a, 16). Groups such as the National Right to Life Committee are premised on these liberal arguments against abortion. They fundamentally believe that the Constitution is designed to guarantee equal rights (as well as equal political rights) to all citizens including fetal life, which is a core liberal argument (Mason 2002a).

Opposing abortion based on these liberal arguments led to a strategic, logical path of defense—accessing political institutions to try to establish and defend the rights of the unborn. Catholic-sponsored efforts manifested in traditional political arenas such as lobbying Congress and setting out to challenge the Supreme Court's *Roe* decision. The anti-abortion movement supported politicians' attempts to overturn the Court's decision by introducing the 1974 right to life amendment in Congress (Staggenborg 1991; Tribe 1992). This legislation was ultimately unsuccessful, but abortion foes were able to pass the 1976 Hyde amendment.

Henry J. Hyde, a Republican representative from Illinois, sponsored a congressional pro-life amendment, attached to the appropriations bill for the following fiscal year, aimed at prohibiting Medicaid funding of abortions. Hyde's amendment passed through the House but was defeated in the Senate due to the absolutism of the bill. Both houses remained deadlocked over the amendment for several months until they finally agreed to a compromise. An exception was included in the rider to allow Medicaid funding for terminating pregnancies that would result in "severe and long-lasting physical health damage" if continued to term (Garrow 1994, 630). All other therapeutic abortions were ineligible for Medicaid coverage. The elimination of federal funding for abortions was a significant victory for the pro-life movement—prior to 1976 approximately 300,000 abortions had been funded annually by Medicaid[1] (Tribe 1992).

Building on the Hyde amendment victory, the pro-life movement looked for other means of restricting access to abortion, thus turning to presidential elections and state legislatures, where it focused on supporting pro-life candidates, eliminating public funding of abortion services, and curbing access to abortion services (Byrnes 1993; Blanchard 1994; Tribe 1992). The 1976 presidential campaign was the first post-*Roe* election and the first opportunity for the NCCB to visibly push for an anti-abortion agenda within a national arena. Both candidates, Jimmy Carter and Gerald Ford, paid attention to the NCCB because in the previous election of 1972, Catholic voters played a significant role in the outcome of the election. Catholic voters largely abandoned the Democratic Party and played a pivotal role in electing Richard Nixon to the White House. By the 1976 presidential elections, candidates were unwilling to overlook the importance of Catholic voters and their religious leaders' agenda (Byrnes 1993).

Jimmy Carter attempted to build a bridge with the NCCB by emphasizing his personal opposition to abortion even though politically he supported it. Gerald Ford emphasized the disparity between Carter's personal and political beliefs and underscored the difference between Carter's position and the NCCB. Ford and Carter both drew much media attention to the NCCB, which simply elevated its political import in national politics (Byrnes 1993). "That abortion could have a real impact on political strategy when most Americans did not consider it a major issue is a testament both to the organization and prominence of the Catholic Church and, from the politicians' viewpoint, to the power of a visible, vocal and intensely active minority" (Tribe 1992, 150). In the end, Jimmy Carter won the election, and the attention given to the abortion debate served as a precursor for what was to come in electoral politics.

The pro-life movement's initial political strategy of chipping away at *Roe* via restrictions on abortion services at the state level and introducing a constitutional amendment that would undo *Roe* altogether appeared to be making headway. Within state legislatures, the pro-life movement helped sponsor and promote bills intended to restrict access to services. And although abortion rights groups, such as the National Abortion and Reproductive Rights Action League (NARAL), lobbied heavily, anti-abortion measures such as spousal notification, informed consent, and parental notification laws were passed in several states. These early legislative victories, however, did not last long.

Outside of the Hyde amendment victory and visibility in the presidential election, anti-abortionists experienced two significant defeats in 1976. The first defeat was issued by the Supreme Court in the *Planned Parenthood v. Danforth* (428 U.S. 52, 1976) decision. A lawsuit was filed on behalf of two abortion providers in Missouri, contesting the state's law requiring spousal consent for married women seeking abortion services and its absolute parental consent law that did not include a bypass mechanism. These two restrictions were struck down by the Court, in a six to three margin, along with a prohibition against saline abortions at twelve weeks or more gestation. The Court ruled that the Missouri laws were unconstitutional because they "delegated to third parties an absolute veto power which the state does not itself possess" (Markels 2005).

The Court embraced Missouri's definition of fetal viability as "when the life of the unborn child may be continued indefinitely outside of the womb by natural or artificial life-supportive systems." This definition paved the way for future restrictions on first trimester abortions by moving away from the trimester framework established in *Roe* (Nossiff 2001, 151). Even though the Court opened the door for pro-life–sponsored legislation at the state level, the movement viewed *Danforth* as a significant defeat, effectively undoing much of the anti-abortion progress at the state level (Tribe 1992; McKeegan 1992).

Along with attempts to restrict abortion services at the state level, the constitutional amendment was also proving to be more difficult to pass than originally envisioned by the pro-life movement. Congress was willing to ban funding for abortion services, but it was becoming increasingly clear that it was unwilling to pass a constitutional amendment prohibiting abortion. For a couple of years, anti-abortionists tried to enact a constitutional amendment without Congress's approval by employing Article V and moving the issue to the state level where the movement had experienced more success. Yet by 1978 only thirteen states had called for a convention to amend the Constitution to overturn *Roe* (Tribe 1992).

Radical Changes in the Pro-Life Movement: The Influx of Fundamentalists

By the end of the 1970s, the predominantly Catholic membership in the anti-abortion movement was beginning to be augmented by an influx of fundamentalist Protestants, which quickly had the effect of radicalizing the movement

(Blanchard 1994). Even though the surge in fundamentalist members was new to the movement, they were not new to American culture.[2] Evangelicals were responsible for two large revival movements across the nation in the eighteenth and nineteenth centuries (usually referred to as the First and Second Great Awakening) (Watson 1997). In both of these awakenings, fundamentalists enlisted a particular style of preaching—mass evangelism. Evangelism was intended to stir emotions through preaching and singing and to cause an immediate conversion (being born again) to attendees or at a minimum compel Christians to reconnect and recommit to their faith (Watson 1997).

The aftermath of the Second Great Awakening is particularly salient to the visible resurgence in fundamentalism during the 1980s. Evangelicals provided a template for national values and a collective identity during a time—the antebellum period—where defining what it meant to be an American was unclear and open to debate. Prior to the Civil War, evangelicals were well adapted to American life both intellectually and socially. After the Civil War, rapid changes were occurring such as urbanization, industrialization, massive immigration, and a growth in the Roman Catholic Church membership (Watson 1997).

All of these late nineteenth-century changes were on a collision course with fundamentalists' social and intellectual reality. Evangelicals were confronted with modernity and their perception of an impending cultural crisis, which they were attempting to resist through a return to fundamentalism. Karen Armstrong explains fundamentalist movements in her book *The Battle for God* (2001).

> [Movements] engaged in a conflict with enemies whose secularist policies and beliefs seem inimical to religion itself. Fundamentalists do not regard this battle as a conventional political struggle, but experience it as a cosmic war between the forces of good and evil. They fear annihilation, and try to fortify their beleaguered identity by means of a selective retrieval of certain doctrines and practices of the past. To avoid contamination, they often withdraw from mainstream society to create a counterculture; yet fundamentalists are not impractical dreamers. They have absorbed the pragmatic rationalism of modernity, and, under the guidance of their charismatic leaders, they refine these "fundamentals" so as to create an ideology that provides the faithful with a plan of action. Eventually they fight back and attempt to resacralize an increasingly skeptical world. (Karen Armstrong, quoted in Jon Krakauer 2004, *Under the Banner of Heaven,* 144)

Fundamentalists' resistance to change resurfaced in the 1920s over the teaching of Darwinism in the schools. The antievolution cause suffered a debilitating defeat at the 1925 Scopes trial, where their champion—William Jennings Bryan—was humiliated when he exposed fundamentalists' belief in religious literalism.[3] Evolutionists ridiculed Bryan's disbelief and mistrust of science, and his literalist interpretation of the Bible left him, and fundamentalists, looking like antiquated, narrow-minded people whose reliance on literalism as a belief system were out of step with modern times. Literalism

> encourages a closed, usually (though not necessarily) politically conservative view of the world: one with a stop-time notion of history and a we-and-they approach to people, in which *we* are possessed of truth, virtue, and goodness and *they* of falsehood, depravity, and evil. It looks askance at figurative language, which, so long as its symbols and metaphors are vital, can open—promiscuously in the eyes of the strict literalist—the world and its imaginative possibilities." (Vincent Crapanzano 2000, quoted in Jon Krakauer 2004, *Under the Banner of Heaven*, 140)

Shortly after the Scopes trial evangelicalism lost much of its credibility, leaving many fundamentalists to withdraw into a subculture composed of their own networks of private education, publishing, broadcasting, missions, and evangelism[4] (Watson 1997; Wilcox 1996). Even today, scores of fundamentalists self-consciously view themselves as outsiders to mainstream culture (Press and Cole 1995). Their identity is shaped and solidified around their belief that they are marginalized in society, a belief that is not completely unfounded. Antagonistic sentiment toward fundamentalists has been growing in American society and becoming more polarized among different segments of society. Antifundamentalist attitudes have declined in Catholic, Protestant, cultural traditionalist, and self-identified Republican populations, but antipathy toward fundamentalists has increased among the cultural progressivist and secularist populations (Bolce and De Maio 1999).

After a roughly four-decade absence, fundamentalism started to reappear in American society and would soon emerge as a recognizable political force. The 1976 presidential campaign functioned as a catalyst for fundamentalists' participation in politics. Jimmy Carter, a born-again Southern Baptist, encouraged evangelicals to become politicized and simultaneously symbolized the arrival of fundamentalism into national politics (Wilcox 1996). Religious leaders soon realized that fundamentalists could be encouraged to participate politically, and they could be molded into a largely unified voting block to support conservative candidates; resources started to be funneled to form such groups (Wilcox 1996).

Fundamentalist groups started forming throughout the late 1970s and 1980s and were part of a larger movement called the Christian Right (also referred to as the New Right). One of the most visible groups to emerge was the Moral Majority, headed by Jerry Falwell who was a Baptist Bible Fellowship pastor. From 1978 to 1984, the Christian Right went through an incredible expansionist period and experienced rapid growth and public visibility (Watson 1997; Viguerie 1981). These new fundamentalist groups used inflammatory and confrontational rhetoric to mobilize potential members and solidify the identity of active participants. These groups' agendas were far more encompassing than the early anti-abortion groups'. Even though abortion opposition was a core issue for the New Right's development, fundamentalist groups also opposed gay and lesbian rights, the equal rights amendment, pornography, welfare spending, and minimum wage increases. They supported prayers in school, tuition tax cuts for religious schools, abstinence-only sex education, and increases in defense spending (McKeegan 1992; Wilcox 1996; Watson 1997; Viguerie 1981).

Evangelicals are credited with getting the Republican Party to adopt an anti-abortion stance in their platform, and by the 1978 elections they received accolades for their contribution to defeating several pro-choice politicians (Staggenborg 1991). The Christian Right was taken very seriously in the 1980 presidential election and was credited with bringing Ronald Reagan to the White House. Yet, despite having a pro-life president in office, the anti-abortion movement was facing mounting internal tensions and outward setbacks.

Changing Rhetoric of Pro-Life Politics

Unlike the NRLC or the NCCB, fundamentalist organizations argue against abortion on conservative rather than liberal notions of equality. These groups see equality in terms of divine creation, not in terms of an egalitarian society where all citizens are granted equal rights (Mason 2002a). This position is clearly articulated by Barry Goldwater in *Conscience of a Conservative* (1960), where he states that only God views people as equal, but in all other respects, humans are unequal.

Pro-life rhetoric had noticeably changed in the 1980s. As the decade progressed, anti-abortion discourse became firmly entrenched in religious content, and the rhetoric of fundamentalists soon came to dominate the rhetoric used by most of the pro-life movement.[5] Activists warned that the legalization of abortion was bringing God's wrath on America. Apocalyptic, evangelical, and paramilitary rhetoric soon evolved in the pro-life movement due to the influx of Christian conservatives into the movement (Mason 2002a, 2002b).

Anti-abortion groups began routinely to portray legalized abortion as government-sponsored mass killings. Their rhetoric and literature compare the services taking place at abortion clinics to the Holocaust, and they liken their efforts to end abortion to the abolition movement. Themes of war, genocide, and resistance abound in their literature and common vernacular (Risen and Thomas 1998; Blanchard 1994; *Economist* 1995). Abortion clinics are referred to as "abortion-mills" that provide a service to the community by "brutally killing babies" (*Voice* 2000). Although the pattern of anti-abortion discourse emerged from the more militant factions of the movement (such as the Army of God, Lambs of Christ, and Missionaries to the Preborn), the use of inflammatory rhetoric is not limited to "extreme" members of the movement (Kaplan 1995; Munson 2005).

Activists who engage in direct action within the rescue branch of the movement quickly adopted the terminology put forth by more extreme groups. "Baby" is used in lieu of "fetus," clinic escorts are referred to as "deathscorts," and American culture has been replaced with "death culture," "culture of death," or "abortion culture." Abortion practices are discussed in terms of "murder," "baby killing," or "child killing," and "mass murderer" and "killer" are descriptions reserved for medical practitioners (Kaplan 1995; Mason 2002a, 2002b). Anti-abortion terminology encourages pro-life supporters to completely identify with a fetus; "My heart was overwhelmed with grief and love for the babies, fury and rage toward the criminals . . . and . . . deep shame and embarrassment before God" (Kaplan 1995, 131, quote from convicted clinic bomber John Brockhoeft). This vein of anti-abortion discourse has also been embraced by more moderate activists and pro-life defenders. Participants operating within the political system rely on inflammatory rhetoric to voice their views. For example, talking about "partial-birth" abortions,[6] Nebraska attorney general Don Stenberg stated, "It shocks the conscience that in the United States of America a human child can be literally pulled from the womb and cruelly killed by having his or her skull punctured and brain suctioned out" (Pro-Life Infonet 2000).

Visual rhetoric is used in conjunction with pro-life linguistic rhetoric. Groups use graphic slide presentations, videos, and television commercials designed to persuade the public and political elites that abortions are immoral (Mason 2002a; Press and Cole 1995; Henshaw 1995a; Luker 1984). One of the most notorious pro-life videos, *Silent Scream*,[7] supposedly documenting an actual abortion, was sent to members of Congress and the Supreme Court. Ronald Reagan claimed it was a "chilling documentation of the horrors of abortion" (Russo and Denious 1998; Houston 1985).

Most recently, anti-abortion groups such as the Center for Bio-Ethical Reform and Life Dynamics Incorporated tour college and high school campuses displaying professionally produced banners, measuring around six feet by thirteen feet, depicting aborted fetuses (Mason 2002a; Kaiser Foundation 2006). At times, the fetal images are shown in conjunction with Jewish victims of the Holocaust and lynched men hanging from trees. Magnifying fetal images is used to establish the similarities between legalized abortion and genocide through visual exaggeration and distortion (Mason 2002a). The Center for Bio-Ethical Reform tours college campuses raising awareness for its Genocide Awareness Project (GAP). The organization is very upfront about its objective with the GAP campaign.

> As part of its Genocide Awareness Project, The Center for Bio-Ethical Reform exhibits large photo murals comparing aborted babies with Jewish Holocaust victims, African Americans killed in racist lynching, Native Americans exterminated by the U.S. Army, etc. Our purpose is to illuminate the conceptual similarities which exist between abortion and more widely recognized forms of genocide. This is important because perpetrators of genocide always call it something else and the word "abortion" has, therefore, lost most of its meaning. Visual depictions of abortion are indispensable to restoration of that meaning because abortion represents an evil so inexpressible that words fail when we attempt to describe its horror. (Gregg Cunningham, executive director of the Center for Bio-Ethical Reform, 2006)

Blending the Old with the New

The influx of fundamentalists into the pro-life movement marked a departure from its predominantly Catholic roots. The infusion of Protestants and fundamentalists into the movement caused substantial tension with Catholic pro-lifers. Catholics and Protestants have historically had a tumultuous relationship in the United States, which carried over into the anti-abortion movement (Munson 2002). As these new participants became more influential, the Catholic Church became uneasy with their far-reaching conservative platform. Catholicism opposes abortion, but the Church is not uniformly conservative on many social issues (Tribe 1992). The strain between Catholics and fundamentalists went into a brief remission with the election of Ronald Reagan (viewed as a large victory for the New Right), but within a few months their relationship began to unravel. The ideological, methodological, and theological differences were no longer contained between the two groups, and by the end of 1980 they felt an outright animosity toward each other (Grant 1991; Risen and Thomas 1998).

The internal conflict within the pro-life movement was publicly evidenced in the two conflicting pro-life bills introduced in Congress during 1982 (Grant 1991; Garrow 1999). The Helms Human Life Statute (the Helms bill) and the Hatch Human Life Federalism Amendment (the Hatch amendment) were being deliberated in Congress. The difference between the two pro-life amendments was the absolutist position taken in each bill. Helms's bill sought to overturn *Roe* by imposing a federal statutory ban on all abortions, whereas the Hatch amendment proposed overriding *Roe* by returning abortion decisions to the states (Tribe 1992). The Hatch amendment was more moderate and was endorsed by the Catholic Conference of Bishops in 1981, who reasoned that Christians had an obligation "to advocate the improvement of such laws at every stage of the legislative process" (Tribe 1992, 163). For absolutist proponents, the Hatch amendment was completely unacceptable, and they felt it simply highlighted the continued insignificance of the unborn because if the Hatch amendment passed, elective abortion services would remain legal in several states. Neither the Helms bill nor the Hatch amendment passed, representing a significant defeat for the pro-life movement, as well as underscoring the tension within the movement.

The pro-life movement continued to experience other setbacks. In the 1982 elections, pro-life candidates had minimal success defeating pro-choice candidates. Anti-abortion legislation did not gain any significant support in Congress the following year and was again defeated. Most of the anti-abortion restrictions passed at the state level were struck down by the Supreme Court (Staggenborg 1991). Adding to its woes, the anti-abortion movement was coming under fire for a rash of clinic bombings and an escalation in violence directed at clinics in the early 1980s[8] (Blanchard 1994; Grant 1991).

Several of the pro-life movement's problems stemmed from the inexperience, naïveté, disorganization, and absolutism found in the Christian Right (Johnson 1999). Similar to other social movements, in its infancy the pro-life movement had severe growing pains. The Christian Right insisted on taking pure political positions and refused to compromise, which is very limiting and problematic when operating in an institutional system premised on political compromise (Rozell and Wilcox 1996). Religious prejudice coupled with individualism retarded coalition development across different denominations. Early activists directed most of their attention to national politics and sought out personal media attention instead of focusing on developing a substantial grassroots movement (Rozell and Wilcox 1996; Watson 1997). Moving toward the end of the decade it appeared as though the pro-life movement was floundering and heading for disbandment.

Reinvigorating the Movement: The Rise of Rescue

The pro-life movement was reinvigorated in the mid-1980s by the emergence of new leaders. These new leaders turned the focus away from national politics to grassroots direct action, bringing new enthusiasm (grounded in scriptural language) and a youthful edge to the movement (Johnson 1999; Risen and Thomas 1998). The rise of the rescue branch of the pro-life movement changed the scope of the abortion debate and continues to shape it today.

Joseph Schiedler was an early pioneer of direct action tactics within the pro-life movement. Before the Supreme Court handed down the landmark *Roe* decision, Schiedler was already operating the Chicago branch of the Pro-Life Publicity organization (Grant 1991). He went on to found the Pro-Life Action League in 1980 and was an early champion of implementing direct action tactics in the campaign to end abortion (Ginsburg 1998). In 1985 Schiedler published *Closed: 99 Ways to Stop Abortion,* a book designed to teach pro-life activists how to end abortion. He has long been an advocate for protests and rescues, sidewalk counseling, and distributing anti-abortion literature at clinics (Grant 1991; Johnson 1999).

Schiedler soon gained national recognition and was on the lookout for fellow recruits who believed in using direct action tactics. Late in 1985, Schiedler's most

famous recruit contacted him. Randall Terry came of age during the social tur-
bulence of the 1960s and 1970s. He grew up in a liberal, middle-class, church-
going family and was an honor roll student as well as a talented musician (Ginsburg 1998; Risen and Thomas 1998). Terry dropped out of high school and
hitchhiked from his home state of New York down to the South to pursue a
career as a musician. His vision of rock-and-roll fame never materialized, and
after getting involved in drugs, seventeen-year-old Terry returned home.
Shortly thereafter, Terry was "saved," joined a charismatic church, and began
preaching to family, friends, and strangers (Ginsburg 1998). Terry soon turned
his energies to abortion protest.

After developing a core group of supporters in Binghamton, New York,
Terry set his sights much higher: taking his direct action tactics to the nation.
Terry and Schiedler strategized and gained support at the Pro-Life Action Net-
work's (PLAN) third annual conference, where members decided to increase
the use of clinic blockades (Johnson 1999). The term *rescue* was initially used in
Philadelphia in 1985 to describe direct action strategies designed to save babies
via shutting down abortion clinics (Munson 2002). Hence, Operation Rescue
(OR) was born. Terry and Schiedler finalized plans for Operation Rescue in
New York, and a five-member national advisory board that included Terry and
Schiedler was elected at the 1987 PLAN conference (Johnson 1999; Risen and
Thomas 1998).

Operation Rescue, a for-profit organization, was officially launched in April
1988 and headed up by Randall Terry (Ginsburg 1998). Terry was a dynamic,
charismatic leader who was able to attract thousands of members to OR. He
knew how to finesse the media and became a master at issuing colorful sound
bites, guaranteeing him time in the press.

Terry's opposition to abortion was firmly entrenched in his larger belief in
fundamentalist philosophy and the "doctrine of necessity," which views scriptural passages as mandates for action and shaped the particular brand of protest
tactics he promoted through Operation Rescue. The "doctrine of necessity"
embraces violence as a justifiable last resort when used to prevent greater acts of
violence (Ginsburg 1998). Operation Rescue ushered in a new era of clinic
blockades, mass protests, and the closing (albeit temporary) of abortion clinics
across the nation.

Under Terry's leadership, the first rescue was staged at a Cherry Hill, New
Jersey, clinic in 1987 (Munson 2002). A mere year later, Operation Rescue made

its national media debut at the 1988 Democratic National Convention in Atlanta and kicked off five months of protest known as "The Siege of Atlanta." Busloads of anti-abortion activists, who were largely recruited from the Christian Broadcasting Network, came from across the country to participate in the protests (Ginsburg 1998). Participants were instructed to withhold their identification from the police and go by the name "Baby Doe" to show solidarity with the unborn while simultaneously clogging up the jails and courts. During the months of July through October, over 1,300 OR protesters were arrested, and their refusal to cooperate with the authorities had the desired effect of backlogging the system (Ginsburg 1998; Johnson 1999). The Siege of Atlanta garnered much media attention leading to a substantial influx of resources into Operation Rescue.[9]

Operation Rescue started to balloon after the Siege of Atlanta, and other rescues were planned throughout the country. Following the Atlanta protests, Randall Terry declared, "We have been completely successful. We have shut down abortion facilities, we have rescued babies, we have maintained a peaceful, prayerful atmosphere. We have injected new vision and hope into the pro-life movement" (Ginsburg 1998, 232). Operation Rescue took its blockades to New York, Philadelphia, Wichita, and Los Angeles, to name a few (Risen and Thomas 1998). These rescues attracted hundreds and oftentimes thousands of protesters to a single abortion clinic. Activists were able to physically shut down the clinic by blockading the building, thereby making it impossible for clinic staff or clients to enter the building (Munson 2002). Operation Rescue's blockades eventually peaked. In 1988 it held 182 blockades, resulting in 11,732 arrests, and in 1989, 12,358 people were arrested at approximately 201 blockades (Johnson 1999).

By 1990, Operation Rescue's activities had significantly diminished—a paltry 34 blockades were held that year, and only 1,363 protesters were arrested (Johnson 1999). The quick decline in activity can be attributed to pro-choice counteractivity. Although abortion rights activists were initially taken by surprise, after a couple of years they had developed fairly successful counterstrategies such as implementing clinic escort services and challenging the legality of Operation Rescue's blockades. The National Organization for Women obtained an injunction against Operation Rescue for trespassing at clinics in New York. Other injunctions were filed against Operation Rescue in California, Georgia, Washington, Pennsylvania, and New York (Johnson 1999; Ginsburg 1998).

Pro-choice organizations began to put political pressure on elected officials, law enforcement agencies, and the courts. Various cities also began to tire of Operation Rescue's antics because they were costing cities considerable amounts of money as well as redirecting law enforcement efforts away from their regular beats to monitor, control, and disperse blockades (Johnson 1999; Risen and Thomas 1998). One city paid around $10,000 in law enforcement and vehicle fees resulting from one day of protesting (Sharp 2005, 41). Some cities were losing patience with Operation Rescue and started issuing fines against its individual members and the organization. In New York City, a trial court ordered Operation Rescue to pay a $50,000 contempt fine after it ignored the court's order prohibiting blockades of clinics in New York City. When Operation Rescue refused to pay the fine it continued to increase. By 1990, Operation Rescue owed $450,000 in fines (Johnson 1999).

Financial troubles were not the only problems beginning to plague Operation Rescue. It started to develop a tarnished reputation leading to a public relations nightmare. Operation Rescue dubbed itself the "civil rights movement of the eighties," and initial media coverage perpetuated this characterization of the group. During the early blockades, Operation Rescue often received favorable media coverage showing the organization engaging in sit-ins, singing freedom songs, and engaging in prayers (Risen and Thomas 1998; Ginsburg 1998). Its efforts were likened to the nonviolent strategies of the civil rights movement, and Operation Rescue frequently received accolades for its dedication to the cause of the unborn.

As pro-choice groups organized and had counterprotesters at clinics, the blockades started to become more antagonistic. Arguing repeatedly erupted between the two sides and often deteriorated into shoving, grabbing, and screaming matches. The physical and verbal aggression was recorded by the media, and Operation Rescue was beginning to be portrayed as the victimizer, particularly as OR members became more aggressive against women trying to enter clinics (Johnson 1999).

Operation Rescue suffered a significant blow from religious leaders. The group's blockades became more outlandish, prompting dozens of Protestant ministers to denounce OR's antics. Reverend Charles Stanley, one of the most influential Baptist ministers in the South, published a scathing critique of Operation Rescue's tactics in a pamphlet entitled *A Biblical Perspective on Civil Disobedience.* Reverend Stanley argued that since the law did not compel women to have abortions, women were acting as "free moral agents responsible before Almighty God for their actions" (Risen and Thomas 1998, 280). He argued that blockading clinic entrances would only be appropriate if women were forced to obtain abortions. The pamphlet also pointed out the dark path aggressive tactics could easily lead to: "if women were to be blocked from entering abortion clinics of their own free will," Stanley asked, then "why not physical restraint of those who are trying to enter, or even destruction of those who are performing the procedure" (Risen and Thomas 1998, 208). Operation Rescue and particularly Terry were stunned by Reverend Stanley's condemnation of the organization and believed his denouncement was a significant turning point for the group's fortunes.

Operation Rescue, which at its peak had a staff of 23 and received over one million dollars in annual donations, was facing financial ruin and disintegrating leadership (Munson 2002; Johnson 1999). Its ability to amass hundreds of protesters was fading. Many rank-and-file members could not keep up with the hectic pace of blockades, arrests, and imprisonment, especially as jail sentences stiffened (Munson 2002; Ginsburg 1998). By 1990, Operation Rescue was down to a core of "professional rescuers" who traveled from city to city living off free food and lodging provided by pro-life sympathizers. The final blow for Operation Rescue came in May 1994 when Congress passed (and President Clinton signed) the Freedom of Access to Clinic Entrances Act (FACE) (18 U.S.C. 248). FACE essentially criminalized clinic blockades and attached severe monetary penalties to those who violated the law. The act also opened the door for individuals who are seeking or providing reproductive services to seek "civil remedies" against offenders—that is, sue (Johnson 1999).

Operation Rescue started to fade into the background of the pro-life movement, but it had a lasting influence on the tactics and structure of the movement. On the more extreme end of activity, Operation Rescue functioned as a network for putting militant activists in touch with each other as well as solidifying their commitment to incorporating violence as a justifiable strategy to end abortion. Many fringe activists, who went on to commit violent acts, befriended each other during the Siege of Atlanta campaign. During their stint in jail, housewife Shelley Shannon (who eventually shot an abortion provider in Wichita, Kansas), John Arena (who was convicted for acid attacks against clinics), and Father Norman Weslin (who went on to become the leader of the extremist pro-life group Lambs of Christ) became acquainted with each other in

1988 (Risen and Thomas 1998). On the more moderate side of tactics, Operation Rescue fostered the direct action branch of the pro-life movement, which continues to be the most publicly visible and culturally influential segment of the pro-life movement.

Modern Structure of the Pro-Life Movement

The direct action arm of the pro-life movement is the most notorious branch of the movement. In reality, the pro-life movement is a combination of different organizations and individuals who share the common goal of wanting to end abortion but disagree on the best approach to achieving their ultimate goal. Munson (2002) describes the three branches of the pro-life movement as streams: direct action, politics, and individual outreach. These three streams are different subsets of organizations and individuals that are fluid, dynamic entities of the same movement.

The direct action stream has been in existence prior to *Roe;* however, it significantly grew in popularity in the decades following the legalization of abortion (Ginsburg 1998; Staggenborg 1991). Although there is not a single, dominant direct action organization, hundreds exist throughout the country. Direct action organizations focus on the immediacy of "saving" babies and women by deterring women from seeking abortion services via direct intervention, which is apparent in the mission statement and stated goals of these organizations (Munson 2002). Direct action organizations are noninstitutional, and the majority are grassroots, operating at the local level. These groups are not trying to directly change legislation, public policy, or court decisions; rather, they are trying to stop abortions in the most direct form—at the clinics. Direct action can take the form of unconventional tactics such as protests, rescues, sidewalk counseling, pickets, or vigils.

The direct action stream keeps the issue visible and salient in local communities, whereas the politics stream of the movement keeps an anti-abortion agenda visible in political institutions. The political branch of the movement consists of organizations and individuals who are trying to shape change through traditional political channels such as lobbying, political campaigns, and litigation (Ginsburg 1989; Munson 2002). These organizations focus on ending abortion via a constitutional amendment or overturning *Roe.* In reality, neither of these has been an attainable goal. Consequently the political arm of the movement frequently expends its effort on smaller legislative and legal victories such as reducing access to abortion services through parental consent laws, waiting periods, informed consent, and "partial-birth" abortion bans.

The dominant organization within this stream is the National Right to Life Committee (NRLC). Its mission is to "restore legal protection to innocent human life," and as a secondary goal the NRLC is "concerned with related matters of medical ethics which relate to the right to life issues of euthanasia and infanticide" (NRLC 2006). The organization does not get involved or take positions on issues indirectly or marginally related to abortion such as contraception, sex education, capital punishment, and national defense (NRLC 2006). The NRLC is the largest and wealthiest pro-life organization in the country (Munson 2002; Blanchard 1994). In 1980 the NRLC had an annual budget of $1.6 million and a membership of 11 million (Blanchard 1994). A mere eight years later its annual income was around $6.5 million, and today they boast an annual budget that exceeds $16.5 million (Blanchard 1994; Munson 2002). The NRLC also has incorporated affiliates in every state in the country (over 3,000 local chapters), and each state affiliate has a representative who sits on the national board of directors. Other major players exist in the politics stream of the movement such as the National Conference of Catholic Bishops and the Christian Coalition. Even though the latter has suffered declining membership and revenue in the past several years, it continues to be an important political player (Munson 2002). All of the organizations in the political stream spend the bulk of their resources on politics—ending abortion through traditional political institutions by means of legislation or litigation.

Finally the third stream of the pro-life movement is the outreach stream, which is composed of crisis pregnancy centers. These centers began before *Roe*; in fact, they were a reaction to the states' liberalization of abortion laws (Hartshorn 2003). Concerned pro-life Catholics believed they needed to offer alternatives to abortion services, hence the advent of crisis pregnancy centers. Birthright was the first formal organization to provide alternatives to abortion; it was founded in Canada in 1968, and it quickly spread to the United States. Birthright follows a strict charter that believes you cannot save a baby without "saving" (or servicing) a mother, and vice versa (Hartshorn 2003).

Today, more than 3,400 crisis pregnancy centers are listed in the United States. Roughly 2,300 of these are pregnancy centers, and approximately 350 of the centers also offer related medical services. About 80 percent of the centers are affiliated with one or more of the nine leading organizations involved in crisis pregnancy centers; the rest are professional social service agencies (for example, Catholic Charities operates about 500 of the centers), Christian maternity homes, (responsible for approximately 350 centers), nonprofit, Christian adoption agencies (another 160 of the centers), hotlines (roughly 30), and freestanding post-abortion programs (about 50) (Hartshorn 2003).

Crisis pregnancy centers offer a variety of services for women experiencing a "problem pregnancy" (also known as an unplanned, unexpected, or unwanted pregnancy) ranging from psychological to emotional to material support (Munson 2002). The driving philosophy behind crisis pregnancy centers is that offering a woman the proper support and guidance will encourage her to forgo an abortion and either keep her baby or place her child up for adoption. This particular branch of the pro-life movement is the least publicized and understood, yet pro-life advocates involved in this aspect of the movement put in the most volunteer hours for the movement (Munson 2002).

Similar to the direct action arm of the movement, the outreach arm has generated some controversy. The primary goals of crisis pregnancy centers are two-part: first, they attempt to attract women who are pregnant and considering an abortion into the center, and second, they aim to convince those women to continue their pregnancies to term (Munson 2002; Staggenborg 1991). All crisis pregnancy centers offer free pregnancy testing, which is often the hook for bringing women into the centers. Once there, women are counseled, especially those who have positive pregnancy tests. The quality of this counseling varies tremendously from untrained volunteers to professionally trained volunteers to paid social workers (Munson 2002). Pro-choice advocates have accused many crisis pregnancy centers of being "bogus clinics" and relying on deceptive advertising practices to entice women in, then using graphic slide shows or films to "counsel" pregnant women (Staggenborg 1991).

The three arms of the pro-life movement serve different functions for the movement. The three-branch structure is in place at the national as well as local level (Munson 2002). While all three streams are working for the same ultimate goal, eliminating abortion, their approaches are varied and unique. There is little overlap between the three streams, for example, volunteers working in the outreach branch may not support the tactics used by the direct action branch. Similarly, direct action organizations rarely work on policy changes or provide counseling and material support for pregnant women.

Successes for the Modern Movement

Together, these three branches of the movement have won some important victories. The outreach division of the movement can measure its success by the tremendous growth in crisis pregnancy centers. In 1971, there were 75 crisis pregnancy centers operating, and today there are over 3,400 (Hartshorn 2003). The politics stream has also experienced considerable success, both at the national and state levels.

Many of the significant national pro-life gains have played out in the Supreme Court. Table 2 contains a summary of the major Supreme Court cases dealing with abortion. By 1989, the constitutionality of states' abortion restrictions was challenged in *Webster v. Reproductive Health Services* (492 U.S. 490, 1989). The *Webster* ruling upheld a state ban passed in Missouri pertaining to the use of public employees and facilities for performing abortions. In a five to four decision, the Court determined that Missouri's ban was keeping with past decisions, such as *McRae,* where the justices stated that "the state need not commit any resources to facilitating abortions." *Webster* marked a sharp departure from its ruling in *Roe;* the Supreme Court upheld many of the anti-abortion restrictions and in turn opened the door for future restrictions. Three of the justices in the majority opinion (Justices Rehnquist, White, and Kennedy) even recommended revisiting the *Roe* decision, and Justice Scalia went so far as to suggest that the Court should overturn *Roe.* Writing for the minority opinion, Justice Blackmun posited that the decision signaled "a chill wind blow" for abortion supporters (Markels 2005).

Two other cases, *Ohio v. Akron Center for Reproductive Health* (497 U.S. 502, 1990) and *Planned Parenthood of Southeastern Pennsylvania v. Casey* (505 U.S. 833, 1992), reaffirmed the Supreme Court's willingness to allow restrictions against abortion services. In the 1990 *Ohio v. Akron* case, by a six to three margin, the Court found that an Ohio parental notification law (requiring notification of one parent plus a judicial bypass option) was constitutional. The Court rejected the argument that the judicial bypass was problematic because it did not guarantee anonymity to the minor, and it upheld a more difficult standard of proof for a minor seeking judicial bypass of the parental notification law.

Planned Parenthood of Southeastern Pennsylvania v. Casey was an even more significant victory for the pro-life movement. In 1992, the Supreme Court upheld and reaffirmed the basic tenets of *Roe*—the validity of a woman's right to choose an abortion—but it substantially altered the standard for reviewing restrictions on abortion. Discarding the trimester framework laid out in *Roe,* the justices determined that restrictions were legal as long as they did not constitute an "undue burden" for women seeking abortion services. An "undue burden" is any law that poses a substantial obstacle to a woman obtaining an abortion. Ruling five to four, the justices supported all but one provision of Pennsylvania's 1989 Abortion Control Act. The Court upheld Pennsylvania's twenty-four-hour waiting period, informed consent provision requiring women be given state-mandated information about abortion and offered materials on fetal development, parental consent, and a reporting and record-keeping provision for abortion providers. Spousal consent was the only part of Pennsylvania's act found by the Court to constitute an undue burden to women.

Since *Roe,* the Supreme Court has heard over two dozen cases pertaining to abortion, many of which have dealt significant setbacks for abortion rights advocates. The Court's decisions fueled the pro-life movement and opened the door for implementing abortion restrictions at the state level. Judicial successes have inspired the pro-life movement to make similar gains through other political institutions, namely, state legislatures.

In 1990, there were 465 abortion-related bills introduced in state legislatures, and the vast majority were anti-abortion bills (NARAL 2006). In 1992 the number of abortion-related bills introduced in state legislatures dropped to 100, but more than doubled to 220 in 1996. Those numbers continued to rise: 245 bills were introduced in 1998, compared to 395 in 2000 and 620 in 2001 (NARAL 2006). The pro-life movement's victories include over 400 anti-abortion measures being enacted in the states within a ten-year time span. Table 3 summarizes the major types of legislation being introduced in the states.

Even though abortion rights groups were mobilized in the states, anti-abortion legislation easily outnumbered pro-choice legislation from 1990 to 2001. For example, in 2000, pro-choice supporters introduced 138 bills, whereas pro-life sympathizers introduced 257 in the same year. The following year, 222 bills were pro-choice and 398 were anti-abortion. Out of the measures that were adopted by states during 2001, there were 39 anti-abortion measures, while 27 were pro-choice measures (NARAL 2006).

At midyear 2005, over 600 bills pertaining to abortion and reproductive

TABLE 2.   Supreme Court Decisions since *Roe v. Wade*

Case	Year	Ruling	Major Findings
Doe v. Bolton 410 U.S. 179	1973	7 to 2	Struck down state residency requirement. Struck down hospital requirement.
Bigelow v. Virginia 421 U.S. 809	1975	7 to 2	Invalidated state ban on advertisements for legal abortion.
Greco v. Orange Memorial Corp 421 U.S. 1000	1975	0[a]	Affirmed lower-court decision that private hospitals, financed by private funds, can refuse to perform elective abortions.
Planned Parenthood v. Danforth 428 U.S. 52	1976	6 to 3	Struck down prohibition against saline abortions at 12 weeks or greater gestation. Forbid absolute parental veto on minor's abortion. Upheld written informed consent and reporting requirements.
Beal v. Doe 432 U.S. 438	1977	6 to 3	State's refusal to use Medicaid funds for non-therapeutic abortions does not violate Title XIX of the Social Security Act.
Maher v. Roe 432 U.S. 464	1977	6 to 3	State's refusal to use Medicaid money for non-therapeutic abortions is constitutional.
Poelker v. Doe 432 U.S. 519	1977	6 to 3	A city-owned public hospital does not have to provide nontherapeutic abortions.
Bellotti v. Baird 443 U.S. 622	1979	8 to 1	Struck down parental consent requirement without a confidential alternative.
Colautti v. Franklin 439 U.S. 379	1979	6 to 3	Struck down requirement that fetal life be saved if viable.
Harris v. McRae 448 U.S. 297	1980	6 to 3	Upheld Hyde Amendment, permitting use of federal Medicaid money only for abortions necessary to save the life of the pregnant woman.
Williams v. Zbaraz 448 U.S. 358	1980	5 to 4	Upheld State's ability to choose not to pay for medically necessary abortions if no federal reimbursement was available.
HL v. Matheson 450 U.S. 398	1981	6 to 3	States may require parental notification for abortion for nonemancipated minor.
City of Akron v. Akron Center for Reproductive Health 462 U.S. 416	1983	6 to 3	Struck down 24-hour waiting period, elaborate informed consent rules, parental or judicial consent for all minors, and hospitalization for all second trimester abortions.
Planned Parenthood of Kansas City v. Ashcroft 462 U.S. 476	1983	6 to 3	Struck down hospitalization requirement similar to Akron.
Simopoulos v. Virginia 462 U.S. 506	1983	8 to 1	Upheld Virginia's hospitalization requirement that includes outpatient clinics.
Thornburgh v. American College of Obstetrics and Gynecology 476 U.S. 747	1986	5 to 4	Struck down Pennsylvania's informed consent rules and standards of care for postviability abortions because they neglected to make maternal health the paramount concern of the physician.

TABLE 2.—*Continued*

Case	Year	Ruling	Major Findings
Webster v. Reproductive Health Services 92 U.S. 490	1989	5 to 4	Upheld state prohibition against allowing state-employed physicians from performing abortions and against performing abortions in a state facility. Upheld requirement that MDs must determine fetal viability for abortions at 20 weeks or greater gestation.
Hodgson v. Minnesota 497 U.S. 419	1990	5 to 4	Upheld notification of both biological parents for minor's abortion as long as judicial bypass is provided. Upheld 24-hour waiting period between parental notification and minor's abortion.
Ohio v. Akron Center for Reproductive Rights 497 U.S. 502	1990	6 to 3	Upheld one-parent notification plus judicial bypass. Ruled that states need not guarantee absolute anonymity to minor seeking bypass. Upheld more difficult standard of proof for minors seeking judicial bypass.
Rust v. Sullivan 500 U.S. 173	1991	5 to 4	Upheld federal prohibition of employees of federally funded clinics from any discussion of abortion with patients.
Planned Parenthood of Southeastern Pennsylvania v. Casey 505 U.S. 833	1992	5 to 4	Upheld *Roe v. Wade* in principle. Discarded trimester framework, adopted "undue burden" standard. Upheld 24-hour waiting period, informed consent rules, reporting and record-keeping requirements. Struck down spousal notification.
Bray v. Alexandria Women's Health Clinic 506 U.S. 263	1993	6 to 3	Federal civil rights statute could not be used to protect abortion patients from protesters.
NOW v. Scheidler 510 U.S. 249	1994	9 to 0	Allowed use of federal anti-racketeering statute (RICO) to sue anti-abortion protesters who engage in violent action with intent to put clinics out of business.
Madsen v. Women's Health Center 512 U.S. 753	1994	6 to 3	Ruled that court-ordered restrictions on abortion clinic demonstrations are constitutional.
Schenk v. Pro-Choice Network 519 U.S. 357	1997	9 to 0	Allow "fixed" buffer zone 15 feet around clinic entrance. Ruled that "floating" buffer zone is unconstitutional.
Mazurek v. Armstrong 520 U.S. 968	1997	6 to 3	Upheld state "physician-only" requirement to perform abortions.
Hill v. Colorado 350 U.S. 703	2000	6 to 3	Upheld state statute that protesters could not approach clinic patients closer than 8 feet, when situated within 100 feet of clinic entrance.
Stenberg v. Carhart 530 U.S. 914	2000	5 to 4	Struck down Nebraska statute criminalizing "partial-birth" abortion.
Scheidler v. NOW 537 U.S. 393	2003	8 to 1	Overturned previous Supreme Court decision. Federal racketeering statute (RICO) cannot be used to sue anti-abortion protesters. Protesters do not violate Hobb's Act.

[a]Supreme Court let lower court decision stand.

TABLE 3. Major Types of State Legislation

Statute or Regulation	States Enacting	Description
Refusal (conscience-based exemptions)	47[a]	A law permitting certain medical personnel, health facilities, or both to refuse to participate in abortion on the basis of conscience (in certain states this law has been declared unconstitutional as applied to public facilities).
Counseling ban/gag rule	18	"Gag rules" preventing health care providers employed by the state or by entities receiving state funds from counseling or referring women for abortion services (one state has ruled this unconstitutional).
Husband consent and notice	9	Unenforceable laws mandating husband consent or notice before a married woman may obtain an abortion. (In *Planned Parenthood v. Casey* the Supreme Court held this provision unconstitutional).
Informed consent/ biased counseling/ waiting periods	33	Mandatory waiting periods providing that a woman may not obtain an abortion until a specified period of time after receiving a state-mandated lecture or materials. Certain states have ruled part or all of this provision unconstitutional or have issued preliminary injunctions prohibiting the enforcement of waiting periods.
		Informed consent laws, many of which require women to receive lectures and state-prepared materials on fetal development, prenatal care, and adoption.
Insurance	17	Prohibit insurance coverage for abortion unless women pay an extra premium. (One state found this provision unconstitutional).
		Provision requiring insurers to provide a policy alternative excluding abortion. Provision prohibiting insurance coverage for abortion in some circumstances where public employees are insured.
		Provision excluding abortion coverage from health care reform programs.
Legislative declaration (anti-choice)/ abortion bans	33	Laws declaring the intent of the legislature, if and when *Roe v. Wade* is overturned, to prohibit abortion. Provision declaring the state's intent of regulating abortion to the full extent constitutionally permissible.
		States' declarations stating their policy to protect the unborn with state laws.
		Resolution in opposition to the Freedom of Choice Act, proposed federal legislation that would codify the U.S. Supreme Court's decision in *Roe v. Wade*. Pre-*Roe* laws left in states' constitutions.
Medical abortion/hospital requirement	21[b]	Law restricting medical abortion.
		Law limiting medical abortion to licensed hospitals with an approved research protocol.
		Law preventing nurse practitioners or physician assistants from prescribing or distributing any drug or medication intended to cause abortion.

TABLE 3.—*Continued*

Statute or Regulation	States Enacting	Description
Abortion access for minors	45	Law prohibiting minors from obtaining abortions without parental consent or notice (some states do not enforce these laws).
Physician-only requirement	45	Law stating that only a physician may perform an abortion. Law stating that no woman may induce an abortion upon herself except under the supervision of a licensed physician.
Postviability restrictions	41	Law restricting the availability of postviability abortion services.
Public facilities	9	Law prohibiting the use of public facilities for the provision of abortion services.
Public funding	30	Provision that excludes abortion from state medical assistance programs except when the woman's life is endangered. Provision that only allows Medicaid programs to fund abortion in cases of life endangerment, rape, or incest.
Targeted regulation of abortion providers	34	A variety of regulations that abortion providers and clinics are required to adhere to, that do not apply to other medical professionals. Often included are elevated physician requirements or mandatory hospital stays. These vary by state.
"Partial-birth" abortion ban	12	Law banning certain types of abortion.
Fetal pain	3[c]	Law would require abortion providers to tell women seeking abortion after 20 weeks gestation that the fetus will feel pain and offer the woman anesthesia for the fetus.
Fetal homicide (Unborn Victims of Violence Act)	33[d]	Establishes fetus as separate victim when pregnant woman is killed. All states have exceptions for legal abortions.

[a]All information for states comes from NARAL, www.prochoiceamerica.org unless otherwise noted in table. Legislative categories encompass variations for each state and include legislation.

[b]Alan Guttmacher Institute, *State Policies in Brief,* February 1, 2006. The number refers to states requiring hospital stays. All information from www.agi-usa.org does not include enjoined legislation.

[c]Center for Reproductive Rights, *Mid-Year Report,* 2005

[d]Alan Guttmacher Institute, *State Policies in Brief,* February 1, 2006

rights had already been introduced in the states. Forty-four bills banning abortion, in the event that *Roe* is overturned, were introduced in twenty-two states during this legislative session; two of the bills were enacted in South Dakota and Texas (Center for Reproductive Rights 2005). The content of the other antiabortion measures ranged from establishing and strengthening personhood rights for a fetus to increasing mandatory counseling and waiting periods for women seeking services to implementing parental notification requirements.

Most recently, the pro-life movement is working with pro-life politicians on introducing the "Unborn Child Pain Prevention Act," which requires doctors to offer anesthesia for fetuses being aborted after twenty weeks of gestation[10] (Hopfensperger 2005). Fetal pain bills were introduced in nineteen states in 2005 and enacted in Arkansas, Georgia, and Minnesota. Within the first two months of 2006, six more states introduced fetal pain bills (Kaiser Network 2006). Table 4 contains a summary of the anti-abortion legislation adopted in each of the fifty states.

Most recently, at the national level, the pro-life movement has received two legislative victories. The first came on November 4, 2003, when President Bush signed into law the Partial Birth Abortion Ban Act. The act bans the dilation and extraction (D&X) abortion procedure, which is performed late in a pregnancy (Katz 2004). The National Right to Life Committee had been lobbying for this ban for over eight years. The bill represents the first direct national restriction on any method of abortion since the Supreme Court legalized elective abortions in 1973 (Johnson 2003). Pro-choice organizations in various states have already challenged the act in court because it lacks an exception for cases where a woman's health is at risk. The act has been ruled on by two different three-judge panels in the Ninth U.S. Circuit Court of Appeals in San Francisco and in the Second U.S. Circuit Court of Appeals in Manhattan. Both courts ruled the ban was unconstitutional; undoubtedly the constitutionality of the act will ultimately be decided by the Supreme Court (Neumeister 2006; Stolley and Uchimiya 2004).

The second significant victory came on April 1, 2004, when President Bush signed the Unborn Victims of Violence Act (also known as Laci and Conner's law). Although the NRLC had been lobbying for this legislation for five years, it received a boost in political support following the highly publicized homicide of Laci Peterson and her eight-month-old fetus, Conner. Laci Peterson's husband, Scott Peterson, was convicted of first-degree murder of his wife and second degree murder of his unborn son in 2004. The bill establishes that if a "child in utero" is injured or killed during the commission of certain federal crimes of violence, then the assailant may be charged with a second offense on behalf of the second victim, the unborn child. The bill recognizes a fetus as a distinct entity from its mother by stating that an assailant can be prosecuted for separate offenses against both a woman and her unborn child, "a member of the species

TABLE 4. Abortion Legislation by State

State	Legislation
Alabama	Abortion ban, Biased counseling, and mandatory delay, Counseling ban/Gag rule, Physician-only restriction, Public funds restriction, Restricts minor's access, TRAP, Postviability restriction, Hospital requirement.
Alaska	Abortion ban, Biased counseling, Physician only restriction, Refusal, Restricts minor's access, TRAP.
Arizona	Abortion ban, Counseling ban/Gag rule, Physician-only restriction, Public facilities restriction, Refusal, Restricts minor's access, TRAP, Postviability restriction, Fetal homicide law.
Arkansas	Abortion ban, Biased counseling and mandatory delay, Insurance prohibition, Anti-choice legislative declaration, Physician-only restriction, Refusal, Public funds restriction, Restricts minor's access, TRAP, Postviability restriction, Fetal homicide law, Fetal pain provision.
California	Physician-only restriction, Refusal, Restricts minor's access, Informed consent, Postviability restriction, Fetal homicide law.
Colorado	Abortion ban, Husband consent, Insurance prohibition, Physician-only restriction, Refusal, Public funds restriction, Restricts minor's access.
Connecticut	Physician-only restriction, Refusal, TRAP, Informed consent, Postviability restriction, Minor specific counseling, Hospital requirement.
Delaware	Abortion ban, Biased counseling and mandatory delay, Physician-only restriction, Refusal, Public funds restriction, Restricts minor's access, Postviability restriction.
DC	Physician-only restriction, Refusal, Public funds restriction.
Florida	Abortion ban, Biased counseling, Physician-only restriction, Refusal, Public funds restriction, Restricts minor's access, TRAP, Postviability restriction, Fetal homicide law.
Georgia	Biased counseling and mandatory delay, Physician-only restriction, Refusal, Public funds restriction, Restricts minor's access, TRAP, Postviability restriction, "Partial-Birth" abortion ban, Fetal homicide law, Fetal pain provision.
Hawaii	Physician-only restriction, Refusal, TRAP.
Idaho	Abortion ban, Biased counseling and mandatory delay, Insurance prohibition, Anti-choice legislative declaration, Physician-only restriction, Refusal, Public funds restriction, Restricts minor's access, TRAP, Postviability restriction, Hospital requirement, Fetal homicide law.
Illinois	Abortion ban, Counseling ban/Gag rule, Husband consent, Insurance prohibition, Anti-choice legislative declaration, Physician-only restriction, Refusal, Restricts minor's access, TRAP, Postviability restriction, Fetal homicide law.
Indiana	Abortion ban, Biased counseling and mandatory delay, Counseling ban/Gag rule, Physician-only restriction, Refusal, Public funds restriction, Restricts minor's access, TRAP, Postviability restriction, Hospital requirement, "Partial-Birth" abortion ban, Fetal homicide law.
Iowa	Abortion ban, Physician-only restriction, Public facilities restriction, Refusal, Public funds restriction, Restricts minor's access, Postviability restriction.
Kansas	Biased counseling and mandatory delay, Counseling ban/Gag rule, Public facilities restriction, Refusal, Public funds restriction, Restricts minor's access, Postviability restriction, "Partial-Birth" abortion ban.
Kentucky	Abortion ban, Biased counseling and mandatory delay, Counseling ban/Gag rule, Husband notice, Insurance prohibition, Anti-choice legislative declaration, Physician-only restriction, Public facilities restriction, Refusal, Public funds restriction, Restricts minor's access, TRAP, Postviability restriction, Hospital requirement, Fetal homicide law.

(Continues)

TABLE 4.—*Continued*

State	Legislation
Louisiana	Abortion ban, Biased counseling and mandatory delay, Counseling ban/Gag rule, Husband consent, Anti-choice legislative declaration, Physician-only restriction, Public facilities restriction, Refusal, Public funds restriction, Restricts minor's access, TRAP, Postviability restriction, Fetal homicide law.
Maine	Physician-only restriction, Refusal, Public funds restriction, Restricts minor's access, Informed consent, Postviability restriction.
Maryland	Physician-only restriction, Refusal, Restricts minor's access, Postviability restriction, Fetal homicide law.
Massachusetts	Abortion ban, Biased counseling and mandatory delay, Insurance prohibition, Physician-only restriction, Refusal, Restricts minor's access, TRAP, Postviability restriction, Hospital requirement, Fetal homicide law.
Michigan	Abortion ban, Biased counseling and mandatory delay, Counseling ban/Gag rule, Insurance prohibition, Physician-only restriction, Refusal, Public funds restriction, Restricts minor's access, TRAP, Postviability restriction, Fetal homicide law.
Minnesota	Biased counseling and mandatory delay, Counseling ban/Gag rule, Physician-only restriction, Refusal, Restricts minor's access, TRAP, Postviability restriction, Hospital requirement, Fetal homicide law, Fetal pain provision.
Mississippi	Abortion ban, Biased counseling and mandatory delay, Counseling ban/Gag rule, Insurance prohibition, Physician-only restriction, Public facilities restriction, Refusal, Public funds restriction, Restricts minor's access, TRAP, "Partial-Birth" abortion ban, Fetal homicide law.
Missouri	Abortion ban, Biased counseling and mandatory delay, Counseling ban/Gag rule, Insurance prohibition, Anti-choice legislative declaration, Physician-only restriction, Public facilities and employees restriction, Refusal, Public funds restriction, Restricts minor's access, TRAP, Postviability restriction, Hospital requirement, Fetal homicide law.
Montana	Biased counseling and mandatory delay, Refusal, Restricts minor's access, Postviability restriction, "Partial-Birth"abortion ban.
Nebraska	Abortion ban, Biased counseling and mandatory delay, Counseling ban/Gag rule, Insurance prohibition, Anti-choice legislative declaration, Physician-only restriction, Refusal, Public funds restriction, Restricts minor's access, Postviability restriction, Fetal homicide law.
Nevada	Physician-only restriction, Refusal, Public funds restriction, Restricts minor's access, TRAP, Informed consent, Postviability restriction, Hospital requirement, Fetal homicide law.
New Hampshire	Public funds restriction, Restricts minor's access.
New Jersey	Abortion ban, Physician-only restriction, Refusal, Restricts minor's access, TRAP, Hospital requirement.
New Mexico	Abortion ban, Physician-only restriction, Refusal, Restricts minor's access, Postviability restriction, "Partial-Birth" abortion ban.
New York	Physician-only restriction, Refusal, TRAP, Postviability restriction, Hospital requirement, Fetal homicide law.
North Carolina	Physician-only restriction, Refusal, Public funds restriction, Restricts minor's access, TRAP, Postviability restriction, Hospital requirement.
North Dakota	Abortion ban, Biased counseling and mandatory delay, Counseling ban/Gag rule, Husband consent, Insurance prohibition, Anti-choice legislative declaration, Physician-only restriction, Public facilities restriction, Refusal, Public funds restriction, Restricts minor's access, TRAP, Postviability restriction, Hospital requirement, "Partial-Birth" abortion ban, Fetal homicide law.

TABLE 4.—*Continued*

State	Legislation
Ohio	Abortion ban, Biased counseling and mandatory delay, Counseling ban/Gag rule, Insurance prohibition, Mifepristone ban, Physician-only restriction, Refusal, Public funds restriction, Restricts minor's access, TRAP, Postviability restriction, "Partial-Birth" abortion ban, Fetal homicide law.
Oklahoma	Abortion ban, Biased counseling and mandatory delay, Physician-only restriction, Refusal, Public funds restriction, Restricts minor's access, TRAP, Postviability restriction, Hospital requirement, "Partial-Birth" abortion ban, Fetal homicide law.
Oregon	Refusal.
Pennsylvania	Biased counseling and mandatory delay, Counseling ban/Gag rule, Husband notice, Insurance prohibition, Anti-choice legislative declaration, Physician-only restriction, Public facilities restriction, Refusal, Public funds restriction, Restricts minor's access, TRAP, Postviability restriction, Hospital requirement, Fetal homicide law.
Rhode Island	Abortion ban, Biased counseling, Husband notice, Insurance prohibition, Physician-only restriction, Refusal, Public funds restriction, Restricts minor's access, TRAP, Postviability restriction, Hospital requirement, Fetal homicide law.
South Carolina	Abortion ban, Biased counseling and mandatory delay, Counseling ban/Gag rule, Husband consent, Insurance prohibition, Physician-only restriction, Refusal, Public funds restriction, Restricts minor's access, TRAP, Postviability restriction, Hospital requirement, "Partial-Birth" abortion ban, Fetal homicide law.
South Dakota	Abortion ban, Biased counseling and mandatory delay, Anti-choice legislative declaration, Physician-only restriction, Refusal, Public funds restriction, Restricts minor's access, TRAP, Postviability restriction, Hospital requirement, "Partial-Birth" abortion ban, Fetal homicide law.
Tennessee	Abortion ban, Biased counseling and mandatory delay, Physician-only restriction, Refusal, Public funds restriction, Restricts minor's access, TRAP, Postviability restriction, "Partial-Birth" abortion ban, Fetal homicide law.
Texas	Biased counseling and mandatory delay, Physician-only restriction, Refusal, Public funds restriction, Restricts minor's access, TRAP, Postviability restriction, Fetal homicide law.
Utah	Abortion ban, Biased counseling and mandatory delay, Husband consent, Anti-choice legislative declaration, Physician-only restriction, Refusal, Public funds restriction, Restricts minor's access, TRAP, Postviability restriction, Hospital requirement, Fetal homicide law.
Vermont	Abortion ban.
Virginia	Abortion ban, Biased counseling and mandatory delay, Counseling ban/Gag rule, Insurance prohibition, Physician-only restriction, Refusal, Public funds restriction, Restricts minor's access, TRAP, Postviability restriction, Hospital requirement, Fetal homicide law.
Washington	Physician-only restriction, Refusal, Postviability restriction, Fetal homicide law.
West Virginia	Abortion ban, Biased counseling and mandatory delay, Refusal, Restricts minor's access, Fetal homicide law.
Wisconsin	Abortion ban, Biased counseling and mandatory delays, Counseling ban/Gag rule, Insurance prohibition, Physician-only restriction, Refusal, Public funds restriction, Restricts minor's access, TRAP, Postviability restriction, Hospital requirement, Fetal homicide law.
Wyoming	Physician-only restriction, Refusal, Public funds restriction, Restricts minor's access, Postviability restriction.

homo sapiens, at any stage of development, who is carried in the womb" (Brownfeld and Emanuel 2004).

Abortion opponents continue to make progress in terms of limiting the accessibility of abortion services by pursuing marginal issues related to abortion. Pro-life organizations have recently attempted to prohibit the use of mifepristone, more commonly known as RU-486, which can be taken to terminate an early pregnancy (defined as forty-nine days or less from conception). The Food and Drug Administration approved RU-486 in 2000, and since it was approved, eight women have allegedly died as a result of using the drug. The FDA responded by adding a warning label to the drug. The United States Conference of Catholic Bishops,[11] along with other groups from the political branch of the pro-life movement such as the National Right to Life Committee, Concerned Women for America, Family Research Council, Democrats for Life, and the Susan B. Anthony List, have lobbied for recalling the drug. Their efforts have materialized into Holly's law (H.R. 1079). Holly's law, named after Holly Patterson, a California woman who died in September 2003 from toxic shock after using RU-486, is being introduced in the 2006 session of Congress. The bill calls for a moratorium on RU-486 while the comptroller general reviews whether or not the FDA adhered to the proper process for approving the drug. A spokesperson for the United States Conference of Catholic Bishops explained the strategy of supporting the bill: "Holly's Law is a very modest bill. It provides only for temporary suspension of the Food and Drug Administration's approval of RU-486. . . . If the FDA bent the rules to expedite approval of RU-486, the agency clearly valued the 'health' of the abortion industry over women's health and should be brought to account" (United States Conference of Catholic Bishops 2006).

Employing a political strategy aimed at incrementally changing abortion policy has also translated into some success in the public opinion arena. The majority of Americans still believe that abortion should be legal in some, but not all circumstances. The pro-life movement has successfully exploited and capitalized on these "middle ground" issue positions that are supported by most citizens by focusing on issues such as parental consent laws, partial-birth abortion bans, and continuing to "humanize" the fetus through fetal pain bills. Pro-life efforts are paying off; opinions are beginning to change in terms of the moral acceptability of abortion (Saad 2004). The majority, 50 percent, of Americans believe that abortion is morally wrong, compared to 40 percent who believe it is morally acceptable (Saad 2004). Even more striking is the change among young people. Although the majority of teens aged 13 to 17 believe abortion is acceptable, one-third believe abortion should be illegal in all circumstances (Mazzuca 2003).

Conclusion

The pro-life movement has grown into a politically savvy movement that has exerted a tremendous amount of influence over the political and cultural landscape in American society. It has achieved significant legislative and legal victories at the national and state levels. Many of the pro-life movement's gains have evolved from a strategy of enlisting multiple political institutions in a campaign to incrementally chip away at abortion. The movement has developed several institutional strategies, one of which is focusing on peripheral issues of abortion such as "partial-birth abortion" and the prevention of fetal pain during abortion services, in conjunction with mounting real threats to the future legality of *Roe*. Focusing on consensus morality issues like fetal pain continues to serve the movement in establishing the fetus as a person in the minds of society while simultaneously winning on an abortion issue that pro-choice supporters are not going to contest.

Over time, this institutional strategy of launching several attacks against abortion—head on and at the margins—in multiple institutional venues at the local, state, and national levels has resulted in substantial and enduring victories for the pro-life movement. In 2005, abortion rights opponents had a significant impact on state legislatures. States enacted more laws to restrict abortion services in 2005 than had been enacted in the previous years (Alan Guttmacher Institute 2006). The introduction of numerous pieces of legislation in January 2006, at the state level, is indicative of what is to come for the remainder of the year; pro-life supporters are likely to push for limiting the availability of abortion services while continuing to emphasize the interests of the fetus. The institutionalized branch of the movement is willing to stay the course by carving away at abortion rights through traditional political institutions.

Yet, in the face of the movement's significant legislative victories and multiple policy gains, the direct action branch continues to thrive and rely on the use of politically harassing tactics. As social movements institutionalize and their interests begin to be represented in political institutions they move away from confrontational tactics because they are no longer necessary—the government is responding to the movements' issues. This pattern has not been the case in the pro-life movement. Legislative and legal victories have not curbed the use of direct action tactics; in fact, the opposite has occurred. Since the early 1990s there has been a tremendous growth in protest activity among the direct action branch of the pro-life movement; anti-abortion opponents picketed clinics over eleven thousand times in 2004 (National Abortion Federation 2006).

The pro-life movement is foremost a morality movement, which creates a unique set of parameters around the movement that are not typical of non-morality movements. Abortion is a black-and-white issue, and for many members of the movement the institutionalized political strategy of compromise, negotiation, and patience fails to address the immediacy of abortion. Activists believe in the urgency of stopping murder today and being front and center in the culture war being waged in society.

The political reality of having twelve years of pro-life support in the White House that never materialized into an outright constitutional or judicial defeat of *Roe* was demoralizing (Blanchard 1994). The movement experienced tremendous frustration resulting from this situation; the ultimate goal of eliminating abortion remained elusive to the movement. Within the direct action arm of the movement, activists turned to a different strategy that enables them to focus on the immediacy of saving lives while avoiding compromise and incremental change. Direct action tactics are cost efficient, timely, and effective in influencing the abortion debate on a daily basis, and they serve the entire movement by providing visibility to the abortion issue, which has been a likely contributor to political actors' responsiveness to the policy initiatives lobbied for by the institutionalized branch of the movement.

In the following two chapters, I explore the growth in prominence of the direct action branch of the pro-life movement. Rather than going through political institutions, the use of political harassment enables the direct action branch to circumvent political actors, compromise, negotiation, and incremental change by taking its fight to those most directly responsible for abortion: providers and women seeking abortion services.

Chapter 4

CREATING A NEW GAME
The Scope of Anti-Abortion Violence
and Harassing Tactics

> The abortion dispute is not merely about conceptual disagreement. It's about
> justice. It's about violence, bloodshed, and victims who need to be defended in
> the midst of a policy permitting 4,000 babies a day to be killed. To "agree to
> disagree" means to cease to defend the absolute rights of the victim. The
> proposal to "agree to disagree" presumes the issue is about people disagreeing
> over abortion, not about people being killed by abortion. It is a false solution.
>
> —Reverend Frank Pavone, national director of Priests for Life,
> speaking at a pro-life event, December 1999

In the past four decades, anti-abortion activities have run the gamut from legal protest to quasi-legal protest to illegal protesting and violence. The trends in activity have waxed and waned throughout the years, often responding to changing strategies and political opportunities. One marked trend is the decrease in extreme incidents of violence such as arson, bombing, and murder following the passage of the 1994 Freedom of Access to Clinic Entrances (FACE) Act (18 U.S.C. 248) and a corollary increase in protest activities around the same time period.

Throughout the 1980s direct action groups of the pro-life movement regularly incorporated confrontational tactics into their repertoire of action. In 1985, among abortion providers, 85 percent reported that they had been subjected to at least one form of anti-abortion harassment,[1] including, but not limited to, picketing, clinic blockades, jamming of telephone lines, invasion of the facility, bomb threats, and distribution of anti-abortion literature. Typically, the harassment was not isolated to one occasion or form; rather it was part of a continual campaign against the provider. For example, 82 percent of providers reported that they experienced multiple forms of harassment (Forrest and Henshaw 1987). In addition, 19 percent of providers received bomb threats, and 16 percent had experienced picketing at their homes or the homes of staff members. By 2000, over half (52 percent) of abortion providers continued to be the targets of at least one form of anti-abortion harassment (Finer and Henshaw 2003). Even more striking is the proportion of providers (82 percent) experiencing some form of anti-abortion activity at large-scale abortion facilities (a large-scale abortion provider is defined as a nonhospital facility that performs 400 or more abortions a year).

The motivation and support for the various types of pro-life activities are not uniform across the movement. The three branches of the movement implement different strategies to achieve different aspects of the same final goal of ending abortion. The political branch focuses on making incremental institutional changes through national and state political institutions, in the hope that this strategy will give way to a permanent, legal reversal of *Roe*. Groups in this branch of the movement focus on supporting bills that make small inroads into criminalizing abortion or, at a minimum, decreasing the accessibility of abortion services. The outreach branch concentrates its efforts on aiding women who are facing unplanned and unwanted pregnancies. Crisis pregnancy centers offer services to help pregnant women and encourage them to keep their children or place them up for adoption.

Direct action groups focus on the immediacy of preventing abortions by trying to influence women seeking services to abstain from getting abortions and encouraging professionals to cease providing the services. Pro-Life Action League, one of the oldest direct action groups in the movement, explains the motivation and urgency of its confrontational tactics in its mission statement.

> We confront the abortionists and abortion promoters wherever they are. We picket and demonstrate outside abortion facilities, pro-abortion events, the offices of abortion organizations like NOW and Planned Parenthood and even abortionists' houses. We infiltrate their meetings and groups. (Pro-Life Action League 2006)

While protesting is certainly endorsed by the direct action branch of the movement, illegal and violent activities are not; the philosophy and actions of extremist groups have been vociferously denounced by the pro-life movement (Schabner 2004; National Right to Life Committee 2004). David Bereit, who heads up one of the most media-featured pro-life direct action groups in the country, explains where his organization draws the boundaries between acceptable and unacceptable activities.[2]

> We always encourage people to practice their faith however they want. We're not there to try and say you have to do things a certain way. And so there'll be people that will be out there praying rosary. There'll be people out there speaking in tongues. There will be people out reading scripture. And we really encourage them to bring your faith and come and pray as you see fit. One thing we very much do is we ask them [activists] to sign a statement of peace because we believe it's important that everybody knows on the front end that that's what we're about; is peaceful solutions. And so, it's a pledge that they will not participate in violent activity. (Interview with David Bereit, December 5, 2003)

Direct action groups of the pro-life movement do not condone violence and illegal activities, but extremist activity is an aspect of the abortion political environment. It is difficult to divorce the rhetorical absolutism as well as the individualized nature of protest activities endorsed by pro-life direct action organizations from the underlying context of violence that has occurred in the fight over abortion politics.

> We are doing all we can to stop the killing and the exploitation. . . . Through prayer vigils outside abortion facilities and sidewalk counseling, we reach out to abortion-bound women and couples with abortion alternatives, confidential counseling, access to pregnancy resources and other help, and witness the value of the lives being destroyed inside. We believe sidewalk counseling is the most important pro-life work God has given us to do. . . . We raise awareness of the injustice of abortion through marches, pickets, prayer vigils, and especially Face the Truth Tours, during which we hold large abortion pictures on busy streets to show what abortion does to the unborn child. (Pro-Life Action League 2006)

The direct action branch of the movement is dedicated to targeting nongovernmental actors in its pursuit of eradicating abortion. Organizations teach direct action strategies to other grassroots groups, training fellow activists how to "become successful pro-life leaders in their communities and save lives through direct action" and teaching activists to learn how to "bewilder the purveyors of abortion" (Pro-Life Action League 2006; American Life League 2006). The form of the activities is personalized, continual, and directed at abortion clinics and women seeking services. Unlike governmental actors, women and health care providers lack the resources to insulate themselves from the tactics. Extremist activities have also been directed at abortion service providers and women seeking services. The combination of violence with the daily acts of confrontation taking place at clinics contributes to an environment of fear, which is what changes the meaning of the activity from unconventional political protest into political harassment. Contextualizing and understanding the scope and implications of harassing behavior must begin with an exploration of the use of extreme violence in the pro-life movement.

Extreme Violence

Extreme anti-abortion violence, while a form of political violence, differs from political harassment. Extremist activity results in greater property and personal losses, but it has not been widely embraced by the pro-life movement, nor is it nearly as popular as unconventional participation (Risen and Thomas 1998; Russo and Denious 1998). Despite the movement's rejection of violence, several radical pro-life groups, following the doctrine of justifiable homicide, endorse and perpetrate extreme violence. During her interviews with extremist members, Luker was told by an activist that "even if lives were lost in violence directed at an abortion clinic, that loss would be outweighed, and justified, by the greater net saving of unborn lives" (1984, 217).

For over two decades, the Army of God has claimed responsibility for pro-life vandalism, burnings, shootings, and bombings spanning from Virginia to Oregon (Mason 2002a). Similar to other extremist resistance movements, the Army of God is a leaderless organization, which in reality is an organization in name only. The Army of God is not a formal organization; it lacks structure and has a limited membership base (Schabner 2004). Over the years, individuals have invoked the name Army of God when perpetrating criminal activity, often as lone agents, against abortion clinics and employees, giving the appearance of a larger and more cohesive resistance movement than actually exists throughout society. Experts estimate that only one to two hundred people share beliefs similar to those espoused by active Army of God members (Schabner 2004). The true number of active members is likely much smaller.

Although it has a limited support base, several of the most notorious anti-abortion extremists have been affiliated with the Army of God. Three men claiming to be Army of God members kidnapped an Illinois abortion clinic owner, Dr. Hector Zevallos, and his wife and held them hostage for eight days in 1982 (Jadhav 2006). In the past couple of years, several Army of God members have been convicted of crimes. Reverend Paul Hill was executed for the 1994 murders of Dr. John B. Britton and clinic escort James H. Barrett outside of a women's reproductive health clinic in Pensacola, Florida. James Kopp was recently convicted of the 1988 murder of Dr. Barnett Slepian, who performed abortion services in Buffalo, New York. Capitalizing on the September 11, 2001, terrorist attacks on the World Trade Center, Clayton Lee Waagner exploited the public's newfound fears of biological terrorism by sending dozens of letters containing faux anthrax to abortion clinics around the nation. He was convicted on fifty-one counts of federal terrorism in December 2003. Figure 1 contains an overview of the number of anthrax, bomb, and death threats directed at clinics from 1987 to 2004. The most notable spike on the graph is a result of the marked increase in anthrax threats at women's health care facilities following September 11, 2001. Over five hundred reproductive health clinics and women's rights organizations around the country received letters alleged to contain anthrax (Alan Guttmacher Institute 2001).

After eluding authorities and being on the FBI's Ten Most Wanted list for five years, in May 2003 another notorious Army of God extremist, Eric Rudolph, was arrested for his alleged role in the 1998 Birmingham, Alabama, clinic bombing that killed a security guard, Robert Sanderson, and severely maimed a nurse, Emily Lyons (Schuster 2003; Mason 2002a; National Abortion and Reproductive Rights Action League 2006). Rudolph is also suspected of bombing a women's clinic in Sandy Springs, Georgia, on January 16, 1997, then bombing a lesbian nightclub in Atlanta on February 21, 1997. Rudolph is also the primary suspect in the 1996 bombing at the Atlanta Olympics, which killed one person and injured 100 others (Schuster 2003; Schabner 2004).

In the context of overall anti-abortion activity, the scope of extreme and criminal activity is not extraordinary; however, the damage in terms of personal and property loss as well as the psychological toll it exacts from abortion clinic employees is very significant. These activities serve to create a credible fear of injury for women and health care professionals. Even though the actual probability of being the target of violence is small relative to other types of pro-life

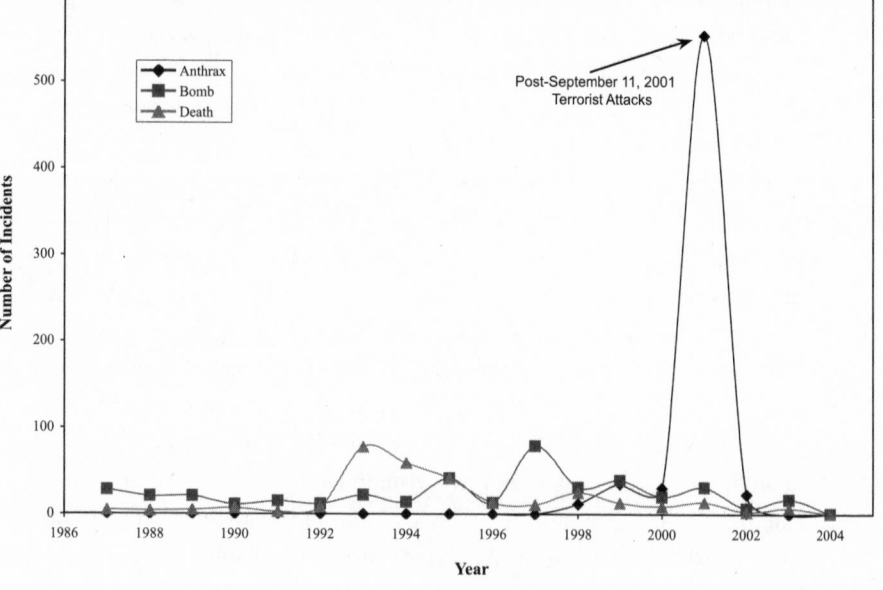

Fig. 1.   Anti-abortion violence threats

activity such as protesting, the numbers are still alarming.[3] Figure 2 displays the extent of anti-abortion criminal activity including attempted arson, invasion of clinic facilities, and vandalism of facilities from the mid-1980s to 2003.

More extreme acts of violence have also been perpetrated by pro-life radicals. The National Abortion Federation has recorded the following incidents directed at abortion providers and facilities between 1977 and 2005: 365 death threats, 87 attempted bombings and arsons, 41 actual bombings, 173 actual arsons, 3 kidnappings, 17 attempted murders, 7 murders, 1,169 acts of vandalism, 373 physical invasions of personal and business properties, 100 butyric acid attacks, 140 assaults, and 655 anthrax threats (National Abortion Federation 2006).

Figure 3 presents an overview of extreme anti-abortion activities including incidents of arson directed at clinics, the bombing of facilities, and the murders of health care professionals. The bulk of extremist activities were perpetrated

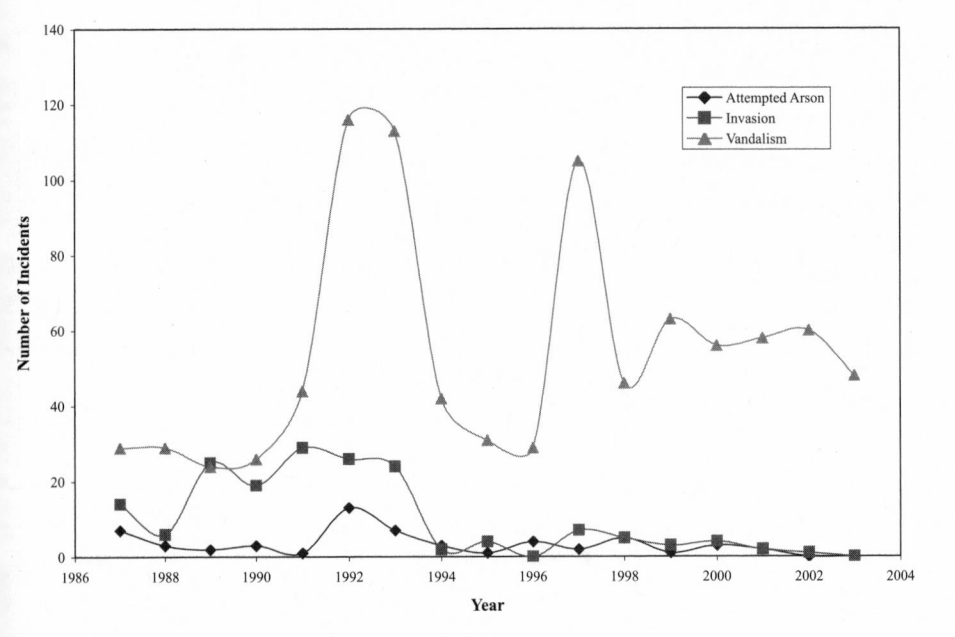

Fig. 2.   Anti-abortion criminal activity

and peaked in the 1980s. For example, 30 arson and bombing incidents occurred in 1984, and another 22 were reported in 1985 (National Abortion Federation 2006). Figure 3 shows a notable exception to this pattern. Acts of arson spiked up in the early 1990s: 19 acts of arson were committed in 1992 and another 12 in 1993. In 1997, bombing activity increased to 6 recorded incidents but tapered off quickly the following year (National Abortion Federation 2006).

Extreme anti-abortion violence has most dramatically resulted in severe injury and death for several doctors and clinic employees (Russo and Denious 1998, 28). Over a nine-year span, pro-life extremists killed three doctors, two clinic employees, a clinic escort, and a security guard (National Abortion and Reproductive Rights Action League 2006). The murders have been isolated to three specific years. The first occurred with the 1993 murder of Dr. David Gunn and the attempted murder of Dr. George Tiller. The next year extremists murdered four people and attempted to murder another eight. Most of these victims

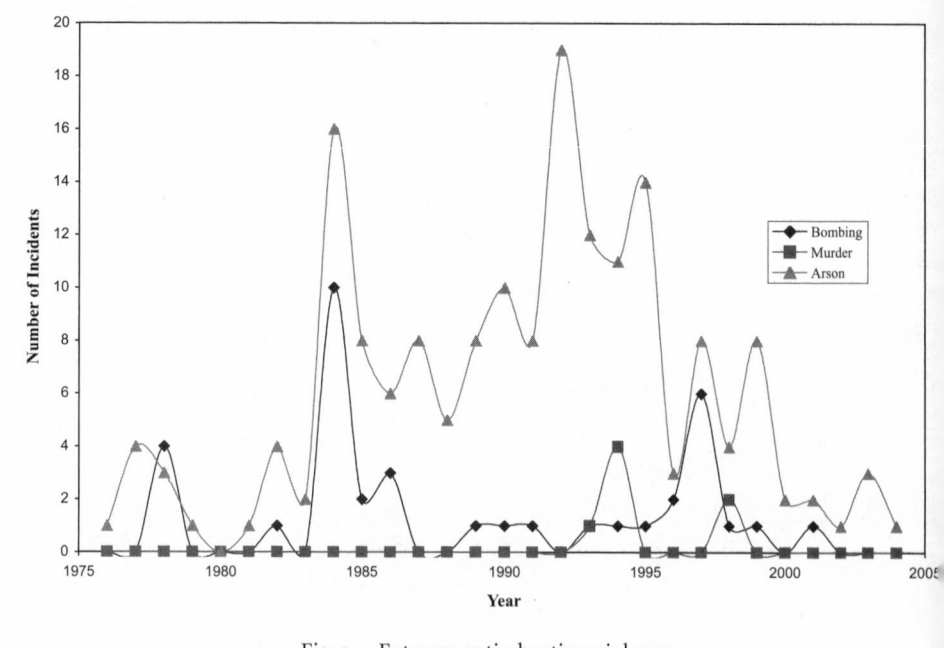

Fig. 3.   Extreme anti-abortion violence

were casualties of a shooting spree committed by John Salvi at two different clinics in Massachusetts. Two clinic employees were killed, and another five were injured[4] (National Abortion Federation 2006).

Extreme violence falls well outside the boundaries of confrontational tactics supported by the direct action division of the pro-life movement. Even though both harassment and extreme violence are intended to achieve the same outcome—eradicate abortion practices—they are motivated by different behaviors. Extreme violence is sporadic, opportunistic, and irregular, frequently committed by a lone participant. Harassment, particularly in the form of calculated protest activity, tends to be more systematic and continual, rarely resulting in the severe physical injury of others (Russo and Denious 1998).

The occurrences of harassment and extreme violence exhibit different patterns; harassment is more predictable than violence.[5] Political harassment and violence should also have a different effect on clinic employees and women seeking abortions. Given the longevity and frequency of political harassment, it should exert more influence over abortion providers and women because it constitutes a continuous threat. The ongoing emotional drain created for clinic employees was frequently reflected in the interviews. One clinic director, whose facility had recently become the target of pro-life protesting, described the toll pro-life harassment has had on the clinic's employees.

> It is effective and it is intimidating and it is scary. It has affected
> them[employees] and that affects everyone. The girls cry when [other
> employees] get something in the mail and you know it affects their families
> and their home lives. It is very effective, very threatening, very threatening.
> (Interview with a clinic director, February 2000)

Extreme violence should not wield as much influence over clinics or their clients because random violence generally does not present a routine and immediate threat to those involved in abortion services. Yet, the threat of extreme violence has become intertwined in the political culture of abortion politics. Threats can be overtly implied by activists at peaceful protests and prayer vigils particularly as pro-life supporters become frustrated with their attempts at ending abortion services. As one group's attempt to obstruct the construction of an abortion facility was failing, the tenor of members' prayers at the construction site became more aggressive and overtly threatening. "Dear Lord, we want to obey the law of the land but it's wrong; and we pray that you will understand if we have to break the law, but the law is flawed" (Protester at prayer vigil, September 1998). The implied threats exist in the same political context where extremists have made the possibility of violence credible by perpetrating acts of violence against clinics and individuals. One in five clinics experienced a form of extremist activities in 2000, including blockades, invasions, bombings, arsons, chemical attacks, stalking, physical violence, gunfire, bomb threats, death threats, and arson threats.

Regularized protesting is embedded in this larger abortion political culture where threats of violence are credible. This context creates an environment of fear and even paranoia at abortion clinics, which can easily exacerbate employees' perception of the threat posed by pro-life protesters and exhibited at routine protests (Lonsway et al. 2001).

> When I first started working here I laughed about it, you know I joked
> about it. I had never been around anything like this. And I didn't take it as

seriously and I would always joke. But I don't know now. . . . It's—this is just a gut feeling—it's got to go somewhere. So it is either gotta stop and go away or something's gotta happen. That's what I see. And it's not going to stop and go away. (Interview with clinic employee, June 2000)

The heightened sense of fear can also color the perception of harm created by nonviolent political protests as evidenced in the beginning of the following quote from an abortion provider.

I think standing out there is harassment, because the only reason for being there is to intimidate. . . . The fact that they attack women and scream obscenities and scream things and write down license plates—basically, they are trying to terrorize these women that are going in there or to some- how dissuade them. (Interview with a physician, November 2003)

Political Harassment

Together, anti-abortion harassment and violence coexist in abortion politics, although harassment is much more common. Figure 4 documents the down- ward trend in pro-life extreme violence and the upward trend in anti-abortion protest. For example, 45 percent of abortion providers reported receiving bomb threats in 1985, but by 2000 only 15 percent of providers were reporting the same crime. Figure 5 isolates protest activity and clearly shows the exponential increase in anti-abortion protests starting in 1995. In 1995, the National Abor- tion Federation reported 1,356 protests. This number jumped to 3,932 in 1996, then nearly doubled the following year to 7,518 protests, and reached 11,640 in 2004 (National Abortion Federation 2006). Unlike extreme violence, political harassment is much more patterned.

Large, nonhospital abortion providers (facilities performing 400 or more abortions a year) disproportionately bear the brunt of anti-abortion harass- ment. Among facilities performing fewer than 30 abortions annually, only 10 percent experienced one or more incidents of harassment, including activities such as picketing; picketing with physical contact or blocking of clients; vandal- ism; picketing the homes of staff; and bomb threats. Comparatively, 70 percent of clinics performing 400 to 900 abortions per year were the targets of similar harassment, and 100 percent of facilities providing 5,000 or more abortions a year were targets of anti-abortion harassment (Henshaw and Finer 2003; Coz- zarelli and Major 1998; Grimes et al. 1991).

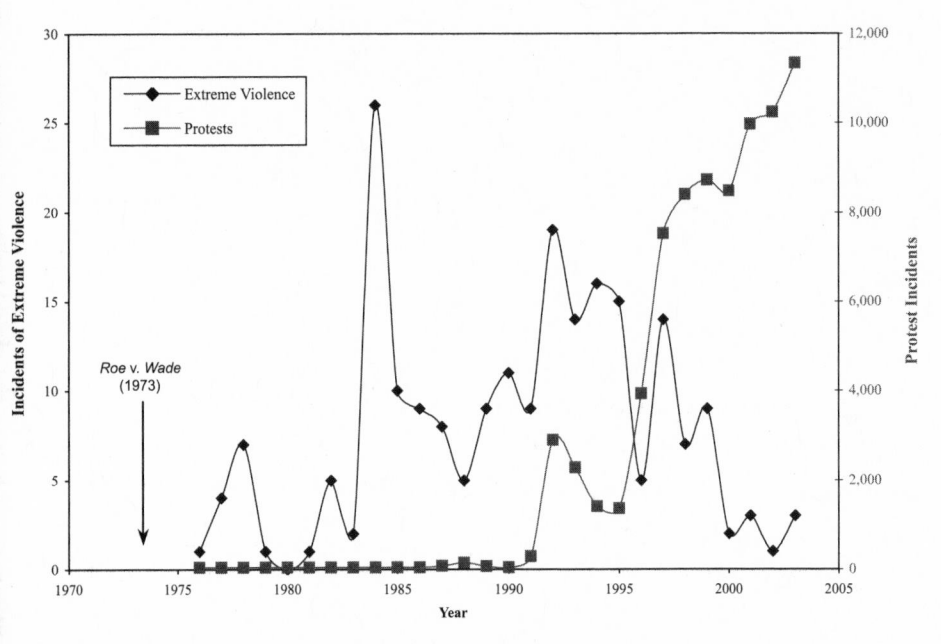

Fig. 4.   Protest and extreme violence

Examining large-scale abortion facilities provides a more accurate picture of where and how anti-abortion harassment is taking place. Clinics providing 400 or more abortions a year accounted for 94 percent of all abortions performed in 2000, and 82 percent of these facilities experienced anti-abortion harassment in the same year (Henshaw and Finer 2003). Since 1996, the proportion of large-scale providers reporting more severe forms of harassment has diminished; 14 to 28 percent of providers reported exposure to more extreme forms of harassment, which represents a marked decline in extremist activities. But the proportion of providers experiencing picketing continued to increase during this time span. In 2000, 82 percent of large-scale facilities were the objects of anti-abortion protesting and 61 percent of these facilities experienced 20 or more incidents of picketing a year (Finer and Henshaw 2003). For example, Hope Clinic in Granite City, Illinois, which is the only clinic in southern Illinois and one of only two clinics in the St. Louis region, is a constant target for protesters. Small Victories, a pro-life organization, has had nearly a daily presence at the clinic for more than a decade (Jadhav 2006).

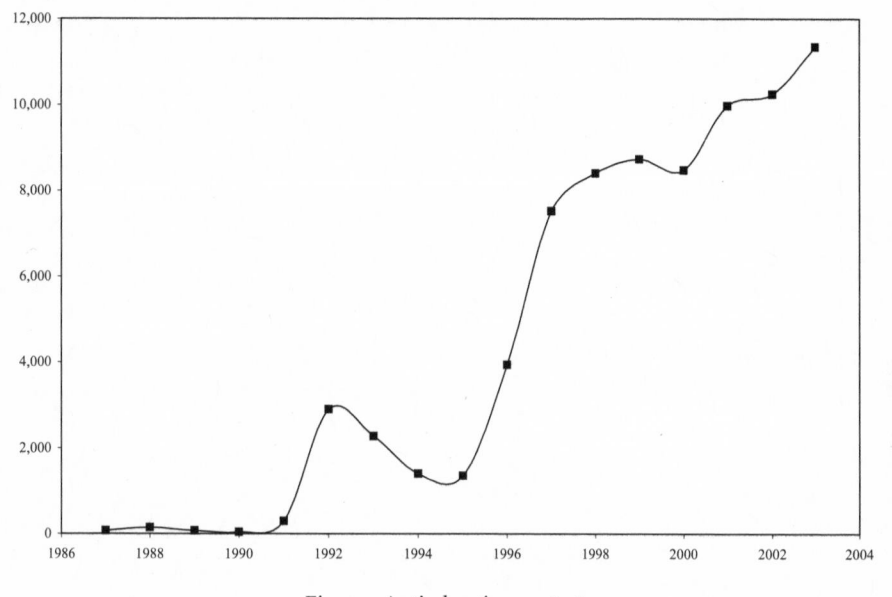

Fig. 5.   Anti-abortion protest

Among large-scale abortion facilities, those operating in the Midwest were most likely to be harassed (91 percent), while those in the western region of the United States were least (78 percent). Although western facilities were the targets of fewer protests, the high percentage of facilities experiencing picketing indicates that geographical region does not insulate facilities from pro-life direct action tactics. The intensity and persistency of protest is difficult to ignore and likely to have negative consequences for those most intimately involved in the abortion conflict—abortion providers and women seeking services.

Harassment and Abortion Providers

The confrontational tactics used by the pro-life movement have had adverse consequences for providers (Hern 1994; Luker 1984; Faux 1990; Blanchard and Prewitt 1993; Paige 1983; Blanchard 1994; Joffe 1995) and mixed effects on women seeking abortion services. In a 1993 survey conducted by the Alan

Guttmacher Institute (AGI), 30 percent of abortion providers named anti-abortion activity as the most important factor hindering their ability to perform services (Henshaw 1995a). Most episodes of anti-abortion harassment and violence are directed at abortion facilities. From 1977 to 1988, providers were the targets of 98 percent of pro-life direct action tactics (Grimes et al. 1991).

Harassment frequently creates problems with hiring and retaining staff members at facilities. Direct action groups encourage and teach activists to create an environment of low morale for clinic employees by regularly picketing at the facility. The American Life League has online instructions for pro-life activists detailing the steps to take to prevent an abortion clinic from opening in their local community, or if the clinic already exists in the community, the instructions teach activists how to shut it down.

> The single most effective thing you can do to fight an existing Planned Parenthood facility is to establish a regular (at least weekly) picket. This single act will lower PP's business, tarnish its community image, and result in increased public attention to its programs and philosophies. All these effects will work to your benefit. The more frequently you can picket PP's offices, the better. However, you should at least plan a weekly, two-hour picket. When you picket weekly, you do not need large numbers. The frequency will have its effect and will cause *morale and business problems* for PP. (American Life League 2006; emphasis added)

This strategy was very effective at creating staffing issues for Planned Parenthood in Bryan, Texas. Many of the clinic employees had worked at Planned Parenthood for years; the director had worked at the facility for eighteen years, the nurse for eight years, and many other staff members had an employment history with the clinic spanning three to ten years. Once Planned Parenthood announced its plans to start offering abortion services the environment surrounding the clinic dramatically changed. The opening of the new facility in 1999 was ushered in with continual pro-life protesting. In the early stages of the protest activity, the clinic employees were managing the stress of the new environment and remained committed to working at the clinic.

> You know, they have not run anybody off. People have asked us that. I mean we get very upset and get very scared, but we talk about it. I am not going to let them control my life. People have asked me if I wear a bullet-

proof vest. My friends, and even the police, think I should. But I refuse. I won't do it. If it comes to that, then it's time for me to quit. I just don't want it to escalate to that. (Interview with a clinic employee, January 2000)

Within three years, the clinic's director was the only employee remaining from the original facility. All other employees had left largely as a result of the strain of the weekly, and often daily, harassment.

Harassment also discourages physicians from providing services at clinics. During every interview I conducted with physicians, I was told that harassment functions as a deterrent for many doctors they know, who would, in the absence of pro-life protest, be willing to provide abortion services. The shortage of abortion providers forces many clinics to rely on physicians that are willing to travel to their facilities to perform services because they cannot permanently staff the clinics. One provider who lives in Washington, DC, spends one to two weekends a month flying to Texas to help out at several reproductive health facilities around the state because he believes in providing care for women and, just as important, he feels a sense of injustice about the limitations harassment places on abortion services.

I can tell you all kinds of stories about the desperation of women, who find themselves, for a number of different reasons, in need [of abortion services]. But that's my specialty, taking care of women. So that's what I do. . . . I have been flying in from DC now because there is a problem with finding providers [because] Texas is, well, these guys got guns for one thing. Some people are afraid of them. I'm not afraid of them. I mean I don't do it just to spite them, but you know, they are a small percentage and I don't want to see them win and close this place. I guess I don't have anything to lose. I don't have a family or anything so I'm not worried about that. I know that some doctors are worried that their homes are gonna get picketed. But I'm like, fine go ahead, picket my house. (Interview with a physician, December 2003)

Aside from staffing issues, harassment also has a detrimental monetary impact on clinics, abortion providers, and employees. As a result of the harassment and violence, many clinics have to implement costly security systems, lose their fire and casualty insurance, and experience high fees for legal services (Hern 1994; Forrest and Henshaw 1987). Facilities often have to deal with unanticipated costs resulting from pro-life harassment including new expenses or a reallocation of clinics' resources. For example, Debbie McCall was initially hired to handle public relations and fund-raising for Planned Parenthood, but her job quickly evolved into dealing with security concerns and monitoring the activity of the protesters who had come to the clinic.

It is my job to be able to tell you if I look out front to be able to say it is safe today because so and so are here and they do such and such. Now it is also my job to be able to tell you if someone new walks in. I can tell you who they all are and what they do. And which ones to be concerned about and which ones we don't have to be concerned about. (Interview with Debbie McCall, Director of Community Services for Planned Parenthood, May 1999)

The average cost of damage resulting from violent activities is $141,000 for a facility (Grimes et al. 1991). Relatedly, the communities where frequent harassment is occurring also incur expenses. For example, the 1991 anti-abortion summer protest in Wichita, Kansas, which lasted forty-two days and was orchestrated by Operation Rescue, cost the city $846,447 and kept three Wichita clinics closed for a week (Cozzarelli and Major 1998, 87; Johnson 1999).

Even the smaller-scale protesting has a monetary impact on communities. Since opening its doors for abortion services, the Bryan, Texas, police department has responded to over 229 calls (from 1999 to 2003) from both Planned Parenthood and pro-life protesters. Police spend an average of 45 minutes responding to each call, which diverts a considerable amount of their limited time to mediating abortion politics (Bryan Police Department 2004). Financially, each call costs the city approximately $19, which quickly adds up, particularly in smaller communities where law enforcement agencies have limited budgets. This officer explained his department's frustration with the diversion of limited resources given to the abortion conflict in his town.

The clinic came to our attention because of the volume of calls for services that we had down there. It started out small, maybe 34 or so a quarter. And when we ran the numbers again, we just watched it climb and climb and climb. And the calls were coming from both protesters and from people inside the clinic, so we were getting it from both sides. We decided that it was a problem because of the amount of time it was taking away from the officers . . . That is a point we try to impress on both sides: every time we have to send an officer down to deal with the clinic issue or the protester issue, that officer is not enforcing the laws, or dealing with more serious crimes. (Interview with a police officer, December 2003)

A more severe result of the harassment is the loss of abortion providers. The remarks made to me by one physician are quite telling. This physician was not an abortion provider, but she was motivated by her personal experience to volunteer to help with abortion services at a clinic relatively close to her home. As a young woman, she experienced an unwanted pregnancy and was moved by the "kindness, understanding, and support" she received from a clinic while she was figuring out what to do about her pregnancy. Years later, she wanted to "repay society" by helping other women who were facing an unwanted pregnancy. Her comments illustrate the deterrent effect that anti-abortion harassment has on other physicians as well as the toll her involvement has exacted on her and her family.

I mean who wants to be shot at. Who wants to be worrying about letter bombs or getting anthrax? I was even experiencing hateful e-mail, hateful harassment—you know people screaming stuff at me, sending postcards to my house, my husband's work, my home, my fellow physicians and clinic workers. (Interview with a physician, November 2003).

Between 1985 and 1988 there was an 8 percent decrease in the number of abortion providers, with a more dramatic drop of 18 percent between 1988 and 1992. The decline continued throughout 1992 to 1996; the number of providers fell another 14 percent (Henshaw 1998a, 1995a). The downward trend persisted from 1996 to 2000, and during this time period the consolidation of abortion provisions at specialized clinics also continued (Finer and Henshaw 2003). The decline in providers was more pronounced among small-scale providers compared to large-scale providers; however, given the small caseload of these providers the decline had little effect on the overall abortion rate (Finer and Henshaw 2003).

Deterring new providers and pushing existing providers out of business is part of the direct action branch's strategy of eliminating abortion by going after the perceived source: the supplier of services. The Pro-Life Action League takes credit for closing down eight abortion clinics in Chicago and over a hundred across the country (Pro-Life Action League 2006). The prevalence of anti-abortion harassment appears to be an obvious factor contributing to the decrease in abortion providers. Singling out this set of nongovernmental actors seems to be an effective strategy for dealing with the immediacy of the movement's goal of saving babies by stopping abortion. But saving babies is also achieved by "saving" women who are seeking out abortion services, which is the second set of nongovernmental actors targeted by direct action groups in the movement.

Harassment and Women Seeking Abortion Services

Angela and Daniel Michael have been protesting at an abortion clinic for over ten years; Angela has been involved with pro-life direct action activities for thirteen years. She was initially asked by a friend to protest once a month at the local abortion clinic. "When I saw those women coming in there like cattle, it broke my heart" (Jadhav 2006). Angela soon turned her protesting into a full-time campaign against the clinic and got her husband involved a few years later. The couple spends about forty hours a week working at their organization, Small Victories; their mission includes having a year round presence at the local abortion clinic. The couple started Small Victories because according to Angela, "When you stand there [the abortion clinic] and tell them don't kill your baby, you've got to give them options" (Jadhav 2006). The Michaels see the larger American culture being responsible for producing a society where abortion is tolerated; their job is to save babies by saving women. Since 2000, the Michaels claim they have saved 1,628 women from having abortions at Hope Clinic.

Pro-life groups' use of unconventional tactics is intended to prevent women from obtaining abortions by converting them to a pro-life stance through individual persuasion.

> I think it is the personal, the one-on-one. That is the only way. I think when it comes to the abortion issue it is a lot like religion in the sense that if you are going to change someone's mind—some people change their mind by reading an article or seeing a picture—or lots of time it's by discussion, debating and talking about things. That's why I think the most important way to make a difference is just one-on-one talking. (Interview with a pro-life activist, January 2000)

Groups believe that many women seek abortion services out of misinformation and a lack of knowledge about abortion. The key, according to one pro-life leader, is for direct action groups to educate women about abortion.

As people get more educated about what abortion is, they will naturally get more strong and see that the pro-abortion people try to keep away the facts of what abortion is and how it works and what it does to a woman—both psychological and physical. I think that as people learn the truth they are going to wake up. (Interview with a pro-life leader, October 1999)

Education takes place in a variety of ways: through prayer vigils, singing, visual aids, and sidewalk counseling. Pro-life groups cite sidewalk counseling as the most effective technique in directly saving women and their babies from abortion. Direct action groups have been using sidewalk counseling strategies for decades, but it started to grow in prominence as activists around the country were exposed to the technique and encouraged to use sidewalk counseling by other pro-life groups.

Sidewalk counseling is exactly what the name implies—standing on the sidewalk outside an abortion clinic, counseling women and couples on their way inside. It is a last attempt to turn their hearts away from abortion and offer real help. . . . The main motivation for sidewalk counseling is concern for the woman facing a problem pregnancy and her unborn child. But this ministry is also about confronting the reality of abortion—not as a philosophical concern but as a real human tragedy taking place today. (Pro-Life Action League 2006)

Pro-choice activists view sidewalk counseling in a different light. Instead of showing concern for women, many abortion rights supporters view it as harassment of the women entering clinics. Debbie McCall described the transition she witnessed when protesters began incorporating sidewalk counseling into their protest campaigns at Planned Parenthood. Debbie initially felt a respect for the protesters' commitment to their beliefs and commitment to peaceful prayer.

There are your regular protesters that come and sing, say their prayers and rosaries. Some places they are so regular you can set your watch by them. That's their level of commitment and that's fine and I respect them for that. . . . Here you have this person who was out there every day because she really believed in this. I even took bottles of water out to her because she would be out there all day long. And we would tell her to go home when we were locking the gates at night. She really believed in what she was doing and you had to respect that—respect her for that. (Interview with Debbie McCall, Director of Community Services for Planned Parenthood, December 1998)

A few months later, local pro-life activists started to be trained in sidewalk counseling techniques and began using it at the clinic, which changed the clinic's perception of the protesters' activities.

They would try to do what they call sidewalk counseling, which that is when they started yelling at people to get their attention. They say hateful, hurtful things to people and that's not sidewalk counseling, that's judging them. (Interview with Debbie McCall, Director of Community Services for Planned Parenthood, May 1999)

For clients, their encounters with sidewalk counseling often elicit a negative response. One young college student who was visiting a women's reproductive health clinic to pick up her monthly contraception was visibly agitated after being stopped by a sidewalk counselor on her way into the clinic. The exchange with the protesters brought back the negative experience Rebecca had with sidewalk counselors two years earlier, at a different clinic, when she was trying to enter a facility to obtain an abortion. She made the following comments about the sidewalk counselors.

Are you going to adopt all of these kids that you don't want to see aborted? What's gonna happen to them? How egotistical of them to decide what is right and what is wrong. Why aren't you helping out at a soup kitchen or why aren't you helping with unwanted kids. It's because they love to judge. They love to judge. They judge the people that won't live their way. They want to tell me what to do with my body and they are supposed to be the light in the tunnel. (Interview with a client, March 2000)

Another client also expressed anger after her encounter with sidewalk counselors as she entered a clinic facility.

You know what is frightening is that they want to deny safe medical attention to someone. You know if a drunk driver got hurt and needed medical attention would they deny him that because he fucked up? You know, shit happens, accidents happen. It's not like people are wanting to use abortion as birth control. They need to spend less time talking about abortion and go help and worry about the kids that are out there who are messed up because their parents don't want them. (Interview with a client, March 2000)

Clients encountering pro-life protesters exhibit anger, and according to Cheri Daniels, Hope Clinic's nursing director, who aborted a pregnancy when she was twenty-one, clients experience guilt, but not for the reason pro-life activists assume. "I went through what a lot of them feel guilty for—relief. It's a huge relief not to be pregnant when you don't want to be pregnant" (Jadhav 2006). Beyond the immediate response of clients, gauging how much influence harassing, pro-life tactics exert on them is difficult to assess, particularly in terms of protesters' success in preventing abortions.

The decision to abort an unwanted pregnancy is typically a private decision that occurs at a woman's home, not at the time she enters an abortion clinic. Consequently, determining how many women decided not to abort because of their exposure to pro-life arguments is impossible (Cozzarelli and Major 1998). Abortion rates have been decreasing over time, but it is difficult to tease out the impact harassment has had on this downward trend. Figure 6 displays the number of protests recorded since the mid-1980s with the number of abortions per 1,000 women between 1973 and 2000. The decline in abortion rates predates the dramatic increase in anti-abortion protesting. In figure 7, the abortion rate trend is easier to view. Since 1980 abortion rates have been trending downward, with a more dramatic decrease in rates since 1990. A more plausible explanation of the decline can be attributed to a variety of factors such as a lower level of sexual activity among teenagers and improvements in contraceptive usage rates rather than protesters persuading women to change their minds at clinic entrances (Finer and Henshaw 2003).

While determining how many women forwent an abortion due to harassment is essentially impossible to assess, studies have calculated how many women decided not to abort once at an abortion clinic, after being exposed to pro-life tactics. A Buffalo, New York, study examining how many women left an abortion clinic after being approached by pro-life protesters documented that out of 400 women confronted by protesters all 400 women entered the clinic (Cozzarelli and Major 1994). Although this study only examined one clinic the results seem fairly generalizable because of the multiple reasons women factor into their decision to abort an unwanted pregnancy; women are not flippant about their decision.

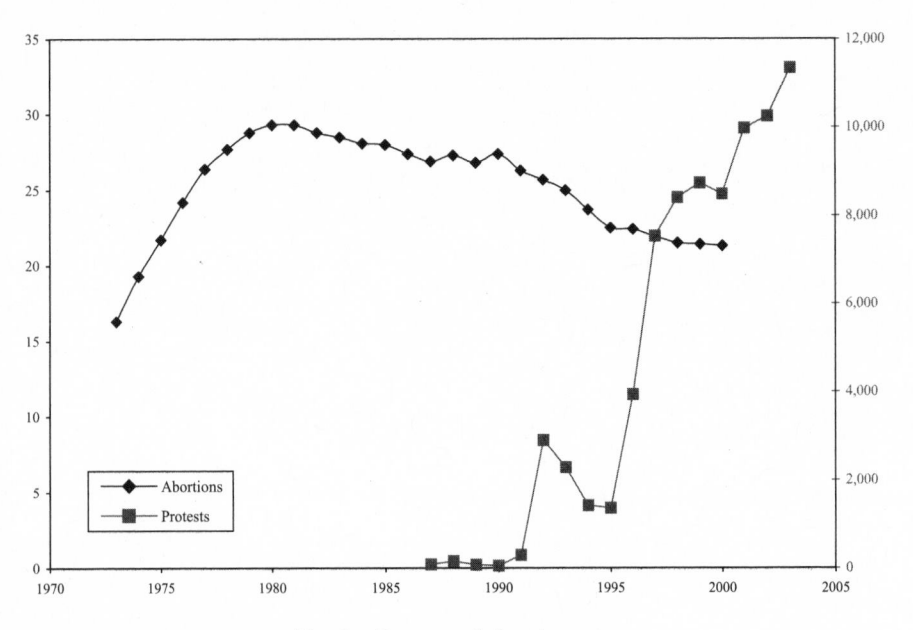

Fig. 6.   Protest and abortion rates

Most women seeking abortion services point to several complex social, economic, and health circumstances that contribute to their decision to abort an
unplanned and unwanted pregnancy (Singh, Bankole, and Haas 1998; Torres
and Forrest 1988). Despite the increasing number of state-enforced anti-abortion restrictions, women continue to seek out abortion services. For example,
twenty-four states have implemented mandatory counseling and waiting periods for women seeking abortion services. In six states, women are required to
have an in-person counseling session (as opposed to receiving the information
in the mail, over the phone, or via fax and the internet) followed by a mandatory waiting period. This particular combination of mandatory counseling and
waiting periods effectively forces women to make two trips to the clinic, which
delays the provision of services (Alan Guttmacher Institute 2006). The added
presence of pro-life protesters at the clinic has also been pointed to, anecdotally,
as contributing to a further delay in the amount of time women wait until seeking services. During an interview with an abortion provider, I asked him if he
thought the protesters had an impact on his patients.

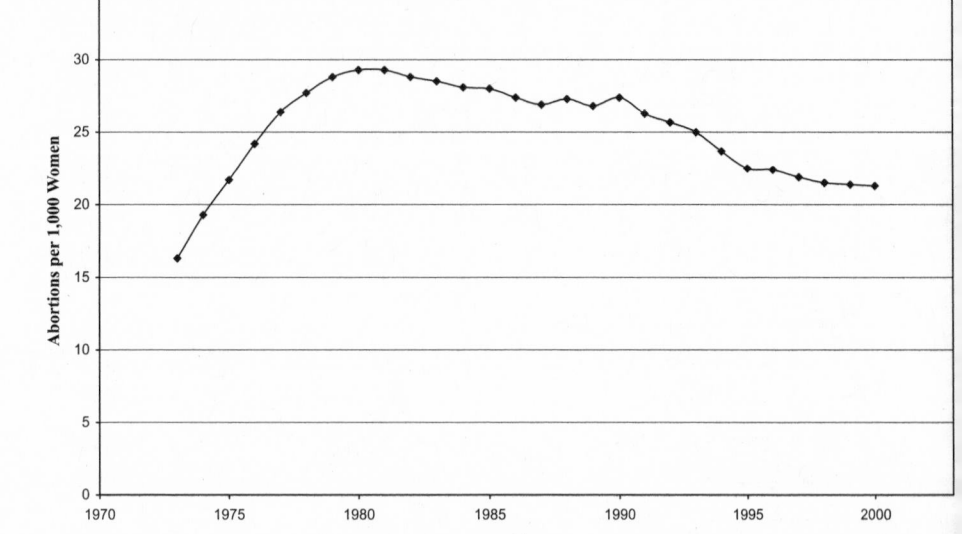

Fig. 7.   Abortion rates

Oh, no doubt about it. They do. I know they do. I've had patients say that they didn't come last week because there were people out here and some of them had said something to them. But they did come back. I was impressed with that. They gave it another try. Some of the stories, I mean these people out here [pro-life protesters] have no idea what other people's lives are like. I don't think they even care. I could be wrong about this, but I would be surprised if they even cared. They think their view is the only way, the right view. (Interview with a physician, December 2003)

Instead of preventing women from aborting, harassment may contribute to an increased delay in the delivery of services and have other adverse consequences on women. One study examined an abortion clinic for three months and found that pro-life protesters confronted 96 percent of the women seeking services. Thirty-six percent of the women reported that they were upset by the confrontation, and 34 percent indicated that they were not at all upset (Cozzarelli and Major 1994, 1998). Another two-year longitudinal study of 615 women who obtained abortions found that 87.7 percent of the women saw protesters when they entered the clinic, 76.5 percent said the demonstrators talked to them, and 42.2 percent stated that the protesters tried to prevent them from entering the clinic (Major et al. 1998; Cozzarelli and Major 1998).

Generally, women's reactions to the harassment fell into two broad categories: feelings of anger and feelings of guilt. Relatedly, a survey of 142 women obtaining abortions and 51 individuals who were accompanying the women reported that 82 percent of the respondents expressed the belief that the protesters were invading their privacy, 81 percent felt the protesters should mind their own business, and 35 percent felt their religious freedom was being challenged (Nasman 1992). A 15 percent minority of women felt the protesters were trying to help and only 1 percent of the respondents reported being interested in what the pro-life activists had to say (Nasman 1992). Direct action tactics may be most influential on this small group of women.

Out of the women in the study, the most detrimental effect of harassment on women seeking services appeared to be in post-abortion adjustment (Russo and Denious 1998, 26–27). Although the evidence is limited to a few studies, scholars and practitioners have observed women displaying signs of physical distress after encountering protesters (Hern 1991; Cozzarelli and Major 1994). Emotional distress can easily escalate for clients when their sense of anonymity is challenged by protesters' use of personalized and invasive legal tactics. The director of an abortion clinic noted the latest tactic used by pro-life activists. "They have brought the video cameras in and regular cameras in, and they are on everybody from the time they come in to the time they go" (Interview with an abortion clinic director, September 1999). Another clinic employee described the distress one young woman, who just had an abortion, and her family experienced as they were leaving the clinic and were confronted by protesters who were armed with video cameras and recording footage of them.

One little girl became hysterical when she was leaving with her parents and saw the video camera. And her dad became furious and I told him, it's not worth it. They are not worth it. Just get in your truck and drive off. So the trauma that family had to go through, I wanted to cry over that. But they [protesters] don't care. They are yelling. They like to scream to parents that their grandchildren are calling out to them for protection and they call out

to young ladies that their babies are calling out for them to spare their life.
(Interview with a clinic employee, June 2000)

Women who were confronted with demonstrators that attempted to block
their entry into the clinic were the most agitated, which related to increased levels of depression thirty minutes after their abortions (Cozzarelli and Major
1994). Women who reported "feeling strong" after their brush with demonstrators tended to have more positive post-abortion adjustments.

The scope and magnitude of anti-abortion harassment is well documented,
but the consequences of the tactics are not. A few studies have confirmed the
detrimental monetary affects of harassment and violence on providers and suggest that harassment may be a factor in the decline of practicing abortion
providers nationwide. For the other group of harassment targets, overall, the
limited research indicates that harassment does not appear to influence
women's decision to abort, except perhaps at the margins. Rather than preventing women from having an abortion once they are at the clinic, harassment
seems to be more influential on women in terms of their well-being after
obtaining an abortion.

Conclusion

Confrontational tactics are purposefully used by the pro-life movement in an
attempt to immediately stop abortion by transforming those directly involved
in abortion services—providers and women seeking abortions—into adopting
a pro-life framework. I have argued that these direct action tactics are politically
motivated forms of harassment that contribute to the pro-life movement's ability to achieve its goal of preventing abortion services. Political harassment is a
cheaper and more immediate means of reducing access to abortion services
compared to the resources expended on changing abortion politics through traditional institutional means.

Operating within the political system is resource intensive, requiring political sophistication, organizational resources, expert knowledge of the political
system, time, and money. The direct action branch of the pro-life movement is
not attempting to change policy; it is circumventing the political system and
trying to change behavior directly. Engaging in political harassment outside of a
clinic is not nearly as resource intensive as pursuing anti-abortion policy goals,

and it provides activists with the perception that they are making a difference in the daily fight to eliminate abortion. In this regard, harassment is an inexpensive strategy, particularly when it's directed at nongovernmental actors who do not have resources comparable to the state's, to curb or eliminate dissident activity. Yet, the overall efficacy of this strategy has not been systematically assessed.

Several surveys, case studies, interviews, and media accounts suggest that pro-life direct action tactics exert a negative impact on women and providers, but much of this research has been constrained by several factors such as the limited size of the studies. To measure the extent of the movement's influence on providers and women, in the following chapter, I empirically examine the effect of anti-abortion political harassment on those nongovernmental actors who are most intimately involved in the abortion conflict.

Chapter 5

DOES HARASSMENT PAY OFF?

Assessing the Success of Anti-Abortion Tactics

> You also have to remember that no matter how uncomfortable someone is with a picture or a poster, the real uncomfortable issue for us is that babies are being murdered. . . . The ultimate issue is that they believe that killing an unborn child is a good thing, and I think it is murder.
> —Interview with a director of a pro-life organization, October 1999

Political Harassment

Pro-life activists frequently express the collective goal of banning abortion or prohibiting access to abortion services (Paige 1983; Luker 1984). Unconventional tactics are among the tools used by the direct action branch of the movement to achieve this goal. Activists aim these tactics at nongovernmental actors because from their perspective, the urgency of "saving lives" necessitates immediate action. Abortion opponents from this arm of the movement are not willing to wait patiently for political compromise and negotiation. Although policy change certainly moves the movement toward its ultimate goal of crim-inalizing abortion, incremental change does not address the immediacy of its mission.

Targeting nongovernmental actors presents an alternative, and more direct, solution to ending abortion. Unconventional activities, directed at nongovernmental targets, introduce costs into the political environment that pose a unique burden to the targets. These tactics are not intended to influence governmental authorities directly, rather they are intended to change the behavior of the individuals openly involved with abortion services—women and providers. This transference of costs onto nongovernmental actors is an alternative strategy employed by the pro-life movement.

Because the pro-life movement's unconventional tactics are continual, individualized, and personalized, they need to be reconceptualized as a form of political harassment that exists along a continuum of political activity where traditional forms of participation are on one end of the spectrum and extreme violence is on the other. Political harassment falls along this continuum when certain conditions are at play. I define political harassment as persistent verbal or physical collective challenges intended to change the behavior of others, to have political significance, to create a reasonable fear, and to be directed at non-governmental actors because of their beliefs.

Political harassment can include legal activities such as political protest, however, when directed at nongovernmental actors within a political context that is underlined with fear, the dynamics of the activity changes from benign unconventional activity to political harassment. The motivation for using political harassment is different than the motivation for using conventional tactics or extreme violence. Political harassment is intended to change nongovernmental actors' behavior *immediately* while operating within the parameters of acceptable democratic political behavior (Munson 2005). In other words, even though political protest is not an illegal activity it can potentially be a useful tactic for achieving pro-life groups' goals when it's directed at individuals who do not have the political resources to dilute the activity.

All three branches of the pro-life movement denounce explicitly violent and illegal activity. But quasi-legal, questionable, and legal (yet harassing) activities are openly endorsed by the direct action division of the movement. The volume of anti-abortion protesting at clinics is indicative of the underlying, politically harassing component of the activity, which does not occur in a vacuum. Other types of quasi-legal tactics are used in conjunction with protests, which can change women's and providers' perceptions of the harm and threat posed by these tactics. For example, employees of reproductive health care facilities and, less frequently, their clients, receive personalized letters from pro-life groups chronicling their professional and personal lives. These letters have been sent to employees' and their family members' places of employment, their homes, and even their colleagues' homes. Health care providers have been featured on wanted posters displayed in their communities. Wanted posters typically contain information about the abortion provider and clinic employees such as their names, work and home addresses, along with a pro-life slogan.

Clients have also been targeted through the mail. One pro-life organization in Texas started recording the license plate numbers of cars in a Planned Parenthood's parking lot and sent out the following letter to the registered car owner.

IT'S NOW THE LAW IN TEXAS . . . AND IT'S CALLED <u>PARENTS RIGHT TO KNOW</u>

Dear Parents:

The recent visit by a member of your immediate family to the Planned Parenthood Abortion Facility near the [university] campus suggests that someone very dear to you may be facing the most serious personal crisis in her young life. And while the willful death of an innocent child is always tragic, the death or serious injury of a young woman resulting from an abortion gone bad is tragedy beyond description. As of 1 January 2000 parents here in Texas now have a **legal right under Texas law** to demand full disclosure from abortion facilities, so please call the [town name deleted] Planned Parenthood Abortion Clinic at [Phone number of clinic listed] today. You have every reason to be concerned about who their abortionist is, what are his medical credentials, his medical liability, where else he performs abortions and what his medical malpractice record looks like. The young woman you love so very much deserves your protection and your loving intervention. Exercise the legal right afforded parents under Texas law and call the clinic today.

Displaying wanted posters and sending letters to people are not explicitly illegal activities, and these tactics are endorsed by many members and leaders of direct action groups.[1] In an interview with one of the more active and visible priests, who was taking a leading role in a pro-life direct action group, he expressed his views on sending literature to clients and their families, and explained where he drew the line between appropriate versus inappropriate protest: "I draw the line at shaming a young lady." The priest expressed his belief that there is a difference between "shaming a person and that person being ashamed." He felt that the mail campaign was acceptable as long as the letters being sent were "factual." The priest explained that if a person is uncomfortable with her loved ones and neighbors knowing where she works, when she visits an abortion clinic, or what she does with her personal life then that was an indication that she was ashamed of herself. He thought the letters provided a service by reaching out to family and friends and providing them with an opportunity to help clinic employees and young women restructure their lives and start living as a Christian (Interview with a priest, March 2000).

The regularity of these types of activities coupled with their personalized tenor introduces obstacles to those intimately involved with abortion practices. Political harassment should have a different outcome compared to the more aggressive and clearly illegal activities committed by anti-abortion extremists. Political violence is sporadic, impossible to predict, and relatively easier to dismiss by nongovernmental actors compared to the more patterned and frequent nature of political harassment. Chapter 4 detailed the breadth of political harassment and violence as well as the qualitatively documented impact it has on women and providers. In this chapter I conduct a more systematic quantitative analysis of political harassment and the threat of extreme violence to determine if they have a measurable impact on women and providers.

The Two Targets of Anti-Abortion Political Harassment

The simplest way to stop abortions is to eliminate the demand for them. Protests, demonstrations, and other confrontational activities are designed to increase the costs of obtaining an abortion by making it more difficult for women to enter clinics and dissuading them from receiving services by counseling them to convert to a pro-life perspective. By increasing the costs of seeking out abortion services, pro-life activists are attempting to change the behavior of women. The abortion rate is used as the dependent variable to capture any potential influence harassment has on women. If harassment, which is expected to be more systematic and patterned than violence, is an influential tactic, abortion rates will be negatively related to the incidence of anti-abortion harassment. The threat of extreme violence is not expected to exert any measurable influence over this group of antagonists because clients are unlikely to be aware of these less publicly visible actions.

Abortion providers are the second set of nongovernmental targets for the pro-life movement. The logic is that if providers can be convinced to stop offering abortion services, no abortion services will be performed.[2] Given both the visibility of providers and their direct link to abortion services, they are the most obvious antagonists to the pro-life movement. Providers are also easier targets because, unlike women who usually obtain an abortion once in their lifetime (Henshaw, Konan, and Smith 1991), providers are in continuous service at the same location. The interaction between anti-abortionists and providers is typically continuous and repeated; consequently anti-abortion activists have more opportunities to exert negative influences over providers. Accordingly, anti-abortion activists from the direct action branch expect that if they are successful the use of unconventional tactics should decrease the number of abortion providers. The threat of extreme violence, which is not endorsed by the movement, should not be as influential on abortion providers due to the sporadic nature of the activity. Abortion providers are the second set of antagonists that will be modeled as a dependent variable in the analyses.

Data

The Alan Guttmacher Institute (AGI) produced a series of surveys in 1985, 1988, 1992, 1995, and 2000 measuring the scope of anti-abortion activities at clinics. These unique surveys are the only national source of information pertaining to the number, types, and geographical distribution of abortion providers in the United States (Henshaw and Finer 2003). AGI has conducted thirteen of these surveys and started including questions on the 1985 survey gauging the extent of anti-abortion activity (throughout the country) in a variety of forms. Even though the Alan Guttmacher Institute surveyed all abortion providers in the United States, for confidentiality purposes data were only released for abortion providers who performed 300 or more abortions a year. Data are available for roughly 70 to 80 percent of the providers in the United States. Although AGI surveyed individual clinics, in order to protect clinics and employees, the data were aggregated (and *only* made available) at the state level.[3]

Each survey asked providers if they experienced various forms of anti-abortion activity, as well as the frequency of the activity. Respondents had four categories to choose from: zero incidents a year, one to four incidents a year, five to nineteen incidents a year, and twenty or more incidents a year. The following analyses use two categories: one to four incidents a year and five to nineteen incidents a year.[4] The question measuring harassment and violence was worded identically on all five surveys: "How many times did each of the following anti-abortion activities occur at your facility in 19__?" Each year's survey had both similar and unique choices. For example, in 1985 providers were asked how many times they experienced a clinic invasion; this particular question was not asked in subsequent surveys.

Only the common measures of harassment and violence are used in the analyses as independent variables. The data used in the following analyses are the percentage of abortion facilities in a state experiencing five forms of harassment, illegal activity, and the threat of violence. These common measures include: picketing clinics, picketing at the homes of clinic staff members, picketing clinics with physical contact, vandalism, and bomb threats. Appendix A contains the exact survey questions and choices given each year. Other state-level, dependent and independent variables were obtained from a variety of sources (see appendix B for a complete description of data sources).

Methods

To determine the effect of political harassment, illegal activity, and the threat of extreme violence on women and providers, I conducted four sets of analyses of the fifty states. The first two models test the impact of pro-life harassing tactics on the abortion rate at differing frequencies. Since the persistency of harassment may have a differential influence on the abortion rate, all models are estimated twice; the first model includes the one to four incidents a year category and the other model is estimated with the five to nineteen category. I end up with five models for each frequency category, producing a total of ten models for each set of antagonists. The basic structure of the models is represented by:

$$Y = \beta_0 + \beta_1 X_1 + \beta_2 X_2 + \ldots + \beta_8 X_8 + \varepsilon.$$

The second set of analyses examines the impact of these same tactics on abortion providers, estimated with both frequency categories, which also produces a total of ten models. Similarly, the basic structure of the models is represented by:

$$Y = \beta_0 + \beta_1 X_1 + \beta_2 X_2 + \ldots + \beta_7 X_7 + \varepsilon.$$

The data are cross-sectional coupled with irregular (and limited) time periods. I estimate the models using multivariate regression analysis, with dummy variables to capture the variation in the estimated regression coefficients over time (Chatterjee, Hadi, and Price 2000; Gujarati 1995). Multivariate regression analysis is a conceptually simplistic method for investigating relationships among variables. Regression analysis examines a dependent variable against a set of explanatory (or predictor) variables and establishes whether or not a functional relationship exists among variables.[5]

Regression analysis is governed by a set of assumptions that need to be fulfilled in order to produce valid inferences and conclusion.[6] Multicollinearity and heteroscedasticity are problems frequently created when the assumptions governing the predictor variables and errors are violated in regression analysis (Chatterjee, Hadi, and Price 2000; Gujarati 1995; Tabachnick and Fidell 2001). All models were checked for both.[7] Diagnostic tests revealed that neither issue presented a serious threat in the models.[8]

Another potential problem created by the cross-sectional and irregular time intervals of the data is a violation of the assumption of independence of the observations. Regression analysis assumes that all observations are equally reliable and play a roughly equal role in determining the results and influencing the conclusions generated from the regression analysis (Chatterjee, Hadi, and Price 2000, 88). Yet, the models in the analyses are incorporating multiple measures for a single state at several time points, which potentially means that the results for a particular state in one year are related to the state's results for the previous time period, but not adequately accounted for by the dummy variables included in the models for time. To guard against this potential violation, each model was also estimated as a change variable model. This allowed me to determine, for example, if the changes in the harassment measures were related to changes in the outcomes. For example, using change variables helps assess if the change in protest activity corresponds with a change in the abortion rate or number of providers. I do not include these models in the text, but the similarities and differences between the models using regular variables compared to the models using change variables are listed in the notes.

Model 1: The Impact of Harassment, Illegal Tactics, and the Threat of Violence on the Abortion Rate

Dependent Variable: The Abortion Rate

One of the foremost goals of anti-abortion direct action groups is to stop women from obtaining abortions. If the harassing tactics of anti-abortionists are successful, they should be related to a decrease in the abortion rate. The abortion rate is measured as the number of abortions per 1,000 women age 15 to 44.

Posner (1992) has estimated that 70 percent of the abortions occurring today would have occurred prior to the legalization of abortion. Faced with substantial legal and medical risks, many women obtained high-risk, illegal abortions in the pre-*Roe* era. Since these obstacles were not a deterrent to abortions before 1973, harassment, illegal activities, and the threat of violence are unlikely to be leading factors in shaping a woman's decision to abort an unwanted pregnancy.

Out of the five forms of harassment, picketing is expected to be potentially the most influential because it is the most common and visible tactic used by pro-life groups. Women have the most exposure to protesting activities compared to the other forms of harassment. Women in need of abortion services are less likely to be dissuaded from seeking those services due to illegal incidents of harassment and threats of extreme violence. It is unlikely that a client would be aware that these activities were taking place at the clinic and therefore would be the least affected by these more aggressive but less visible actions. Political harassment certainly creates an intimidating environment and places more obstacles in the way for women seeking services. But the decision to resolve an unwanted and unplanned pregnancy is relatively inelastic.

Independent Variables

Anti-Abortion Harassment, Illegal Activities, and the Threat of Violence

The key variables of interest are harassment, illegal activities, and the threat of violence. Five common measures that tap into these three forms of pro-life tactics are used in this—and subsequent—analyses. These measures fall along a continuum of political participation from activities that are politically harassing to activities that are illegal and extreme.

Harassment is measured by two variables. The first variable is the number of times a provider experienced picketing at his or her facility in the past year; the second is the number of times picketing occurred at the homes of staff members. Both of these activities fall within the definition of political harassment, but protesting (whether at the clinic or a staff member's home) is not illegal as long as protesters stay outside of any legally established buffer zones and private property boundaries.

The second two variables capture tactics that are illegal: acts of vandalism and picketing with physical contact. Vandalism is clearly illegal, and picketing with physical contact is grouped in with illegal activities because many protests, particularly prior to the FACE Act, degenerated into pushing, shoving, and other forms of physical contact that fall within the purview of assault.[9] The final measure used in the models to reflect the threat of extreme violence is the number of times a provider received a bomb threat in the last year. Several of the harassment measures are skewed or kurtotic; therefore they are logged to reduce the problem (Chatterjee, Hadi, and Price 2000, 155–63). The following harassment measures are logged: picketing the homes of staff members (1–4 times a year and 5–19 times a year); picketing with physical contact (5–19 times a year); vandalism (5–19 times a year); and bomb threats (5–19 times a year).

Financial Resources

Other factors that either aid or hinder access to abortion are expected to influence the abortion rate. Income plays a role in a woman's ability to obtain abortion services. Prior to the legalization of abortion, wealthier women had access to abortion services, and this pattern is still prevalent today (Luker 1984; Frost 1996). The average cost of $372 for a first-trimester abortion is affordable for women who possess the necessary financial resources; for poor women, the cost is prohibitive (Henshaw and Finer 2003).

Women with resources are also more likely to avoid an unwanted pregnancy compared to women with fewer financial resources. Studies have demonstrated that Medicaid funding of abortion has an important impact on poor women—allowing them to terminate an unwanted pregnancy rather than carrying it to term (Meier and McFarlane 1994; Henshaw and Kost 1996; Cook et al. 1999). Income, measured as personal income per capita, and funded abortions, measured as the rate (per 10,000 women) of publicly funded abortions, are included in the analysis.[10] Income is expected to have a negative relationship with the abortion rate, while funded abortions are expected to be positive. The funded-abortion variable is logged to correct for skewness and kurtosis.

Access Variables

Immediately following the legalization of abortion, anti-abortion groups introduced numerous bills attempting to either overturn or curb the use of abortion services (Halva-Neubauer 1993). Abortion restrictions in a state can hinder access to abortion services through, for example, waiting periods, two clinic visits, or notification requirements. Women who have to travel long distances to obtain services or who lack resources are vulnerable to being adversely affected by state abortion laws, which can delay abortion services or prompt young women to travel out of state for services (Henshaw 1995a, 1995b). Abortion restrictions are measured as a straight count of the number of anti-abortion restrictions in a state and are expected to have a negative relationship with the abortion rate.[11] The number of abortion providers in a state is also likely to affect access to abortion services. A shortage of health care providers makes it more difficult to obtain abortion services. Abortion providers are measured as the number of abortion providers in a state per 10,000 population, and it is expected to be positively related to the abortion rate. The abortion provider variable is logged to correct for skewness and kurtosis.

Demographic Variables

Several demographic variables are expected to affect the abortion rate and are included in the models: the percent Protestant fundamentalist (this variable is logged), the percent Black population, and the percent urbanism in a state. Protestant women obtain abortions at a slightly lower rate than the overall population.[12] Protestants account for 37 percent of abortion clients yet are 54 percent of the general population (Henshaw and Kost 1996). Protestant population is expected to have a negative relationship with the abortion rate.

African American women are more likely to experience an unwanted pregnancy compared to white women. Their disproportionate number of unplanned pregnancies reflects the higher incidence of poverty among African American women. Being financially impacted is associated with a higher contraception failure rate and nonuse among Black women, which consequently leads to a disproportionately higher abortion rate relative to white women (Henshaw and Kost 1996). A positive relationship is expected between the Black population and the abortion rate.

Finally, urbanism is another important demographic variable expected to be positively associated with the abortion rate. Eighty-seven percent of the counties in the United States do not have abortion providers; the proportion of women living in counties that do not have an abortion provider increased from 28 percent to 34 percent in 2000 (Henshaw and Finer 2003). Most rural communities do not have abortion providers, whereas 86 of the 276 metropolitan areas in the United States do not have abortion providers. The majority of abortion providers are located in metropolitan areas, making it relatively easier for women living in urban states to access abortion services compared to women residing in rural states (Henshaw and Finer 2003; Henshaw 1995a; Henshaw and Kost 1996).

Results

After initially running the models, diagnostics showed Nevada was an outlier.[13] The models were reestimated with a dummy variable included for Nevada to eliminate the influence it was exerting in the models. Examining both sets of models (those looking at one to four yearly incidents of pro-life activities, and those looking at five to nineteen yearly incidents), the harassment variables measuring the percentage of facilities experiencing picketing has a negative and significant relationship with the abortion rate, even when controlling for multiple variables.

Starting with table 5, the regression coefficients indicate that a 1 percent increase in facilities experiencing picketing one to four times a year is associated with a .049 decline in the abortion rate per 1,000 women, controlling for the resource, access, demographics, and control variables. The t-score for the coefficient is 3.06 with a .002 associated significance.[14] In the four remaining models in table 5, none of the other harassment variables is statistically significant at the .05 level or better.

Other variables tapping into financial resources and access to abortion services are also important to the abortion rate. The funded-abortions variable, which represents a financial resource in the models, is consistently statistically significant across all the models in table 5. The access variable measuring abortion providers is also positive and significant across each model and is one of the most influential variables in the model, second only to the demographic variable for urbanism. The partial slope coefficient is similar across models, averaging about 9.64 for abortion providers and averaging around .287 for urbanism.

The two other demographic variables are also statistically significant across models: Protestant population and African American population. Both of these variables are related to the abortion rate in the hypothesized direction. Protestant population is negatively related to the abortion rate, while the African American population is positively related to the abortion rate. Neither income nor the number of abortion restrictions is statistically significant in any of the models in table 5.

All of the models perform pretty well, reflected by the adjusted R^2-value, which ranges from .796 to .804 in the models. These results are fairly consistent

TABLE 5. Impact of One to Four Yearly Incidents of Harassment on Abortion Rates

Tactics Models	Clinic	Staff	Contact	Vandalism	Bomb
Variables					
Constant	11.17***	6.28*	7.15**	6.57*	6.54*
	(3.05)	(2.66)	(2.74)	(2.70)	(2.71)
Harassment					
Tactics	−.049**	−.877~	−.017	−.007	−.005
	(.016)	(.491)	(.014)	(.015)	(.015)
Resources					
Income	−.00007	−.00005	−.00007	−.00009	−.00009
	(.00021)	(.00021)	(.00021)	(.00021)	(.00021)
Funded	3.75***	3.74***	3.77***	3.68***	3.75***
	(.802)	(.814)	(.817)	(.835)	(.821)
Access					
Restrictions	−.053	.014	.008	−.002	.004
	(.139)	(.139)	(.140)	(.142)	(.141)
Providers	9.03***	9.60***	9.64***	9.92***	9.96***
	(1.29)	(1.29)	(1.32)	(1.31)	(1.32)
Demographics					
Protestant	−5.86***	−5.78***	−5.69***	−5.71***	−5.69***
	(.935)	(.948)	(.950)	(.958)	(.956)
Black	.286***	.308***	.289***	.288***	.291***
	(.036)	(.038)	(.037)	(.037)	(.037)
Urban	.278***	.294***	.287***	.292***	.291***
	(.026)	(.026)	(.026)	(.026)	(.026)
Controls					
Nevada	14.69***	13.05***	13.80***	13.78***	13.75***
	(2.12)	(2.16)	(2.13)	(2.14)	(2.14)
1988	−.419	−.556	−.573	−.351	−.474
	(1.02)	(1.04)	(1.05)	(1.05)	(1.07)
1992	−1.54	−1.79	−1.85	−1.54	−1.80
	(1.50)	(1.52)	(1.52)	(1.55)	(1.56)
1995	−6.49**	−3.57	−3.81~	−2.96	−3.06
	(2.40)	(2.15)	(2.26)	(2.13)	(2.19)
2000	−5.04*	−2.44	−2.54	−1.77	−1.88
	(2.33)	(2.13)	(2.21)	(2.11)	(2.18)
Model statistics					
N	230	230	230	230	230
SEE	4.38	4.45	4.47	4.48	4.48
Adjusted R^2	.804	.798	.797	.796	.796

Note: Number in parentheses is standard error.
~$p < .10$; *$p < .05$; **$p < .01$; ***$p < .001$

TABLE 6. Impact of Five to Nineteen Yearly Incidents of Harassment on Abortion Rates

Tactics Models	Picketing	Staff	Contact	Vandalism	Bomb
Variables					
Constant	7.63**	6.47*	6.54*	6.40*	6.37*
	(2.71)	(2.67)	(2.70)	(2.70)	(2.68)
Harassment					
Tactics	−.034*	−.807	−.253	.242	.522
	(.015)	(.641)	(.513)	(.600)	(.771)
Resources					
Income	−.00001	−.00005	−.00008	−.00009	−.00009
	(.00021)	(.00021)	(.00021)	(.00021)	(.00021)
Funded	3.50***	3.76***	3.79***	3.78***	3.73***
	(.819)	(.817)	(.820)	(.820)	(.820)
Access					
Restrictions	−.009	.027	.015	.004	.002
	(.139)	(.141)	(.141)	(.141)	(.140)
Providers	9.08***	9.90***	9.96***	10.13***	10.11***
	(1.34)	(1.28)	(1.30)	(1.28)	(1.27)
Demographics					
Protestant	−5.58***	−5.97***	−5.67***	−5.61***	−5.67***
	(.942)	(.981)	(.953)	(.962)	(.952)
Black	.293***	.294***	.291***	.286***	.285***
	(.037)	(.037)	(.037)	(.038)	(.037)
Urban	.288***	.296***	.291***	.288***	.289***
	(.025)	(.026)	(.026)	(.026)	(.026)
Controls					
Nevada	14.34***	13.43***	13.67***	13.72***	13.66***
	(2.13)	(2.14)	(2.14)	(2.14)	(2.14)
1988	−.699	−.432	−.576	−.416	−.350
	(1.04)	(1.04)	(1.11)	(1.05)	(1.05)
1992	−1.91	−1.53	−1.88	−1.80	−1.57
	(1.51)	(1.53)	(1.58)	(1.55)	(1.53)
1995	−5.84*	−2.91	−3.32	−2.90	−2.65
	(2.48)	(2.12)	(2.31)	(2.13)	(2.15)
2000	−3.34*	−1.74	−2.08	−1.67	−1.43
	(2.21)	(2.10)	(2.26)	(2.10)	(2.13)
Model statistics					
N	230	230	230	230	230
SEE	4.43	4.47	4.48	4.48	4.48
Adjusted R^2	.800	.797	.796	.796	.796

Note: Number in parentheses is standard error.
$\sim p < .10$; $^*p < .05$; $^{**}p < .01$; $^{***}p < .001$

with the change variable models.[15] Table 6 is also very similar to table 5. In table 6, only the harassment variable measuring picketing (five to nineteen times a year) is negative and statistically significant with the abortion rate. The other measures of harassment—illegal activity and the threat of violence—are not significant, even when these activities occurred more frequently at a facility. Funded abortions, abortion providers, Protestant population, African American population, and urban population are all significant and in the expected direction for all of the models included in table 6. Like the models in table 5, these perform fairly well overall, indicated by the range of adjusted R^2-values from .796 to .800.

Model 2: The Impact of Harassment, Illegal Activities, and the Threat of Violence on Abortion Providers

Dependent Variable

The politically harassing tactics used by anti-abortion direct action groups are intended to stop the provision of abortion services by targeting abortion providers. Providers are the second set of nongovernmental actors who are forced to deal with the costs of pro-life activities on a routine basis. Out of the two antagonists, providers (relative to women seeking services) are more vulnerable to being negatively affected by anti-abortion harassment. Harassment and illegal activities are expected to be more influential on providers compared to the threat of extreme violence.

Bomb threats may initially serve as a scare tactic, but eventually their novelty wears off, particularly as the actual probability of being the victim of an anti-abortion bombing is very small. Bomb threats also command the attention of governmental agencies that investigate, protect, and work on behalf of those being threatened with a bomb attack. This is not the case when it comes to harassing activities. Providers have to manage harassing protests at their clinics and homes, which is personalized and individualized, without the intervention of the government. The continuous strain created by these anti-abortion activities is expected to exert more of an influence on providers than illegal activities do. The number of abortion providers per 10,000 population in a state is the dependent variable in this set of models; this variable is logged to eliminate skew and kurtosis.

Independent Variables

Anti-Abortion Harassment, Illegal Activities, and the Threat of Violence

The key variables of interests in these models are anti-abortion activities. All five of the measures tapping into harassment, illegal activity, and the threat of violence will also be used in the provider models. Anti-abortion activities are expected to influence the number of providers in a state negatively.

Demand Variables

Similar to other physicians, abortionists provide a medical service for women. Although providers deal with an emotionally and politically charged service, they nonetheless provide a service, therefore they should be influenced by the demand for their services.[16] The abortion rate is the most obvious demand variable and is included in the analysis. It is measured as the abortion rate per 1,000 women aged 15 to 44 and is expected to have a positive relationship with abortion providers. Two other variables, the percentage of the population that is African American and the percentage living in an urban area, are included in the models. Both variables should be negatively related to the number of providers because more white women receive abortions (Henshaw and Kost 1996) and fewer providers are needed in urban areas (Risen and Thomas 1998).

Political Variables

In addition to the demand variables, three variables tapping into the political environment of a state are included: the number of abortion restrictions, the Catholic population, and NARAL membership. These measures reflect the receptivity (or lack of it) to abortion services. The first variable directly taps into political actors' support for abortion services. Over the past several years, states have implemented restrictions that place legal constraints on the conditions in which an abortion may be performed. In order to comply with these new constraints, facilities must assume extra financial costs and increased time commitments, which may influence the clinic's decision whether to continue operating (Finer and Henshaw 2003). For example, one provider in South Carolina closed due to the new burdensome requirements implemented in that state. Abortion restrictions are expected to be negatively related to abortion providers.

The Catholic Church has long played a vocal and financial role in the abortion debate (Tribe 1992) and is expected to exert a negative influence over providers. This variable is measured as the percentage of the Catholic population in a state. Finally, the number of National Abortion Rights and Reproductive Action League (NARAL) Pro-Choice America members per 10,000 population represents a measure of support for abortion providers.[17] NARAL is primarily a single-issue group that is extremely vocal in maintaining and improving abortion rights. NARAL has a national and state political presence; it has affiliates in every state. NARAL members offer support to providers politically and practically—in terms of court proceedings, legislation, and offering escort services at clinics. NARAL membership is expected to be positively related to abortion providers.

Results

Diagnostics indicated that Hawaii was an outlier in the models; therefore they are reestimated with a dummy variable for Hawaii. Looking at table 7, the models overall perform well, which is reflected in the range of adjusted R^2-values from a low of .722 to a high of .731. In sharp contrast to the effect of anti-abortion harassing tactics on the abortion rate (where only picketing at clinics exerted a negative and significant impact), table 7 suggests that the effect of those same activities (committed one to four times a year) on abortion providers is often negative and statistically significant. Three of the measures are significant at the .05 level or better: picketing the homes of staff members, picketing with physical contact, and bomb threats. For example, one of the harassment models indicates that a 1 percent increase in picketing at staff members' homes is associated with a .052 percent decrease in abortion providers, controlling for the demand, political, and control variables. Vandalism is negatively related to abortion providers but only marginally significant, with a p-value at .065. These results are very similar for the results found in the models using change variables. In those models, the impact of harassing tactics was even greater; both picketing and vandalism were statistically significant in the change models, indicating that an increase in the level of these activities is statistically associated with a decrease in abortion providers.[18]

All of the demand and political variables were related in the hypothesized direction and statistically significant. The abortion rate and NARAL membership are the most influential variables included in the models. The results of table 8 indicate a bit of a different pattern.

The models in table 8, similar to those in table 7, perform pretty well overall.

TABLE 7.   Impact of One to Four Yearly Incidents of Harassment on Abortion Providers

Tactics Models	Picketing	Staff	Contact	Vandalism	Bomb
Variables					
Constant	−.182*	−.244***	−.164**	−.232***	−.219***
	(.086)	(.061)	(.068)	(.063)	(.063)
Harassment					
Tactics	−.001	−.052**	−.002**	−.001~	−.001*
	(.001)	(.018)	(.001)	(.001)	(.001)
Demand					
Abortion rate	.013***	.012***	.012***	.013***	.013***
	(.002)	(.002)	(.002)	(.002)	(.002)
Black	−.004**	−.003**	−.004**	−.004**	−.004**
	(.001)	(.001)	(.001)	(.001)	(.001)
Urban	−.003**	−.003**	−.003**	−.003**	−.003**
	(.001)	(.001)	(.001)	(.001)	(.001)
Political					
Restrict	−.018***	−.017***	−.017***	−.017***	−.017***
	(.005)	(.005)	(.005)	(.005)	(.005)
Catholic	−.004***	−.004***	−.003***	−.003***	−.004***
	(.001)	(.001)	(.001)	(.001)	(.001)
NARAL	.025***	.026***	.025***	.024***	.025***
	(.003)	(.003)	(.003)	(.003)	(.003)
Controls					
Hawaii	.515***	.522***	.502***	.516***	.515***
	(.092)	(.088)	(.088)	(.090)	(.089)
1988	−.016	−.020	−.031	−.014	−.034
	(.037)	(.037)	(.037)	(.037)	(.038)
1992	−.020	.024	.011	.030	−.009
	(.043)	(.042)	(.042)	(.043)	(.043)
1995	−.066	−.034	−.077	−.031	−.053
	(.063)	(.047)	(.050)	(.047)	(.049)
2000	−.052	−.036	−.072	−.028	−.048
	(.065)	(.050)	(.054)	(.051)	(.053)
Model statistics					
N	248	248	248	248	248
SEE	.181	.178	.178	.180	.180
Adjusted R^2	.722	.730	.731	.725	.726

Note: Number in parentheses is standard error.

~$p < .10$; *$p < .05$; **$p < .01$; ***$p < .001$

The adjusted R^2-value ranges from a low of .721 to a high of .730. In these models, where harassment is occurring at a higher frequency, the results change compared to those found in table 7. Vandalism is not even marginally significant this time, and the bomb threats variable becomes insignificant in this model as well. The statistical significance of picketing with physical contact diminishes in table 8. It is only marginally significant in the model with a *p*-value of .060. Picketing

TABLE 8.   Impact of Five to Nineteen Yearly Incidents of Harassment on Abortion Providers

Tactics Models	Picketing	Staff	Contact	Vandalism	Bomb
Variables					
Constant	−.154*	−.263***	−.222***	−.260***	−.252***
	(.070)	(.062)	(.064)	(.062)	(.062)
Harassment					
Tactics	−.002**	−.046*	−.037~	−.038	−.005
	(.001)	(.023)	(.019)	(.023)	(.029)
Demand					
Abortion rate	.012***	.012***	.013***	.013***	.013***
	(.002)	(.002)	(.002)	(.002)	(.002)
Black	−.004**	−.004**	−.004**	−.004**	−.004**
	(.001)	(.001)	(.001)	(.001)	(.001)
Urban	−.003**	−.003**	−.003**	−.003**	−.003**
	(.001)	(.001)	(.001)	(.001)	(.001)
Political					
Restrict	−.018***	−.017***	−.016***	−.016***	−.017***
	(.005)	(.005)	(.005)	(.005)	(.005)
Catholic	−.003***	−.004***	−.004***	−.004***	−.004***
	(.001)	(.001)	(.001)	(.001)	(.001)
NARAL	.024***	.025***	.025***	.025***	.025***
	(.003)	(.003)	(.003)	(.003)	(.003)
Controls					
Hawaii	.477***	.532***	.519***	.533***	.544***
	(.091)	(.088)	(.089)	(.089)	(.089)
1988	−.021	−.020	−.038	−.015	−.019
	(.037)	(.037)	(.038)	(.037)	(.037)
1992	.028	.025	.001	.026	.012
	(.042)	(.043)	(.043)	(.043)	(.043)
1995	−.118*	−.020	−.059	−.021	−.020
	(.058)	(.047)	(.052)	(.047)	(.048)
2000	−.050	−.019	−.048	−.012	−.003
	(.051)	(.050)	(.055)	(.049)	(.051)
Model statistics					
N	248	248	248	248	248
SEE	.178	.180	.180	.180	.181
Adjusted R^2	.730	.725	.725	.724	.721

Note: Number in parentheses is standard error.
~$p < .10$ *$p < .05$; **$p < .01$; ***$p < .001$

the homes of staff members continues to be negative and significantly related to abortion providers. The relationships between picketing clinics and abortion providers changes in table 8. Unlike the previous model, the higher frequency of picketing at clinics appears to be negatively and significantly related to abortion providers. This relationship estimates that a 1 percent increase in picketing at clinics—occurring five to nineteen times a year—is associated with a .002 percent decrease in abortion providers controlling for the demand, political, and control variables. The results of table 8 are very similar to the results found in the regression analyses using the change variables.[19] The remaining results of table 8 are very consistent with table 7. All of the demand and political variables are statistically significant, with the abortion rate and NARAL membership being the most influential variables in the models.

Discussion

The influence of anti-abortion activities on nongovernmental actors is summarized in table 9. Anti-abortion picketing appears to exert a consistently negative influence on the abortion rate. The abortion rate has been declining over time. Much of this decline can be attributed to a variety of factors, some of which are not included in the analyses, such as improvements in contraception, and some factors that have been included in the analyses, such as access to abortion services represented by the number of providers in a state or ease of access captured by the urban demographic variable as well as resources for obtaining services such as funding of abortion for indigent women in a state.

Many obstacles exist for women seeking abortion services such as the distance they must travel to a clinic as well as financial considerations. The majority of abortion clinic patients only receive one abortion in their lifetime (Henshaw, Konan, and Smith 1991); therefore, the pro-life movement usually has one opportunity to influence them. Factors besides harassment carry more influence over a woman's decision to abort, and it is worth remembering that when a woman is committed to terminating an unwanted pregnancy a pro-life presence at a clinic is unlikely to be the most important factor preventing her from carrying through with an abortion; abortion decisions are relatively inelastic. Yet, the results of the analyses suggest that anti-abortion protesting—while not the most influential variable—is also partially associated with the decline in the abortion rate.

The exact nature of the relationship between anti-abortion protesting and the abortion rate cannot be solely determined by these analyses. For example, the picketing may help convince women who are undecided about whether to terminate their pregnancy into keeping the pregnancy by providing immediate alternatives through sidewalk counseling. As mentioned in chapter 4, one study looking at the influence of pro-life protesters on women seeking abortion services found that 1 percent of the women entering the clinic reported being inter-

TABLE 9. Summary of Harassment Tactics and Influence on Antagonists

Type of Tactics	Antagonists	
	Women (Abortion Rate)	Abortion Providers
Harassment		
Picketing clinics		
(1–4 yearly incidents)	X	
Picketing clinics		
(5–19 yearly incidents)	X	X
Picketing homes of staff		
(1–4 yearly incidents)		X
Picketing Homes of Staff		
(5–19 yearly incidents)		X
Illegal Activities		
Picketing and physical contact		
(1–4 yearly incidents)		X
Picketing and physical contact		
(5–19 yearly incidents)		
Vandalism: physical damage		
(1–4 yearly incidents)		
Vandalism: physical damage		
(5–19 yearly incidents)		
Threats of violence		
Bomb threats		
(1–4 yearly incidents)		X
Bomb threats		
(5–19 yearly incidents)		

X = significant relationship at $p < .05$

ested in what the protesters had to say (Nasman 1992). Nonhospital abortion providers estimate that approximately 7 percent of their clients arriving at their facilities are unsure whether they want to resolve their pregnancy through an abortion. The percentage of undecided women is even smaller at large-scale abortion facilities (Henshaw and Finer 2003). Sidewalk counseling and other pro-life tactics used at clinic protests are probably most likely to be influential on this minority group of women who are already unsure about their decision to abort prior to encountering pro-life activists.

Picketing may also function as a deterrent for women. In interviews, doctors, staff members, and patients have commented on the stress that picketing can create for women entering the clinic. The presence of picketing can prolong the time period in which a woman comes in for services, and it can perhaps prevent her from ever coming to the clinic. The volume and visibility of pro-life protesting may also help convince women to forgo an abortion altogether. Protest may essentially function as a public awareness and education campaign. Pro-life sentiment has been growing in society; during the late 1990s and into the twenty-first century, societal support for abortion has been waning (Jelen and Wilcox 2005). The decline in the public's support for abortion may be attributable to the massive protesting campaigns playing out at clinics across the country, keeping the issue visible and in turn changing public opinion about the "wrongness" of abortion.

In reality, the effect of picketing is likely to encompass all of these elements—swaying undecided women, delaying services, changing public opinion, and sometimes preventing women, at the margins, from seeking services. As for the other forms of harassment, they tend to be more sporadic, less visible, and less influential on women seeking abortion services compared to the steady presence of pro-life picketers at the clinics. The analyses produced some evidence suggesting that targeting this set of nongovernmental participants in the fight to end abortion appears to have some payoff for direct action groups as evidenced by the negative relationship between pro-life picketing and the abortion rate.

The second set of nongovernmental targets, providers, has multiple interactions with anti-abortion activists, whereas most women seeking abortion services do not. This interplay makes providers a more vulnerable set of antagonists because they are continually identified and targeted by pro-life groups. Providers are also perceived by pro-life activists as being more culpable in the perpetuation of abortion services because they knowingly offer abortion services, whereas activists believe that women often seek out services resulting from their misunderstanding of what abortion entails (ending a life) and their lack of knowledge about alternatives to abortion.

The repeated interaction between providers and direct action groups creates a different set of opportunities for pro-life activists to exert a negative influence over this set of anti-abortion antagonists. The results from the analyses in tables 7 and 8 are suggestive of pro-life groups' ability to shape the behavior of providers through political harassment. The influence of these tactics changes according to their frequency as well. In table 7, three of the tactics are significantly related to a decrease in abortion providers, and one tactic is marginally related. Out of the measures of harassment, picketing staff members' homes and picketing with physical contact appear to exert the most influence, followed by bomb threats and to a lesser degree vandalism. The impact of these same activities changes as the frequency of their occurrence increases. When these activities are happening five to nineteen times a year, it is the harassment measures that exercise more pressure on abortion providers.

Picketing clinics and picketing the homes of staff members, both of which are legal activities, exert the most power over abortion providers. Picketing with physical contact is a marginally significant tactic. The other measure of illegal activity (vandalism) and the threat of violence (bomb threats) are not significant. The novelty of these actions appears to wear off as they increase in frequency. Bomb threats may initially cause alarm and fear, and even prompt facilities to close, but as the threats fail to materialize, they cease to be credible and, consequently, effective. The shock value of vandalism also appears to wane as it occurs more often. Several factors may account for the insignificance of vandalism. Vandalism is illegal, therefore acts of vandalism warrant intervention by law enforcement agencies on behalf of clinic facilities. This intervention may provide clinics with a feeling of security and the sense that vandals will be accosted and dealt with by law enforcement agencies. Vandalism has also waned over the years. Since 1997 there has been a marked decrease in acts of vandalism committed at abortion clinics. The National Abortion Federation reported 105 acts of vandalism in 1997; this number dropped to 46 the following year and has averaged around 52 acts of vandalism between 1998 through 2005 (National Abortion Federation 2006). The likelihood of a clinic being vandalized is not that great, and it lacks the personalized, individualized, and regularized nature of anti-abortion harassment, which I have argued is more powerful in shaping abortion politics, particularly the behavior of nongovernmental actors who are the targets of the harassment.

Tables 7 and 8 lend empirical support to the trends documented in the literature—the number of providers has been declining. Much like the abortion rate, anti-abortion harassment is not the most powerful factor influencing the number of abortion providers, but it certainly plays a role, particularly the tactics that fall in the definition of political harassment. Picketing at clinics and picketing at staff members' homes constitute persistent verbal collective challenges that are intended to change the behavior of others, have political significance, are embedded in a larger environmental context where reasonable fear has been created, and are aimed at nongovernmental actors.

The individualized and personalized nature of anti-abortion picketing creates large costs for providers in terms of monetary expenses, unwanted attention, stress, and intimidation, to name a few. Unlike the state, which has the authority and resources to counter social movement activities, nongovernmental agencies and actors have little recourse against these activities other than exiting the environment or implementing escort and security services. However, these counteractions do not eliminate or prevent further protest at clinics, as evidenced by the dramatic increase in protest activities in the mid-1990s and into the new decade. From this standpoint, politically harassing tactics—directed at the same target and used repeatedly over time—have some payoff for direct action groups. Transferring the costs of harassing protest activities onto providers creates a situation where the continuation of services may simply become too much, prompting providers to use an exit strategy.

Hospital providers and private practices appear to be less equipped to deal with the harassment, and their numbers have decreased the most (Henshaw and Van Vort 1994). Large, nonhospital providers (performing 400 or more abortions a year) have fared better; their numbers remained fairly stable from 1992 to 1996 (Henshaw 1998a). Facilities specializing in abortion services are better prepared to deal with anti-abortion harassment, but even their greater resources do not completely insulate them from the impact of the harassment. Nonhospital providers are not immune to the effects of harassment. In April 2000 a nonhospital provider announced she was closing her clinic in Denton, Texas, because the continual anti-abortion protesting occurring at her clinic, home, and church simply became too costly (Texas Abortion and Reproductive Rights Action League 2000).

Conclusion

The United States' political foundation is premised on compromise and bargaining, which is problematic for the pro-life movement because it believes abortion is not an issue that can be compromised. As the movement has evolved, it has increasingly participated in the traditional political process. Through its institutional participation, the anti-abortion movement has learned that an immediate, outright reversal to *Roe v. Wade* is unlikely to occur. Consequently the movement has turned to other policy strategies such as supporting legislation geared toward decreasing the accessibility of abortion services via mandatory counseling, waiting periods, and parental notification and consent laws. Despite the significant anti-abortion legislative and legal gains, the ultimate victory of ending abortion remains an elusive and, within the political process, a very difficult goal to achieve.[20]

Engaging in direct action tactics in front of abortion clinics is a different strategy that makes the ultimate goal feel more readily achievable and addresses the immediacy of eliminating abortion for this branch of the movement. Protesting in front of a clinic provides members with an opportunity to convey the horrors of abortion and directly reach out to women who are experiencing crisis pregnancies. Activists are trying to convert women to a pro-life view. Preventing even one abortion from occurring represents a huge victory for these groups. Direct action organizations post counts of how many women they saved from abortion in their newsletters, on their web sites, and at their protests. They are also trying to influence abortion providers by converting them to a pro-life perspective or by "encouraging" them to close down their clinics. Either strategy represents a victory for the movement and recognizes the urgency of preventing "murder" in a direct, confrontational manner.

The individualized and personalized nature of the protest changes it from an unconventional form of participation to politically harassing behavior that has consequences. The analyses examining the impact of political harassment, illegal activities, and threats of violence on nongovernmental actors have added some empirical support to the results discussed in previous, largely qualitative literature. Picketing is associated with a decrease in the abortion rate and number of abortion providers.

The long-term consequences of anti-abortion harassment remain to be seen, but there is evidence suggesting that the political environment continues to become more conducive to anti-abortion policy initiatives, and with the recent election of Samuel Alito to the Supreme Court in 2006, many pro-choice supporters fear the Court now possesses the necessary votes to overturn *Roe.*

Providers are forced to deal with continuous harassment because they offer a legal medical procedure for women. The increasing availability of medical abortions may alter and improve the availability of abortion services, but it is unlikely to have an effect on anti-abortion harassment. The decline in abortion providers is likely to continue. Medical schools are more reluctant to teach abortion procedures, even though abortion is a vital aspect of providing gynecological care. The population of practicing abortion providers is aging, and there is not an adequate replacement pool (Henshaw and Van Vort 1994). William Harrison, a seventy-year-old physician who has provided abortion services for over thirty years in Arkansas, epitomizes the staffing dilemma faced by many clinics. He has recently had several surgeries for a head injury and has been urged by his wife to retire. Harrison continues to practice because he contends "there's no one to take my place" (Simon 2005).

Harassment has been an important tool used by the direct action groups of the pro-life movement. It has been an effective way of contributing to the reduction in the number of abortion providers and has had an impact on women (evidenced in the abortion rate). In its simplest form, political harassment is fairly cheap and easy to implement and, most important for the perpetrators of harassment, it helps them remain committed to achieving their goals.

Chapter 6

THE CHANGING FACE OF THE ABORTION DEBATE

> It is always and everywhere wrong to take innocent human life—even if a potential good is promised. There must be no unwanted humans. If "wanted-ness" becomes the criteria for personhood and legal protection it is the poor, the elderly, and those without a voice who are the next in line. The ability for any person to survive without the need of help from others cannot become the criteria for "humanness" either; to do so will end civilization as we know it. We are made for one another and we are our brother's keeper.
>
> —Rev. Keith A. Fournier, founder and president, Common Good 2002

The pro-life movement shares similar institutional structures and social-psychological dynamics that are present in other social movements. The anti-abortion movement's origin and development have, in many ways, mirrored other social movements. Yet, unlike many movements, the pro-life movement has heavily relied on harassing, confrontational tactics despite the overall institutional progression of the movement and its resultant success operating through legitimate political channels.

Anti-abortion groups have had access and opportunities within national, state, and local political institutions. Shortly following its inception, the right-to-life movement entered national politics and since then has expanded its role as a legitimate political player within multiple institutional venues. Over the years the movement has become more sophisticated and politically savvy. Pro-life strategists have crafted multiple approaches designed to restrict the availability and limit the accessibility of abortion services. Chapter 4 documented several of the important national legislative and legal victories won by the movement in the past few decades. At the state level, the pro-life movement has easily outpaced the pro-choice movement in terms of helping to introduce and pass legislation around the country.

Given the impressive institutional progress of the movement, theory predicts that the pro-life movement would move away from using disruptive, "outsider" strategies and incorporate "insider" strategies. But for the pro-life movement, the shift away from outsider, confrontational tactics has not occurred. Quite the opposite pattern has emerged: the movement started out largely institutionalized and began incorporating confrontational strategies throughout the 1980s. By the 1990s the proportion of providers experiencing some form of anti-abortion activity hovered around 85 percent (Cozzarelli and Major 1998; Henshaw 1995a), and since 1995 the volume of anti-abortion picketing has exponentially increased (National Abortion Federation 2006).

Political Harassment

Confrontational pro-life tactics are used in the same political environment as mainstream, institutionalized tactics and more extreme, radical tactics. Political behavior exists along a continuum, where traditional participation is on one end of the spectrum and acts of violence fall on the other end. All along the continuum, groups are attempting to achieve political outcomes even though their strategies may differ. Protests, sit-ins, and boycotts are all forms of legal, unconventional political participation and have been used by social movements throughout history to achieve favorable outcomes for their causes. These activities are designed to gain the *attention* and *responsiveness* of governmental authorities to movements' issues.

Social movements may experience significant costs resulting from their use of unconventional tactics; costs typically come in the form of a government's attempt to ignore, limit, or eliminate the challenges posed by movements. The confrontational tactics used by the pro-life movement radically depart from this expected pattern. Unlike most social movements, the anti-abortion movement is not trying to gain the government's attention and responsiveness directly through these strategies. By working through traditional political institutions, the pro-life movement has already earned politicians' attention and has also gained significant policy victories through this relationship. Confrontational anti-abortion tactics are aimed at nongovernmental actors and are an attempt to elicit an immediate response from them. I have argued throughout this book that these tactics are politically harassing because they are directed at nongovernmental actors in a political environment ensconced in an underlying fear, and the tactics are intended to change the behavior of others to achieve political goals. Along the continuum of political behavior, the dynamic between protesters and nongovernmental targets is significantly different than that between protesters and the government. Nongovernmental actors lack the resources to insulate themselves, whereas the government commands the authority to respond to the dissidents' activity in a manner deemed appropriate by the state.

Political harassment is used by the direct action branch of the pro-life movement with a very specific political outcome in mind: ending abortion. Protest activities are designed to address the immediacy of the movement's goal by directly confronting women seeking abortion services and those professionals administering the services. The intent of the confrontational activity is not veiled in secrecy. Direct action groups openly discuss their goals: to prevent women from having abortions and to close down abortion facilities.

> There used to be over 2,000 abortion clinics in America. Today, there are 738. Clearly, the pro-lifers are winning this battle. . . . Rest assured, Life Dynamics will not stop until every one of these death camps is closed and the American holocaust is over. (Life Dynamics 2006)

The Outcomes of Political Harassment

Political harassment is not the only strategy used by the pro-life movement, nor is it the most effective. The pro-life movement has created a three-tiered approach to help achieve its mission to end abortion. The political branch operates through political institutions, the outreach branch offers resources and alternatives for women experiencing "crisis pregnancies," and the direct action branch contends with the urgency of ending abortions at clinics. Combined, these three strategies have been successful over the past three decades.

The direct action branch has delivered some victories to the entire movement by using a confrontational and harassing approach to the fight against abortion. Through interviews with pro-choice and pro-life activists, paired with existing research, I have attempted to document the intent, use, and effect of protesting activities on those most intimately involved in the abortion conflict. In chapter 5, I conducted an empirical investigation examining the impact of political harassment on women and providers. Empirically, the evidence suggests that anti-abortion protesting is negatively related to the abortion rate. Anti-abortion confrontational tactics are even more detrimental to abortion providers; the empirical evidence points to a negative relationship between the number of abortion providers and harassment in the following forms: picketing clinics, picketing the homes of staff members, picketing with physical contact, and bomb threats. The more personalized forms of activities (picketing clinics at a higher volume per year as well as picketing at the homes of staff members) appear to have the greatest impact on providers. Empirically, certain forms of political harassment are effective in terms of changing the behavior of the targets of the activities.

From an anti-abortion activist's standpoint, this strategy is very effective because victories are measured one at a time: saving *one life*, preventing *one abortion*, or closing *one clinic*. These daily, small-scale victories have added up over the course of the past two decades and have in part contributed to the decline in abortions and providers. Confrontational tactics allow activists to work toward the goal of eradicating abortion without participating in compromise, which is unacceptable for an activist who deals in absolutism. Political harassment also presents participants with an opportunity to deal with the urgency of ending abortion via directly confronting the sources of the problem in a relatively cost-efficient manner. Political harassment does not demand the amount of resources needed to launch an institutionalized campaign against abortion. Compared to traditional institutional involvement, harassment does not require a similar level of financial resources, organizational capacity, or human capital such as expertise, professionalism, or a full-time commitment to the cause.

The sheer volume of the harassing tactics also serves other goals. It provides visibility to the entire movement and political currency to sympathetic politicians, and it provides a forum for changing the political and social culture of American society. For the larger movement, the direct action branch helps create a continual focus on abortion in the media. Figure 8 contains a simple count of abortion-related stories that have appeared in major newspapers and magazines from 1970 through 2004.[1] The media coverage follows the trajectory of the marked increase in pro-life direct action tactics starting in the 1990s. The magazine articles chronicling the abortion conflict have ranged in the hundreds and newspaper articles have ranged in the thousands per year.

Commanding this scope of media coverage has implications for political

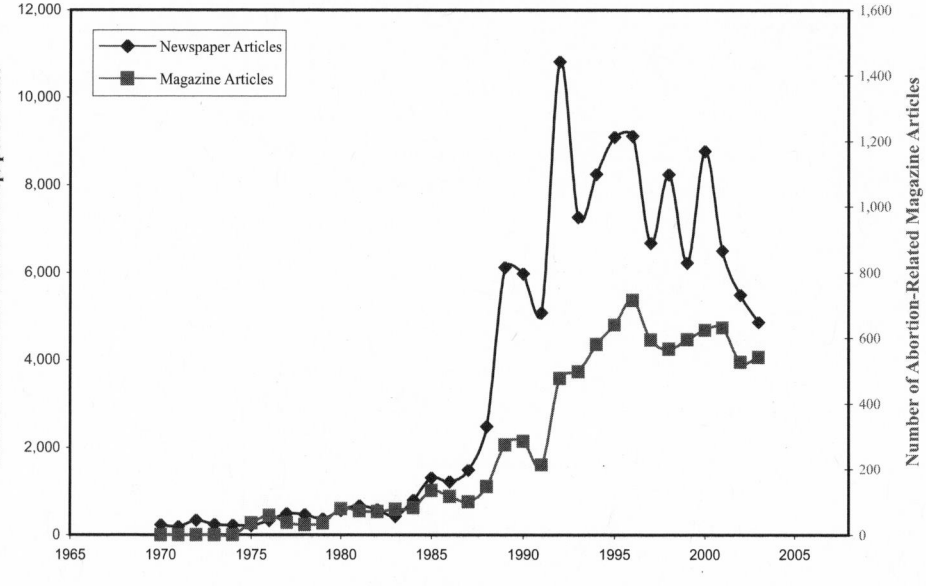

Fig. 8.   Media coverage of abortion issues

actors. Contentious morality politics, particularly those that do not have an overtly economic stake, tend to attract politicians' attention. Under these conditions, politicians are more responsive to morality politics and the changing tides of public opinion that may follow them (Sharp 2005; Mooney and Lee 2000). The direct action branch provides visibility for sympathetic politicians who are frequently featured in pro-life newsletters, on web sites, and as guest speakers at pro-life events. Politicians are rewarded with the support of these groups who are willing to vote based on the single issue of abortion.

The visibility of the abortion issue is rudimentarily reflected in the figures measuring the attention it has generated in two national political institutions: the congressional and executive branches. Figure 9 displays a yearly count of the number of congressional hearings pertaining to abortion-related issues and the length of each hearing.[2] Not only has the number of hearings related to abortion increased, and rather steeply since 1995, the number of House and Senate committees and subcommittees holding hearings on these matters has also dramat-

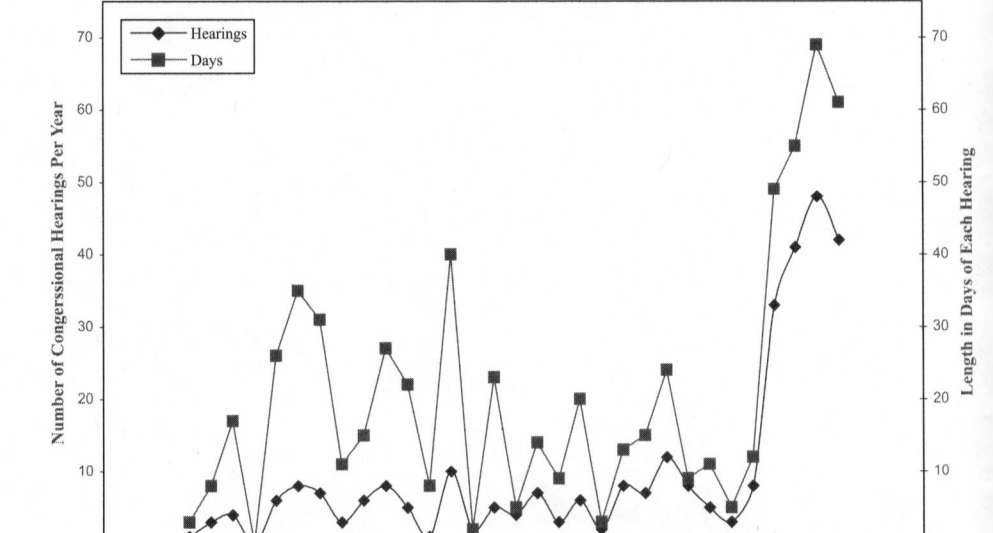

Fig. 9.   Total number and length of congressional hearings

ically increased as evidenced by figure 10. Similar to figure 9, the growth sharply increases around 1995 and correlates to the rise in protest activities around the country as well as correlating with the Republican takeover in Congress following the 1994 midterm elections, which suggests the congressional environment may have become more receptive to pro-life sympathizers.

The executive branch has also been marred in the abortion debate. Figure 11 presents a simplistic graphical representation of annual presidential attention to abortion.[3] Presidents have dealt with the abortion debate and approached it from pro-life and pro-choice perspectives. The figure does not reflect the trend in presidential abortion rhetoric: anti-abortion presidents have adopted the pro-life movement's construction of the debate and adopted much of the rhetoric used by the movement, which is a testimony to the movement's impact on the political landscape. Aside from national political institutions, as chapter 4 documents, pro-life issues are well represented in state legislatures' activities. The rise in anti-abortion bills being introduced at the state level is staggering.

The scope of pro-life protesting may also be influential in changing public

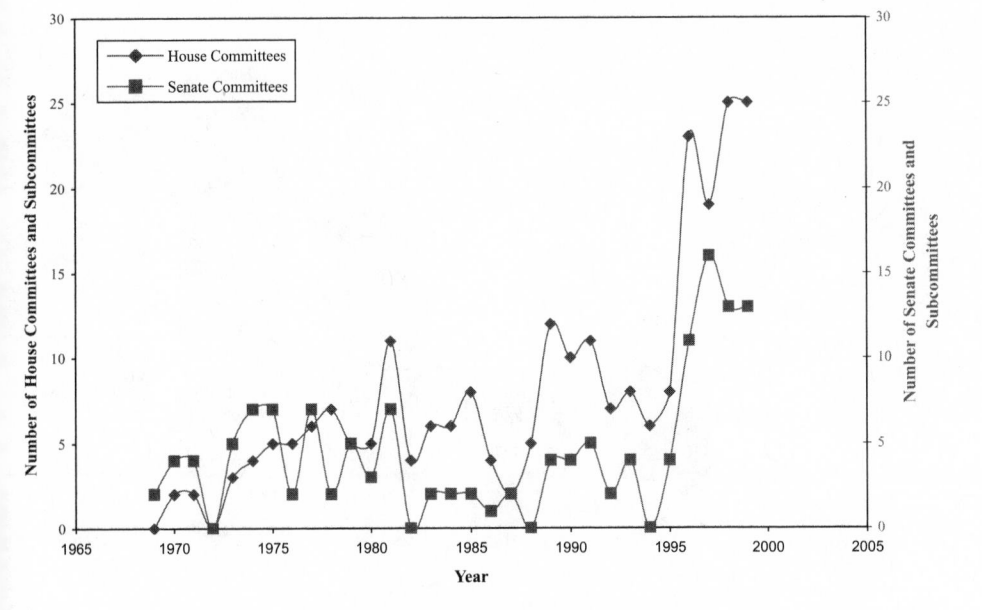

Fig. 10.   Congressional committees addressing abortion issues

opinion toward abortion. Public opinion supporting legalized abortion declined during the 1990s and early years of the new century (Jelen and Wilcox 2005). The decline has not been dramatic, but it is a significant decline, which may be attributable in part to the visibility generated by the protesting strategies used by direct action groups. The entire pro-life movement has made substantial gains in humanizing a fetus at every stage of pregnancy and helping to establish personhood rights for the unborn. Enlarged pictures of aborted fetuses and other graphic illustrations are commonly displayed at protests and may help contribute to a changing, more humanized, conceptualization of a fetus and in turn help sway public approval against the permissibility of using elective abortion services to resolve unwanted pregnancies.

In short, I have argued and attempted to demonstrate that political harassment is used by anti-abortion direct action groups because it works in a variety of ways including generating an immediate response from nongovernmental actors along with creating potential secondary benefits like attracting support from sympathetic politicians and shaping public opinion. Activists can deal

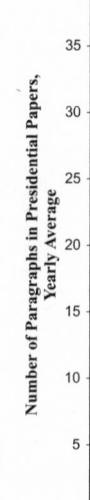

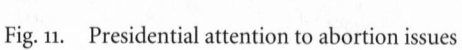

Fig. 11.   Presidential attention to abortion issues

with the urgency of the movement's mission while avoiding political compromise and still operating within a range of (mostly) legal activities. The pro-life
movement is a movement dedicated to achieving moral goals by political means
(Munson 2005). Direct action groups rely on harassing tactics to confront those
most intimately involved with abortion services because members are deeply
disturbed by the wrongness of abortion. Their mission is grounded in their
larger religious beliefs and perceptions of a changing culture that no longer values life but instead embraces individualism, selfishness, instant gratification,
and ultimately a culture of death.

Abortion, Morality, and Politics

The larger cultural conflict occurring between traditionalists and progressivists
in American society underscores abortion politics. As Nieburg (1969) pointed
out long ago, when a group's rudimentary grievances are essentially a struggle
or quest for identity, the group believes the old image must be recovered at any

cost. The anti-abortion movement is a morality movement whose members are "acting defensively in an effort to preserve a moral order that provides meaning for their lives" (McVeigh and Sikkink 2001, 1431). The larger cultural war is reflected in the respective frameworks used by both sides of the issue to describe the abortion conflict; one framework embraces moral absolutism, the other moral choice. One pro-choice activist described her position on abortion in terms of women's autonomy and choice.

> Personally and also for [the clinic] it is 100 percent about women's choice and reproductive rights. You can beat it to death in politics or morals, but it all boils back down to a woman's choice and the well being and health of a woman. And that's it; there is nothing else to say. I mean we can play all of these political games, but that's what it is all about. (Interview with a pro-choice activist, February 2000)

In contrast, a pro-life activist grounded her beliefs about abortion within a larger cultural context that she feels continues to blur the boundaries between morality and individualism.

> I think that there is a greater problem than that people just don't know the facts about abortion. So really I think that it will take more than education really, it will take a change of consciousness. Abortion is part of a larger problem. Everyone is sort of embedded in this idea that people can have whatever you want at whatever expense. (Interview with a pro-life activist, May 2000)

Clinic protests are a means of recovering, promoting, and celebrating an identity that is out of step with a culturally progressive and increasingly individualistic society. Many pro-life supporters deeply believe in the moral wrongness of abortion and truly perceive abortion as a sin against an unborn baby and, importantly, a grave sin against God. Yet, the obvious moral component of the abortion conflict cannot easily be divorced from the moral component governing the alternative understandings and beliefs about gender ascribed to by pro-choice and pro-life activists.

The cultural divide between the two sides is clearly embodied in the differing conceptions they hold regarding sexuality. Abortion discussions are fundamentally linked to ideas of what constitutes illicit, promiscuous sexuality. People's opinions toward abortion are inexorably linked with their attitudes toward women's roles and sexual morality (Hout 1999; McVeigh and Sikkink 2001; Luker 1984). The commingling of sexual morality and abortion is reflected in pro-life activists' opinions of women seeking abortion services. Women seeking abortions symbolize the shifting norms structuring sexuality and the permissibility of engaging in sexual activity outside of marriage. Many anti-abortion participants, encapsulated by this pro-life activist's comments, expressed feelings of unfairness and loss of control because women can engage in sexual activity and avoid the price of unwanted motherhood though abortion.

> There are women who have an abortion because the timing's not right and that a baby would inconvenience them. I feel like they're taking the—I don't think it's the easy way out—but I think that it's a way for them to get an immediate end to a problem. (Interview with a pro-life activist, December 2003)

Liberalized attitudes toward gender and sexuality continue to vie with more traditional views, particularly for pro-life activists who believe much of the early teaching on sexuality remains accurate and useful. Anti-abortion politics are in essence one attempt to remasculinize American culture. Direct action tactics help reestablish patriarchal feelings of control, power, and protection, all of which many activists perceive as being stripped away in society. Confrontational activism resonates with participants who are interested in reversing the trend toward female autonomy and the devaluing of motherhood as a full-time occupation. Participating in direct action tactics speaks to the fear of losing patriarchal control in general and, more specifically, a loss of control over women's sexuality and reproduction (Luker 1984; Stearns 1990; May 1998).

> The abortion warrior can be said to be projecting his fears onto the unborn . . . to a fear of losing one's power in society. . . . The abortion warrior fears loss of power, projects those fears onto the so-called most vulnerable of all people (unborn), and fantasizes about absorbing the evil that threatens the unborn. (Mason 2002a, 26)

The loss of control felt by many pro-life activists was expressed not only in terms of their disdain toward abortion services but also in their antagonism toward family planning services and education. Jim Sedlak, founder of Stop Planned Parenthood International (STOPP) believes that sex education programs are a marketing program for promiscuity and propaganda for pushing a pro-abortion agenda onto women.

> Birth control makes girls and women have sex more often. Although studies say birth control reduces abortion, it doesn't work in practice. In practice it leads to more sex and more abortion. (Interview with Jim Sedlak, December 2003)

Other pro-life activists expressed their disapproval of contraception in terms of marriage. They believe family planning interferes with, and undermines, the traditional power dynamic embedded in marriage.

> The Catholic Church opposes anything that interferes with the procreative and unity of marriage, and contraception does just that. It tears apart the procreative aspect of marriage. And when you tear apart the procreative part then you are tearing apart the unitative part, because as a husband and a wife you are saying that I am not going to give myself to you wholly. You can have everything except my fertility. (Interview with a pro-life activist, October 1999)

Another activist similarly commented on the inappropriateness of using contraception within the context of marriage.

> I am Catholic and the Catholic Church has very specific teachings on abortion and contraception. The Church teaches that you can't control the act of marriage which is a state to create both love and life. So, contraception basically cuts off half of what marriage is supposed to be in the conjugal act. Contraception says well I will give all of myself to you except my fertility. That is removing God from the most important act of love. (Interview with a pro-life activist, January 2000)

The direct action branch of the pro-life movement draws from a cultural setting that is not shared by the majority of society—an identity glued together by fundamentalist beliefs. Fundamentalists can compartmentalize individuals into an "us" versus "them" framework because they tend to insulate themselves from those who do not share their belief system. The direct action division of the movement is operating outside of political institutions where it does not have to compromise, negotiate, or participate in competing abortion discourses. Under these conditions, activists can more readily separate themselves into "us" and "them" categories. The more radical groups' isolation contributes to the ideological solidarity of members, which ultimately serves the whole movement.

The Future of Abortion Politics

The intractability of abortion politics leaves little room for common political ground or promise for ending the conflict surrounding abortion. Moderate abortion supporters in society (those who do not believe in criminalizing abortion services or allowing unregulated elective abortion services) hold ambivalent and confused feelings about abortion because many citizens simultaneously hold conflicting values: they value female autonomy and fetal life (Jelen and Wilcox 2005). These conflicting values surface in the public's attempt to find common ground via supporting measures that restrict the availability of abortion services such as placing limits on the circumstances in which minors can receive an abortion without parental involvement (Jelen and Wilcox 2005).

Politicians have also wrestled with attempts to find commonality between the two sides by supporting restrictions and focusing on prevention. For example, in New York state, Nassau County executive Thomas Suozzi, who ran in the 2006 gubernatorial primary, has proposed a "new argument" in the hopes of "establish[ing] a new middle ground" in the abortion conflict (Dionne 2006). Suozzi's proposal initially included providing $909,000 in county funds to a coalition of eight groups who offer adoption services, housing services for single pregnant women, and sex education—including abstinence-only education—as a means of reducing the abortion rate in New York. Suozzi is optimistic that his plan will "bring together opposing sides" and help create a "world with fewer abortions" (Dionne 2006). On November 1, 2006, Nassau legislators passed Suozzi's initiative and agreed to spend over $800,000 on pregnancy prevention. The funds will be apportioned to seven different agencies, including disparate organizations such as Planned Parenthood and Catholic Charities.

Focusing on reducing the need for abortion services does hold some promise for moderate politicians and citizens; however, for activists on both sides of the debate, the search for middle ground is very unlikely to solve the conflict surrounding abortion because the conflict is over much more than simply trying to reduce the abortion rate. The abortion debate, as currently constructed, is an intractable issue, which as I have argued, is a large contributing factor to the rise of the direct action branch and corollary growth in using harassing tactics. For direct action activists, compromise is exactly the problem produced when operating within the political system. Direct action groups are able to circumvent and avoid compromise.

Members of the direct action branch are more likely to hold absolutist positions in the abortion debate, which also carries over into their views about the best route to take in reducing the need for abortion. The prospect of finding middle ground through the common desire to reduce the need for abortion is a dubious prospect. Sex education has increasingly become a contentious morality and political issue that has been tied to the abortion conflict (Doan and Williams 2003). Abstinence-only education has been applauded as the key to reducing the abortion rate by pro-life activists and scoffed at by pro-choice activists who view it as completely ineffective.[4]

Finding middle ground is also unrealistic particularly as the abortion conflict continues to expand and becomes linked with other morality issues such as stem cell research, genetic cloning, euthanasia, and infertility technology. All of these issues have presented another forum for discussing abortion in different contexts and political venues, and contributes to activists' belief and resolve that the need to protect the sanctity of life from conception to death is a paramount battle in modern society. Abortion politics will continue to be salient and divisive in American society, especially as pro-choice supporters' fear of a Supreme Court reversal of *Roe* becomes more of a probability with the changing, increasingly conservative, composition of the Court.

Political harassment probably will not decline in the coming years because the movement is seeing some payoff from the activity, which should continue to fuel direct action groups' reliance on it. Unless *Roe* is overturned, it is unlikely that groups will move away from engaging in confrontational tactics at abortion clinics. Even if *Roe* was overturned and abortion decisions were returned to the states, pro-life activism would continue to have a market in the states where abortion services remained legal. After all, many local and national direct action groups promise to continue their fight against abortion until "every one of these death camps is closed" around the country (Life Dynamics 2006).

Another trend in abortion politics, which is likely to continue, is the onslaught of anti-abortion bills being introduced within state legislatures. In many regards, the volume of activity and the "guerrilla style" approach to anti-abortion legislation mirror the style of tactics taken by the direct action faction of the pro-life movement. Several Supreme Court cases have helped spur the growth in anti-abortion policy, namely, the *Webster* and *Casey* decisions. The scope of protesting has helped create a political environment where institution-alized forms of harassment such as inundating state legislatures with anti-abor-tion bills are becoming more common.

Overwhelming the opposition in this institutionalized style is also emerging in terms of lawsuits being filed against abortion providers by anti-abortion groups. For example, several abortion providers in North Dakota and Califor-nia were sued by pro-life groups for distributing literature disputing pro-life groups' claims that there is a statistically significant link between abortion and breast cancer[5] (Center for Reproductive Rights 2004). Several pro-life organiza-tions encourage women who have been "harmed by abortion" to contact them for legal support. Life Dynamics offers free legal consultation with one of its purported 700 attorneys, representing all fifty states, who are willing to file mal-practice lawsuits against abortion providers for abortion-related injuries, assault, or noncompliance with state laws (Life Dynamics 2006).

> If you were injured during an abortion procedure or if you suspect that a condition you are suffering from could somehow be related to a past abor-tion procedure then call toll-free, (800) 401–6494. You have the right to seek compensations for your injuries and suffering. If you have been sexu-ally harassed or sexually assaulted by an abortionist or a clinic employee, then you are entitled to seek legal redress. . . . Also, please recognize that physical injury or assault is not the only cause of action available to you. All underage girls who obtain an abortion, birth control pills, a pregnancy test, or treatment for a sexually transmitted disease may be able [to] sue a doctor or clinic that provided any of these without complying with their state's mandatory reporting laws. Likewise, a parent of an underage girl could pur-sue a similar lawsuit. (Life Dynamics 2006)

The exact nature of the relationship between direct action harassment, pol-icy and litigation harassment cannot be determined from this project. The com-bined impact of these anti-abortion strategies is likely to disproportionately fall on abortion providers and clinics, and contribute to a continuing reduction in the number of practicing abortion providers.

Conclusion

From a broader perspective, the impact of the pro-life movement on the politi-cal landscape in American society has been vast and has ushered in a new brand of activism. But more than providing an in-depth look at abortion politics, examining this morality movement and its use of confrontational tactics presents an opportunity to generate a more nuanced approach to examining the reasons for and efficacy of incorporating political harassment into a strategy to achieve a movement's goals. Developing a theoretical argument for why and how unconventional but legal tactics can be a harassing form of rational political behavior moves us toward a broader definition of political participation, one that changes the calculation of costs and benefits of protest activities.

In turn, identifying and understanding why confrontational tactics can be used as a political resource enables us to examine the efficacy of these tactics in terms of costs and benefits to a social movement and its antagonists. Conceiving of political participation as a continuum, with conventional activities such as working on a campaign on one end while on the other is extreme violence like bombings and murders, allows us to examine the myriad forms of participation that fall into gray areas; behavior that is not traditional participation or violent participation. We can also begin to account for why the same behavior (here, legal political protest) can have different implications and consequences in different contexts.

APPENDIX A: SURVEY QUESTIONS

1985 SURVEY QUESTIONS

1. How many times did each of the following anti-abortion activities occur at your facility in 1985?

(1) Picketing; (2) Picketing with physical contact or blocking of patients; (3) Picketing with noise loud enough to be heard inside in patient areas; (4) Invasion by demonstrators; (5) Distribution of anti-abortion literature inside your facility; (6) False appointments made to disrupt scheduling; (7) Jamming of telephone lines; (8) Tracing of license plates to identify your abortion patients; (9) Vandalism: jamming of locks, physical damage; (10) Picketing the homes of staff members; (11) Death threats; (12) Bomb threats.

1988 SURVEY QUESTIONS

1. How many times did each of the following anti-abortion activities occur at your facility in 1988?

(1) Picketing; (2) Picketing with physical contact or blocking of patients; (3) Vandalism: jamming of locks, physical damage; (4) Picketing of homes of staff members; (5) Bomb threats; (6) Demonstrations resulting in arrests.

1992 SURVEY QUESTIONS

1. How many times did each of the following anti-abortion activities occur at your facility in 1992?

(1) Picketing; (2) Picketing with physical contact or blocking of patients; (3) Vandalism: jamming of locks, physical damage; (4) Picketing of homes of

staff members; (5) Bomb threats; (6) Demonstrations resulting in arrests; (7) Chemical attacks (e.g., butyric acid); (8) Tracing of license plates to identify your abortion patients; (9) Stalking (following) of staff or patients; (10) Blockade (attempt to block doorways so that patients can't enter).

1995 SURVEY QUESTIONS

1. How many times did each of the following anti-abortion activities occur at your facility in 1995?

(1) Picketing; (2) Picketing with physical contact or blocking of patients; (3) Picketing of homes of staff members; (4) Vandalism: jamming of locks, physical damage; (5) Bomb threats.

2000 SURVEY QUESTIONS

1. How many times did each of the following anti-abortion activities occur at your facility in 2000?

(1) Picketing; (2) Picketing with physical contact or blocking of patients; (3) Picketing of homes of staff members; (4) Vandalism: jamming of locks, physical damage; (5) Bomb threats.

APPENDIX B: DATA SOURCES

Abortion Providers: number of abortion providers as reported in various issues of *Family Planning Perspectives*, which is published by the Alan Guttmacher Institute. Note: the journal changed its name to *Perspectives on Sexual and Reproductive Health* in 2002.

Abortion Rate: the abortion rate per 1,000 women aged 15–44 as reported in various issues of *Family Planning Perspectives*, which is published by the Alan Guttmacher Institute. Note: the journal changed its name to *Perspectives on Sexual and Reproductive Health* in 2002.

Abortion Restrictions: the number of the following restrictions against abortion services in a state. Pre-*Roe* Criminal Abortion Law; Mandatory Waiting Periods; Limits on Public Funding of Abortions for Poor Women; Conscience-Based Exemptions; Counseling Bans; Husband Consent or Notification Requirements; Requiring the Payment of Extra Insurance Premiums; Limits on Public Employees' Insurance Coverage; Informed Consent (forms of communication); Informed Consent (fetal development information); Informed Consent (the provision of abortion information); Informed Consent (the provision of childbirth information); Informed Consent (the presentation of alternatives to abortion); Viability Restrictions; Restrictions on Minors (consent of two parents); Restrictions on Minors (consent of one parent); Restrictions on Minors (parental consent without judicial bypass); Restrictions on Minors (parental notification of both parents); Restrictions on Minors (parental notification of one parent); Restrictions on Minors (parental notification without judicial bypass); Restrictions on Minors (informed consent); Restrictions on Minors (waiting periods); Physician-only Requirement; Restrictions on the Use of Public Facilities; Targeted Regulation of Abortion Providers (TRAP) subjects abortion providers to burdensome restrictions not applied to other medical professionals. Data are from *Who Decides? A State-by-State Review of Abortion and Reproductive Rights*, various years, published by the National Abortion and Reproductive Rights Action League Pro-Choice America.

Black Population: the percentage of the population that is black. Data are from the *Statistical Abstract of the United States,* various years.

Catholic Population: the percentage of a state's population that self-identifies as Catholics. Data are from *Churches and Church Membership in the United States,* various years.

Funded Abortions: the number of publicly funded abortions for the poor. Data are from *Family Planning Perspectives,* various years, which is published by the Alan Guttmacher Institute. Note: the journal changed its name to *Perspectives on Sexual and Reproductive Health* in 2002.

Income: per capita income per person. Data are from the *Statistical Abstract of the United States,* various years.

NARAL Membership: the number of National Abortion and Reproductive Rights Action League Pro-Choice America members in each state. Data were obtained directly from NARAL. Contact information at www.naral.com or (202) 973-3000.

Protestant Fundamentalists: the percentage of a state's population that self-identifies as Protestant Fundamentalists. Churches classified as Protestant Fundamentalists are Churches of God, Latter Day Saints, Churches of Christ, Church of the Nazarene, Mennonites, Conservative Baptist Association, Lutheran Church Missouri Synod, Pentecostal Free-Will Baptists, Pentecostal Holiness, the Salvation Army, Seventh-Day Adventists, Southern Baptists, and Wisconsin Evangelical Lutheran Synod. Data are from *Churches and Church Membership in the United States,* various years.

Urbanism: the percentage of the population living in urban areas. Data are from the *Statistical Abstract of the United States,* various years.

NOTES

Chapter 1

1. I refer to movements and activists (on both sides of the abortion conflict) in a variety of ways throughout the book. I generally adopt the names used by the respective movements. I try to use neutral names and vary the names (for example, anti-abortion or pro-life) for the purposes of prose.

2. For four years I followed (via observation, frequent visits, and media coverage) the development of a Planned Parenthood facility in Bryan, Texas that began offering abortion services in 1999. The quotes used throughout this book are taken from interviews I conducted with activists, volunteers, employees, and pro-life and pro-choice supporters from local and national organizations. The quotes appear the way they were articulated by the respondents during the interviews; grammar mistakes in the quotes are not edited. I conducted interviews between September 1998 and August 2000; and again during the period of November 2003 through March 2004. During this span of time, the Brazos Valley Coalition for Life changed executive directors. David Bereit became the second executive director of the coalition while I was conducting my research (the coalition currently is led by another director). To protect the individuals involved in this research, many of the names, organizations, and locations have been changed and are noted in the text by generic organizational terms. If a name appears in quotation marks, it indicates a pseudonym for the person being interviewed. However, many individuals wanted me to use their names and organizational affiliations, which is also noted in the text.

3. The Nature Conservancy is a private, nonprofit group that purchases land for conservation purposes and uses market-based approaches to achieve solutions to environmental problems.

4. Other models of political violence have grown out of resource mobilization theory, in particular, the McAdam political process model, which focuses on three variables: the dissident group's level of organization, the perceived probability of success of collective protest, and the political opportunities available to the group in securing their demands (see McAdam 1982).

5. I purposely refer to women's health care clinics instead of abortion clinics because the former are often targets of anti-abortion protest activity even when the facility does not offer abortion services.

Chapter 2

1. This is a simplification of the multiple issues tied to reproduction. For example, it is nearly impossible to divorce the politics of fertility control—in a historical perspective—from issues of race, class, equality, eugenics, poverty, elitism, health, overpopulation, and infanticide. A thorough historical overview of fertility politics is, however, beyond the scope of this chapter. For more information related to the subject see, for example, Brodie 1994; Donovan 1995; Tone 2001; Luker 1996; Solinger 1998.

2. For a more detailed look at the history of birth control please see Tone 1997, 2001; McCann 1994; Brodie 1994; Douglas 1970.

3. The women's movement of the 1800s often advocated abstinence as a form of birth control. Unlike the modern women's movement, these early feminists embraced domesticity, and although they posed a threat to traditional Victorian mores, they did not represent a threat to the family structure (Gordon 1976).

4. The Hippocratic oath refers to one of the earliest medical documents mentioning abortion. The oath was written by Hippocrates, an ancient Greek physician frequently referred to as the "Father of Medicine." It is estimated that Hippocrates lived sometime between 460 and 377 B.C. The Hippocratic oath states: "The regimen I adopt shall be for the benefit of my patients according to my ability and judgment, and not for their hurt or for any wrong. I will give no deadly drug to any, though it be asked of me, and I will counsel such, and especially I will not aid a woman to procure abortion. Whatsoever house I enter, there will I go for the benefit of the sick, refraining from all wrong-doing or corruption, and especially from any act of seduction, of male or female, of bond or free. Whatever things I see or hear concerning the life of men, in my attendance on the sick or even apart therefrom, which ought not to be noised abroad, I will keep in silence thereon, counting such things to be as sacred secrets" (*Encyclopedia Britannica*, 14th ed., s.v. "Medicine, Custom of (Ancient medicine)," 197). Students take the oath when they graduate from medical school.

5. English common law refers to "the body of unwritten law that governed the behavior of men and women in England before the practice of having laws enacted by legislative bodies came into regular use" (Rubin 1994, 5). Common law was based on the traditions of English people, ancient legal writings, and the Bible. Judges relied on common law to settle legal disputes.

6. *Quickening* was a term used to describe the point in a pregnancy when a woman can feel the fetus move. There is a lot of variability as to when this occurs, but on average a woman can feel fetal movement around the fourth to sixth month of pregnancy. Consequently, there was little regulation of first and second trimester abortions during this time period (Luker 1984).

7. Kentucky was the exception. In Kentucky, the courts ruled that abortion was illegal (Rubin 1994).

8. The reluctance of governmental involvement stimulated the AMA to establish boards and bureaus designed to investigate illegal abortion services. For decades the AMA acted as an extension of the government. It attempted to investigate, regulate, prosecute, and enforce anti-abortion laws. For a more detailed account of the AMA's "policing" role see Reagan 1997.

9. Women have always been active in political affairs in the United States; however, they were excluded from formally participating for over one hundred years after the United States won its independence from Britain in 1776. At the U.S. Constitutional Convention in 1787, states were granted the authority to decide women's suffrage. New Jersey was the only state to retain voting rights for women, but the state eventually revoked women's voting rights in 1807. After being involved in the abolitionist movement in the 1830s, women turned their efforts to women's suffrage. In 1848, the first Women's Rights Convention was held in Seneca Falls, New York. Elizabeth Cady Stanton proposed equal suffrage, which was a radical notion at the time; the proposal was adopted at the convention. Nearly one hundred years later, on August 26, 1920, the Nineteenth Amendment giving women the right to vote, which was also referred to as the Susan B. Anthony Amendment, became law (Timeline of Women's Suffrage in the United States 2005). Given the newness of women's voting rights coupled with the prevailing cultural norms of the time, Margaret Sanger's efforts to sway the League of Women Voters and the National Woman's Party into putting birth control reform on their agendas were met with resistance (McCann 1994; Kennedy 1970).

10. Although Margaret Sanger was a tireless advocate for birth control reform and lobbied for contraception as a means of liberating women from the burden of uncontrolled fertility, she eventually formed a political alliance with the eugenics movement, forever tainting her reputation. The eugenics movement built on the prevalence of racism in America by providing a "scientific" rationale for the practice of discrimination in society, directed at minorities, immigrants, the poor, and the physically and mentally disabled. Eugenicists advocated for population control, limited reproduction, and abortion reform. They also promoted large families among those deemed fit. For example, John D. Rockefeller Jr. had six children and so did Frederick Osborn (he was the first strategist for the American Eugenics Society and the first administrator for the Population Council). Later population control supporters continued the tradition: former president George Bush, multimillionaire entrepreneur Ted Turner, and financier George Soros each raised five children (Meehan 1998). The eugenics movement had many academics, scientists, socialites, and politicians in the movement. This assortment of players was helpful in pushing for abortion reform as early as the 1930s. The Eugenics Publishing Company produced a book in 1933 that called for abortion reform via the relaxing of anti-abortion laws. In the 1960s eugenicists gave large sums of money to the Association for the Study of Abortion and also contributed money to the winning side in *Roe v. Wade* (Meehan 1998).

11. Alan Guttmacher became the president of the Planned Parenthood Federation. He was a strong proponent of abortion rights and supported the use of elective abortions decades before it was legalized. As early as 1941, Dr. Guttmacher was referring his

patients to an illegal abortionist. He believed that access to abortion services helped women. Women's rights and health were not Dr. Guttmacher's only motivation for supporting abortion. He was also a member of the eugenics movement and served as the vice president and a board member for the American Eugenics Society (Meehan 1998).

12. Margaret Sanger was one of the first activists to publicly link birth control reform (specifically access and availability) to women's rights. In her early years of advocacy, Sanger saw controlled family planning as the key to improving women's lives in terms of their emotional, physical, and financial health. Sanger also advocated for abortion reform, but at that point in time her advocacy for abortion liberalization was tainted by her connection to the eugenics movement, and she approached it from a eugenics perspective rather than tying abortion rights to women's rights. The Society for Human Abortions was one of the first organizations to explicitly link abortion rights to individual rights.

13. The National Association for the Repeal of Abortion Laws (NARAL) changed its name after abortion was legalized in 1973 to the National Abortion Rights Action League. In 1993 the organization changed its name to the National Abortion and Reproductive Rights Action League, to reflect its concern with broader issues pertaining to reproductive rights. By 2003, the organization changed its name to the National Abortion and Reproductive Rights Action League Pro-Choice America. It has used the same acronym, NARAL, throughout its various name changes. Currently, the organization is referred to as NARAL Pro-Choice America (National Abortion and Reproductive Rights Action League Pro-Choice America 2006).

14. Abortion was not a partisan issue during the 1960s to late 1970s. The Republican and Democratic parties have become more internally consistent about the abortion issue over time. For a more detailed look at the issue evolution of abortion (how abortion became a partisan issue) see Adams 1997 and Stimson 1991.

15. Norma McCorvey publicly revealed her identity as Roe in 1984. McCorvey has written two autobiographies about her life. The first one, *I Am Roe: My Life, Roe v. Wade, and Freedom of Choice*, candidly details McCorvey's struggles with sex abuse, domestic violence, drug and alcohol abuse, and her lesbian identity. McCorvey had three children, all of whom she gave up for adoption. She worked as a counselor at several abortion clinics in Dallas, Texas. In 1995, Operation Rescue moved into the building next door to the clinic where McCorvey was working. She soon converted to Christianity, was baptized on August 8, 1995, and renounced abortion (Korosec 2004; Cartwright 2004). She went from being a staunch pro-choice supporter to a staunch pro-life supporter. McCorvey wrote about her transformation in her second autobiography, *Won by Love*. McCorvey's conversion was a victory for the pro-life movement; however, the relationship between McCorvey and the movement continues to be strained at times. Despite McCorvey's conversion to Christianity and renouncement of lesbianism, she continues to reside with Connie Gonzales, her longtime partner of over thirty years (Cartwright 2004). Their living arrangement poses a problem for pro-life members who believe lesbianism is immoral. Shortly after converting, McCorvey transformed her garage into an office and started an anti-abortion ministry named Roe No

More. In 2003 McCorvey and her lawyer, Allan Parker (president of the Justice Foundation), filed a petition using Rule 60 (Federal Rules of Civil Procedures: Rule 60: Relief from Judgment or Order) to have *Roe v. Wade* overturned. A federal district court in Texas along with the Fifth U.S. Circuit Court of Appeals rejected the suit. McCorvey and Parker have appealed to the Supreme Court (Bluey 2005).

16. Henry McCluskey Jr. had an openly and active gay client, Alvin L. Buchanan, who was arrested in a bathroom at Dallas's Reverchon Park and two months later in a department store restroom. Buchanan was arrested and convicted for violating the sodomy statute, which criminalized all acts of oral or anal sex for homosexuals and heterosexuals, regardless of marital status. In late May 1969, McCluskey appealed Buchanan's conviction in *Buchanan v. Batchelor* (Charles Batchelor was the chief of police in Dallas). He filed an appeal in a Texas court and also filed a federal case, alleging that the nineteenth-century sodomy statute was unconstitutionally overbroad (Garrow 1994). The Court's ruling in *Griswold,* where the Court ruled in favor of shielding marital privacy from governmental intrusion, paved the way for a victory in *Buchanan v. Batchelor* (U.S.L.W. 3057, June 19, 1970). The three-judge panel cited *Griswold* in their ruling in determining that the sodomy law was unconstitutionally overbroad. They ruled that moral disapproval of sodomy "is not sufficient reason for the State to encroach upon the liberty of married persons in their private conduct" (Garrow 1994, 402). The judges also noted another case that had been decided in the Seventh Circuit Court of Appeals, which the Supreme Court did not disturb. The case was *Cotner v. Henry,* which freed a man from prison who was convicted of having anal sex with his wife.

17. For a detailed account of the court cases leading up to the *Roe* decision please see Garrow 1994; Epstein and Kobylka 1992; Craig and O'Brien 1993, chapter 1.

18. The Supreme Court ruled that the only regulation the government could impose during the first trimester of pregnancy was requiring a licensed physician to perform the abortion (Tribe 1992).

19. Similar to many new social movements, the pro-life movement had both organizational and goal-setting problems. During the late 1970s and early 1980s the movement underwent a transformation, incorporating new participants—most notably, the New Right. See chapter 3 for more information on the pro-life movement's organizational problems and growth.

20. Fundamentalism has a long history in the United States. Politically, fundamentalists were active until the Scopes trial. After the court defeat, many fundamentalists retreated from the political scene until the late 1960s. In the past three decades, as social issues have increasingly taken center stage, fundamentalists have reemerged in the political arena. Scholars have assessed the impact of fundamentalism on political institutions. For a recent example, please see Morone (2003), and Songer and Tabrizi's (1999) work on the impact of fundamentalism on justices' decision making in the courts.

21. The political branch of the pro-life movement has national organizations that are professionalized and institutionalized. Pro-life groups also affiliate with multiple-issue groups or can be multiple-issue groups themselves. The pro-life, multiple-issue

groups' agenda varies and may include any (or all) of the following issues: "opposition to abortion, feminism, the Equal Rights Amendment, gay rights, domestic violence legislation, busing, 'secular humanist' school books, the Supreme Court ruling against prayers in public schools, pornography, welfare spending, and reductions in military spending" (Johnson 1999, 244).

22. The pro-life movement has used other issue frames in the abortion debate. However, the most enduring has been framing abortion as a morality issue.

23. Although Focus on the Family is a pro-life organization, it also addresses other social issues, from a conservative standpoint, that more broadly compose a New Right agenda.

Chapter 3

1. On the same day the Hyde amendment was approved by Congress, pro-choice advocates filed a lawsuit in a New York federal court challenging the legality of the legislation. The day the Hyde amendment was to be enacted, District Judge John F. Dolling Jr. enjoined the enforcement of the bill. Between 1977 to 1980, the Supreme Court heard arguments in four cases (*Maher v. Roe, Beal v. Doe, Poelker v. Doe*, and *Harris v. McRae*) pertaining to government funding of abortion services. Three of the cases were decided on the same day in 1977. In *Maher v. Roe*, the Supreme Court ruled, in a six to three margin, that the state's refusal to fund abortions through Medicaid is constitutional. Justices voted six to three in *Beal v. Doe* that the state's refusal to fund nontherapeutic abortions did not violate Title XIX of the Social Security Act. The third case in 1977, *Poelker v. Doe*, ruled that city-owned, public hospitals did not have to provide nontherapeutic abortions. The final funding question was settled in *Harris v. McRae* when the Court upheld the Hyde amendment by a five to four ruling in 1980 (Garrow 1994; McFarlane and Meier 2000). In the 1977 decisions, the Court affirmed *Roe* by stating that its rulings did not show a "retreat" from *Roe*, but it also supported state restrictions on funding because the Court believed prohibiting the use of governmental financing of abortion services did not undermine women's constitutional rights.

2. There are important religious distinctions between the self-designations people use to describe themselves. For example, within the Religious Right, Christian Coalition, or Moral Majority, individuals identify themselves by denomination, as Baptists, Pentecostals, charismatics, Presbyterians, fundamentalists, or simply Christians (Watson 1997). I recognize these differences, and for simplicity I use the terms *evangelicals* and *fundamentalists* interchangeably.

3. The creationism versus evolution debate has not been resolved and continues to resurface in debates regarding the appropriateness of each curriculum in the context of science classes taught in public schools. The most recent iteration of this debate is articulated as the theory of intelligent design instead of creationism. Intelligent design posits that there are numerous inconsistencies and features in nature that are best explained as resulting from an intelligent designer, as opposed to a purely neo-Darwinian theory of natural selection and random mutations (Abbey 2005). The teaching of intelligent design in public schools is being challenged in the courts as a violation of the separation

between church and state. Americans United for Separation of Church and State won a lawsuit in Pennsylvania challenging the constitutionality of teaching intelligent design in public schools. Following the victory, the group filed a similar suit in Kern County, California, on behalf of eleven parents whose children are educated in the El Tejon School District, where intelligent design is taught as an evolution theory in a philosophy course (KGET News 2006).

4. This brief history of fundamentalism is only a glimpse and does not adequately explain the nuances and distinctions between different types of fundamentalists (such as separatist-fundamentalism, accommodationist-evangelicalism, or the Pentecostal-charismatic movement). For a more comprehensive history of fundamentalism see Watson 1997; Wilcox 1996.

5. The perceived domination of fundamentalists within the pro-life movement is largely a result of biased media coverage to the extent that media focus on sensational, dramatic, and personalized stories, rather than a true reflection of their contribution to the movement. Consequently, the direct action branch of the pro-life movement received an abundance of attention because of its reliance on confrontational and outlandish tactics, which has led to the erroneous, general perception that the other two branches of the movement (the political branch typified by the NRLC and the individual outreach branch typified by crisis pregnancy centers) do not play as pivotal a role in the movement. This is only a perception rather than an accurate portrayal of the movement (Munson 2002).

6. Partial-birth abortion is not a medical term or procedure. Partial-birth abortion is a term used by pro-life groups to refer to late-term abortions. The procedure that best approximates the multiple descriptions of "partial-birth" abortions is an intact dilation and extraction (D&X). This procedure is very rare, accounting for approximately .003 to .005 percent of all abortions in 1996 (Henshaw 1998a).

7. After its release, subsequent analysis of the film by both pro-choice groups and physicians led to the questioning of the film's scientific validity, accuracy, and truth (see, for example, Prescott 1989 and *Nightline,* February 12, 1985).

8. All three branches of the pro-life movement (the political, direct action, and outreach) reject the use of violence. Following extremist activity, public outcry often points to the whole movement and holds it accountable for the crimes committed by anti-abortion extremists.

9. Even though substantial contributions flooded into Operation Rescue, many pro-life groups and prominent Christians disapproved of its tactics and strategy.

10. The Unborn Child Pain Prevention Act poses problems for doctors who specialize in prenatal medicine. Their science cannot give an unequivocal answer to the question of when a fetus can feel pain. Prenatal specialists contend that this legislation introduces many questions that have not been determined scientifically (Hopfensperger 2005). For example, does this legislation require anesthetizing a fetus during in utero surgery? If so, who would be responsible for administering the anesthesia and in what dose? How would physicians know if it was effective? Does this act demand the use of anesthesia during a labor delivery that requires the use of forceps?

11. In 1917, United States Catholic bishops formed the National Catholic War Council (NCWC) to provide spiritual care to servicemen during World War I. By the early 1920s the word "Conference" replaced "Council" to reflect the consultative rather than a legislative nature of the organization. In 1922, the National Catholic Welfare Conference was established to address national social issues such as immigration and education. In 1966, two other organizations were created: the National Conference of Catholic Bishops (NCCB) and the United States Catholic Conference (USCC). Each organization attended to separate concerns. The NCCB focused on Church issues as specified by the Vatican, while the USCC attended to Church issues in the context of larger societal issues. These two organizations were combined to form the United States Conference of Catholic Bishops (USCCB) on July 1, 2001 (United States Conference of Catholic Bishops 2006).

Chapter 4

1. Pro-life groups claim that they have experienced harassment and violence directed at them from pro-choice activists. According to Human Life International, there have been 1,139 documented incidents of pro-abortion violence in the United States and Canada, which they claim is not surprising since "anyone who would gruesomely kill an innocent preborn baby and then unblinkingly defends such a crime is capable of any kind of violence" (Human Life International 1999). The figure includes actions such as practicing witchcraft, using obscene language, being anti-Christian and anti-God, displaying sex toys in public, women dying from legal abortion, vandalism, and assault (Human Life International 1999).

2. David Bereit was the executive director of the Brazos Valley Coalition for Life. Under his leadership, the Coalition for Life became a model for many pro-life grassroots organizations across the country because of the intensity, consistency, and longevity of its activities directed at Planned Parenthood, which is located in Bryan, Texas. The Bryan, Texas, Planned Parenthood quickly became the most heavily protested clinic in the country because of the daily presence of the coalition at the clinic. This level of activity has lasted for three years (the coalition has been in existence for over seven years) and continues to be the pattern in 2006. David Bereit helped catapult the coalition into the national media spotlight with its role in the Austin, Texas, boycott of the Planned Parenthood facility that was under construction as well as his efforts in organizing and successfully carrying out the coalition's "40 Days for Life Campaign." David Bereit was approached about taking a national pro-life leadership position to duplicate the efficacy of the Coalition for Life in communities across America. He accepted a position in spring 2005 with the American Life League, which is the nation's largest pro-life education organization. Bereit is the national director of American Life League's STOPP program. The STOPP program is dedicated to ending Planned Parenthood (Coalition for Life Newsletter 2005; American Life League 2006).

3. These numbers reflect only those incidents reported to the National Abortion Federation (NAF), therefore, the actual number of violent incidents is probably higher.

4. John Salvi was convicted and sentenced to two life terms. He did not serve his

prison time because he committed suicide in his jail cell in November 1996 (National Abortion Federation 2006).

5. Given the nature of extremist activities, it is difficult to predict or find a common pattern to the activity. However, David Nice (1988) attempted to model extremist activity in the form of bombings. He looked at thirty bombing incidents and concluded that bombings predominately occurred in states that had a high ratio of abortions to live births, states that had not passed a resolution banning abortions in the event that *Roe v. Wade* is overturned, and states that had a higher crime rate against women, which indicated a state culture that was more tolerant of violence directed at women (Nice 1988).

Chapter 5

1. The legality of using wanted signs continues to be debated. In 1995, the American Coalition of Life Activists (ACLA) started to compile personal information about abortion providers including their work and home addresses. Neal Horsely published the information on the Internet at a web site called the Nuremburg Files. Pictures of the providers accompanied the information about them. When a provider was murdered by a pro-life extremist his name was crossed out on the web site. For those providers injured by extremists, their names were grayed out. Several abortion providers filed a lawsuit in Portland, Oregon, against the coalition and Horsely, charging that they violated the federal racketeering act and the Freedom of Access to Clinic Entrance Act of 1994. A jury awarded the doctors $107 million in damages for "true threats" against the doctors. However, a three-judge panel of the Ninth Circuit U.S. Court of Appeals in Pasadena, California, ruled that publishing the names and addresses of doctors who provide abortion services was protected by the First Amendment. Writing for the three-judge panel, Judge Alex Kozinski stated that the ACLA's speech was "pungent, even highly offensive" but it did not directly threaten the doctors, therefore, "unless ACLA threatened that its members would themselves assault the doctors, the First Amendment protects its speech." The court also distinguished between "true threats" and threats that were "threatening on their face but could only be understood, under the circumstances, as hyperbole or jokes." The court ruled that the defendants can only be held liable for "true threats" like blackmail or extortion because they "authorized, ratified, or directly threatened violence." This ruling, however, has not ended this debate; not all legal scholars agree with the logic of the ruling (*News Media and the Law* 2001, 20–21). In addition, the Patriot Act has changed the scope of what is defined as "terrorist" behavior and activity. The Nuremburg Files web site was shut down by the Federal Bureau of Investigation and the U.S. Immigration and Customs Enforcement agencies following the new federal policies enacted after the terrorist attacks committed on September 11, 2001 (Christian Gallery 2006).

2. In reality, eliminating abortion providers will likely just cause individuals seeking abortions to obtain them from nontraditional practitioners. The evidence on the number of illegal abortions performed in the United Sates before legalization suggests that abortion options were always pursued (Degler 1980).

3. The Alan Guttmacher Institute provided these data to me on the condition of

maintaining confidentiality and anonymity to protect abortion providers. Consequently, AGI aggregated the data at the state level and only made state-level data available. Furthermore, per my agreement with AGI, I cannot publish research that would reveal information about specific individuals or organizations, which precludes using county or metropolitan area data. Finally, I cannot share the AGI data with others; therefore, any variables used from the AGI surveys are not available from the author.

4. Although each survey had four categories, I only have all four categories for a few of the surveys. Therefore I use the common categories I have data for across all five years.

5. Regression analysis is a popular estimation technique because it is robust and can be applied to data sets where the independent variables are correlated with one another as well as correlated to the dependent variable, in varying degrees. Regression modeling does more than assert correlation; it allows a researcher to test for causal relationships that are specified a priori to the analysis. Although causality can never be proven, regression analysis allows the research to test for evidence of a causal relationship between an explanatory variable and a dependent variable. "The flexibility of regression techniques is, then, especially useful to the researcher who is interested in real-world or very complicated problems that cannot be meaningfully reduced to orthogonal designs in a laboratory setting" (Tabachnick and Fidell 2001, 111). The regression equation takes the following form: $\hat{Y} = A + B_1X_1 + B_2X_2 + \cdots + B_kX_k$. The multiple regression equation represents the best prediction of the dependent variable from several continuous variables. A regression equation fits a line that minimizes the sum of squared deviations between the predicted and observed values of Y while optimizing the correlation between the predicted and observed Y values in the data set.

6. Several assumptions governing regression analysis must be reviewed in order to ensure that estimates are valid, before drawing inferences and forming conclusions. Given the robustness of regression analysis, minor violations of the underlying assumptions do not invalidate the conclusions and inferences drawn from the analysis in any significant way; however, major violations of regression assumptions can significantly distort and invalidate them. The standard regression assumptions consider the form of the model, the errors, the predictors, and the observations. For a more detailed explanation see Tabachnick and Fidell 2001; Chatterjee, Hadi, and Price 2000; Gujarati 1995.

7. SPSS 13.0 was used for estimation. All models were checked for multicollinearity with Tolerance and VIF statistics, as well as auxiliary regressions. White's test was used to test for heteroskedasticity. Variables were also checked for normality in distribution; those variables that were significantly skewed or kurtotic were logged. Finally, diagnostics revealed the presence of outliers in certain models. Extreme cases exert too much influence over the regression equation and disrupt the precision of estimation of the regression weights (Tabachnick and Fidell 2001, 117). An outlier was present in every model. In each model where abortion rate was used as the dependent variable, Nevada was an outlier. In the abortion provider models, Hawaii was consistently an outlier. Dummy variables for Nevada and Hawaii were included in a reestimation of the models to diminish the influence being exerted by these outlying cases.

8. I ran models for each separate year, which included all of the harassment and violence measures for that particular year. For example in 1985 the survey included questions such as how many times the facility experienced invasion into the clinic by demonstrators and how many times the facility experienced the jamming of phone lines intended to disrupt scheduling. These unique measures are not included in the pooled models but are included in the individual yearly models. All of the yearly models are estimated two times to reflect the two distinct frequency categories (1–4 incidents a year, and 5–19 incidents a year). The yearly results are fairly consistent with the pooled model results. The unique individual measures for each year produced dozens of models that yielded results that were fairly consistent and similar to the pooled models; therefore I do not report them.

9. Vandalism includes physical damage and the jamming of locks. Vandalism is illegal, and the evidence for the activity is more straightforward compared to picketing with physical contact. Vandalism leaves visible proof that it has occurred, whereas picketing with physical contact can be a matter of opposing protesters' claims of assault against each other. Even though the illegality of picketing with physical contact is more difficult to assess, it is nonetheless a violation of the law, and so it is included with vandalism, under the general theme of illegal activity perpetrated by pro-life participants.

10. Most of the data for the number of funded abortions comes from the Alan Guttmacher Institute; however, the measures used in the 1995 and 2000 models come from McFarlane and Meier 2000 and Cook et al. 1999. In 1985, the number of funded abortions was estimated for Connecticut. The estimation was based on the amount of money the state allocated for abortions and is consistent with the approximately $500 per abortion estimated by Cook et al. (1999). In 1985, no data were available for Alaska, Mississippi, Montana, Wisconsin, and Wyoming. In 1988, the number of funded abortions used in the analysis is from the Alan Guttmacher Institute for the previous year, 1987. The data was not available for 1988 so the previous year's estimation was used with the assumption that the number of funded abortions did not dramatically change between 1987 and 1988. For the measure used in the 1988 models, the number of funded abortions was estimated for Hawaii using the Cook et al. (1999) estimation. No data were available for Maine, Ohio, or Wisconsin. In 1992, the number of funded abortions was estimated for Tennessee using the Cook et al. (1999) estimation. No data were available for Arizona, Iowa, or Massachusetts. In 1995, the number of funded abortions was estimated for Connecticut and Massachusetts with the Cook et al. (1999) estimation. No data were available for Arizona, Louisiana, Rhode Island, or South Dakota. Data were not available for 2000, therefore the figure from the previous year in the model (1995) had to be used for estimation.

11. The impact of individual state policies on the accessibility of abortion services is likely to be more nuanced than a straight count of anti-abortion restrictions reflects. Researchers have amassed evidence that points to the obstacles these restrictions create for women seeking services; however, evidence does not clearly indicate that anti-abortion statutes are influential at directly reducing the abortion rate. Although abortion restrictions can contribute to the difficulty of receiving abortion services, for the pur-

poses of the abortion rate models in this chapter, I am interested in seeing if there is a cumulative effect of the restrictions in terms of reducing the abortion rate rather than measuring the increased difficulty these laws may present in obtaining services. Therefore, I include a straight count of restrictions in the models.

12. Although the Catholic Church has been politically vocal and active in the pro-life movement, particularly in the political branch of the movement, in practice Catholic women receive abortions at the same rate as all women (Henshaw and Kost 1996). For this reason, the Catholic population is not included in the abortion rate model. Instead, the Protestant fundamentalist population is included because unlike Catholic women, fundamentalists are less likely to resolve an unwanted and unplanned pregnancy with an abortion.

13. In 1988 Wyoming is excluded from the analysis because no abortion provider performed over 300 abortions.

14. This finding is very similar for the model using the change variables; the picketing coefficient is −.026, with a t-score of 2.284 and .023 significance.

15. The only notable differences in the change variable models are with two variables: income and the African American population. In the regression analyses using change variables, income was statistically significant in all of the models. African American population, while statistically significant in the models reported in the text, was not a significant variable when measured as a change variable in the analyses.

16. Although African American population, urbanism, and restrictions are included as variables in the abortion rate and abortion provider models, the influence they are expected to exert in each of the respective models is different. The variables that influence the abortion rate do not necessarily influence the number of providers in a similar manner. For example, while urbanism tends to increase the abortion rate it has the opposite affect on providers. Fewer providers are needed to deliver services in urban areas (Risen and Thomas 1998).

17. NARAL would not release its membership figures for 2000. Rather than eliminating this important variable from the analysis, the same membership figure is used from 1996.

18. The other differences between the models in table 7 and the parallel change variables models involve two of the political variables: abortion restrictions and Catholic population. In the models reported in table 7 both of these variables are statistically significant in all models. In the regression models using change variables, neither abortion restrictions nor Catholic population shows statistical significance across any of the models. The time dummy variables for 1988, 1992, 1995, and 2000 also differed: they are statistically significant in all of the models using the change variables.

19. In the analyses using change variables, both picketing and picketing with contact were statistically significant. Similar to the differences found earlier, neither abortion restrictions nor Catholic population is statistically significant in the change variable models, but the time dummy variables for 1988, 1992, 1995, and 2000 are significant.

20. Reversing the legality of abortion may have become a more attainable goal early in 2006. Samuel Alito was confirmed and then sworn in as a Supreme Court justice on

January 31, 2006. Alito is known as a conservative who is opposed to abortion rights. Pro-choice advocates fear that his seat on the bench, in conjunction with the other conservative justices, will garner enough votes to reverse *Roe v. Wade* and return abortion decisions back to the states.

Chapter 6

1. The data presented in figure 8 come from a search of the major American newspapers and magazines tracked on the Lexis-Nexis database. The data cover articles from January 1970 through July 7, 2004. This figure is intended to provide a simple visual representation of the visibility of abortion topics in the national media rather than to draw any causal relationships between anti-abortion harassment, media coverage, and politicians' interest in the debate. Abortion-related stories also receive more coverage than reflected in this figure because the count presented in figure 8 does not include local or state newspapers or magazines.

2. The data examined in figures 9 and 10 are taken from the Congressional Information Service (CIS) reports of congressional activity and are also intended to present a simple visual aid regarding the overview of congressional attention to abortion-related issues for the time period roughly corresponding to the empirical analyses, which ends in 2000. These figures are not intended to draw any causal relationships between harassment and congressional attention to abortion. The hearings were initially searched using the keyword *abortion*. A total of 306 hearings dating from 1969 to 1999 are included in the figures. The criterion used to determine whether or not a hearing pertained to the abortion conflict was fairly broad. Hearings were excluded when the word *abortion* was used in a literary context or in regard to nonhuman animals. For example, a 1996 Senate Commerce Committee hearing discussed the problem of spontaneous abortions in dolphins. Even if the main purpose of the hearing was not specifically related to abortion, it was included in the number in an effort to capture attempts at issue expansion.

For example, in 1996, what initially appeared to be an innocuous hearing on global warming turned into a heated debate about abortion. A House committee was addressing the issue of global warming. During a witness's testimony, a pro-life supporter interrupted, arguing that global warming was being used as a way to promote abortion as a solution to overpopulation. In earlier research, I examined the scope of conflict surrounding abortion within national political institutions. I concluded that the political branch of the pro-life movement has repeatedly redefined abortion into several frameworks, which has enabled it to approach multiple institutional venues to address abortion-related issues. This strategy has worked fairly well and has led to several significant policy victories that have limited (both symbolically and in reality) the availability and accessibility of abortion services (Doan 2000).

3. Presidential attention is measured by the number of paragraphs in the presidential papers dedicated to the topic of abortion. The papers were read for content for a different research project (Doan 2000) and are used in chapter 6 as a simplistic portrayal of presidential attention to the issue of abortion. Many other measures of presidential

support/disapproval toward abortion exist; however, looking at rhetoric captures a president's most visible, public discourse on the subject. The topic of abortion first appeared during the Nixon presidency. The figure only reflects presidential attention through 1993. This figure is not intended to be used for drawing any causal relationships between harassment and presidential attention to abortion-related issues.

4. There is little evidence abstinence-only education is an effective way to educate adolescents about disease and pregnancy prevention. Evidence indicates that the efficacy and medical accuracy of abstinence-only education is problematic (Darroch, Landry, and Singh 2000; Landry, Kaeser, and Richards 1999; U.S. House of Representatives 2004). Despite these findings, the Personal Responsibility and Work Opportunity Reconciliation Act of 1996 included a provision for a $250 million, five-year federal grant for abstinence-only education. Abstinence-only education is currently used in roughly one-third of all public schools, and President Bush increased funding for abstinence-only programs in his first term and has promised to continue the funding trend in his second term.

5. The National Cancer Institute (NCI) has conducted several studies investigating the alleged link between abortion and breast cancer purported by the pro-life movement. In March 2003 the NCI held a joint meeting between the NCI board of scientific advisers and board of scientific counselors, where the entire panel unanimously supported the conclusion that there is no scientific link between abortion and breast cancer. The panel stated that its conclusion was "well established," which meets the NCI's highest standard of approval (Boonstra 2003).

REFERENCES

Abbey, Tristan. 2005. "Michael Behe Promotes Intelligent Design." *Stanford Review* 34, no. 3. www.stanfordreview.org.

Adams, Greg D. 1997. "Abortion: Evidence of an Issue Evolution." *American Journal of Political Science* 41:718–37.

Alan Guttmacher Institute. 2001. "Anthrax Threats, Continued Violence Prompt Renewed Attention to Clinic, Client Protection." *Guttmacher Report on Public Policy* 4, no. 6.

Alan Guttmacher Institute. 2006. "State Policies in Brief: Mandatory Counseling and Waiting Periods for Abortion." *Alan Guttmacher Institute*, February 1.

American Life League. 2006. www.all.org.

Aminzade, Ron, Jack Goldstone, Doug McAdam, Elizabeth Perry, William Sewell, Sidney Tarrow, and Charles Tilly. 2001. *Silence and Voice on the Study of Contentious Politics*. Cambridge: Cambridge University Press.

Armstrong, Karen. 2001. *The Battle for God*. New York: Ballantine Books.

Associated Press. 2003. "Boycott Stops Abortion Clinic Project." November 14.

Baierle, S. G. 1998. "The Explosion of Experience." In *Cultures of Politics—Politics of Culture*, ed. S. E. Alvarez, E. Dagnino, and A. Escobar. Boulder: Westview.

Baird-Windle, Patricia, and Eleanor J. Bader. 2001. *Targets of Hatred: Anti-Abortion Terrorism*. New York: Palgrave Macmillan.

Balkin, Jack M. 2005. *What Roe v. Wade Should Have Said*. New York: New York University Press.

Banaszak, Lee Ann. 1996. *Why Movements Succeed or Fail: Opportunity, Culture, and the Struggle for Woman Suffrage*. Princeton: Princeton University Press.

Baumgartner, Frank R., and Bryan D. Jones. 1993. *Agendas and Instability in American Politics*. Chicago: University of Chicago Press.

Bean, Clive. 1991. "Participation and Political Protest: A Causal Model with Australian Evidence." *Political Behavior* 13:253–83.

Beilenson Senate Bill. 1967. Also known as the Therapeutic Abortion Act. California Senate Bill 462. February 27.

Bennett, W. Lance. 2004. *The Politics of Illusion.* 6th ed. White Plains, NY: Longman.

Benson, Michelle, and Jacek Kugler. 1998. "Power Parity, Democracy, and the Severity of Internal Violence." *Journal of Conflict Resolution* 42:196–209.

Berbrier, Mitch. 2002. "Making Minorities: Cultural Space, Stigma Transformation Frames, and the Categorical Status Claims of Deaf, Gay, and White Supremacist Activists in Late Twentieth Century America." *Sociological Forum* 17, no. 4: 553–91.

Blanchard, Dallas. 1994. *The Anti-Abortion Movement and the Rise of the Religious Right: From Polite to Fiery Protest.* New York: Twayne.

Blanchard, Dallas, and Terry J. Prewitt. 1993. *Religious Violence and Abortion: The Gideon Project.* Gainesville: University Press of Florida.

Bluey, Robert B. 2005. "Roe v. Wade: McCorvey Rejects Roe Decision." *Human Events* 24 (January).

Bolce, Louis, and Gerald De Maio. 1999. "Religious Outlook, Culture War Politics, and Antipathy toward Christian Fundamentalists." *Public Opinion Quarterly* 63, no. 1: 29–61.

Boonstra, Heather. 2003. "Critics Charge Bush Mix of Science and Politics Is Unprecedented and Dangerous." *Guttmacher Report on Public Policy* 6, no. 2 (May). www.guttmacher.org/pubs/tgr/06/2/gr060201.html.

Brady, Henry E. 1999. "Political Participation." *Measures of Political Attitudes.* New York: Academic.

Brazos Valley Coalition for Life Annual Newsletter. 2004. www.CoalitionForLife.com. January 14.

Brodie, Janet Farrell. 1994. *Contraception and Abortion in Nineteenth Century America.* Ithaca: Cornell University Press.

Brownfeld, Peter, and Mike Emanuel. 2004. "Senate Passes Unborn Victims Bill." Fox News. www.foxnews.com. March 26.

Brush, Stephen G. 1996. "Dynamics of Theory Change in the Social Sciences: Relative Deprivation and Collective Violence." *Journal of Conflict Resolution* 40:523–45.

Bryan City Police Department, Crime Analyst Division. 2004. 301 South Texas Avenue, Bryan, Texas 77803.

Bullough, Vern L., and Bonnie Bullough. 1994. "A Brief History of Population Control and Contraception." *Free Inquiry* 14, no. 2 (Spring): 1–7.

Burnham, John C. 1973. "The Progressive Era Revolution in American Attitudes toward Sex." *Journal of American History* 59, no. 4: 885–908.

Byrnes, Timothy A. 1993. "The Politics of the American Catholic Hierarchy." *Political Science Quarterly* 108, no. 3: 497–514.

Calhoun, Craig. 1994. "Social Theory and the Politics of Identity." In *Social Theory and the Politics of Identity,* ed. Craig Calhoun, 9–36. Oxford: Blackwell.

Canadian Security Intelligence Service. 2000. "Anti-Globalization—A Spreading Phenomenon." Report # 2000/08. www.csis-scrs.gc.ca/eng/miscdocs/200008.

Cartwright, Gary. 2004. "My Choice." *Texas Monthly,* December.

Center for Bio-Ethical Reform. 2006. "Why Abortion Is Genocide." www.abortionno.org.

Center for Reproductive Rights. 2004. "Yet Another Anti-Abortion Scare Tactic: False Claims of Breast Cancer Link." www.reproductiverights.org.

Center for Reproductive Rights. 2005. "2005 Mid-Year Legislative Summary." www.reproductiverights.org.

Cerulo, Karen. 1997. "Identity Construction: New Issues, New Directions." *Annual Review of Sociology* 23:385–409.

Chatterjee, Samprit, Ali S. Hadi, and Bertram Price. 2000. *Regression Analysis by Example.* 3rd ed. New York: John Wiley and Sons.

Chong, Dennis. 1991. *Collective Action and the Civil Rights Movement.* Chicago: University of Chicago Press.

Christian Gallery. 2006. www.christiangallery.com.

CNN News. 2003. "70,000 Grocery Store Workers Strike." www.cnn.com. October 12.

Coalition for Life Newsletter. 2005. "Making a Difference: Getting Results across the Brazos Valley and Beyond." January 22.

Coleman, James S. 1990. *Foundations of Social Theory.* Cambridge: Belknap Press.

Conover, Pamela Johnston, and Virginia Gray. 1983. *Feminism and the New Right: Conflict over the American Family.* New York: Praeger.

Cook, Elizabeth Adell, Ted G. Jelen, and Clyde Wilcox. 1992. *Between Two Absolutes: Public Opinion and the Politics of Abortion.* Boulder: Westview.

Cook, Philip J., Allan M. Parnell, Michael J. Moore, and Deanna Pagnini. 1999. "The Effects of Short-Term Variation in Abortion Funding on Pregnancy Outcomes." *Journal of Health Economics* 18:241–57.

Cozzarelli, Catherine, and Brenda Major. 1994. "The Effects of Anti-Abortion Demonstrators and Pro-Choice Escorts on Women's Psychological Responses to Abortion." *Journal of Social and Clinical Psychology* 13:404–27.

Cozzarelli, Catherine, and Brenda Major. 1998. "The Impact of Antiabortion Activities on Women." In *The New Civil War: The Psychology and Politics of Abortion,* ed. Linda J. Beckman and S. Marie Harvey. Washington, DC: American Psychological Association.

Craig, Barbara Hinkson, and David M. O'Brien. 1993. *Abortion and American Politics.* Chatham, NJ: Chatham House.

Crapanzano, Vincent. 2000. *Serving the Word: Literalism in America from the Pulpit to the Bench.* New York: New York Press.

Crary, David. 2004. "Abortion Foes Target Planned Parenthood: Activists Focus on Old Enemy on *Roe v. Wade* Anniversary." Associated Press, January 22.

Darroch, Jacqueline E., David J. Landry, and Susheela Singh. 2000. "Changing Emphases in Sexuality Education in U.S. Public Secondary Schools, 1988–1999." *Family Planning Perspectives* 32:204–11, 265.

Davies, James C. 1962. "Toward a Theory of Revolution." *American Sociological Review* 27:5–19.

Dayton, Cornelia Hughes. 1997. "Taking the Trade: Abortion and Gender Relations in an Eighteenth-Century New England Village." In *Controlling Reproduction: An American History,* ed. Andrea Tone. Wilmington, DE: Scholarly Resources.

Degler, Carl N. 1980. *At Odds.* New York: Oxford University Press.

Delio, Michelle. 2003. "E-Mail Mob Takes Manhattan." *Wired News.* www.wired.com. June 19.

Dionne, E. J. 2006. "Nassau County, N.Y., Executive Suozzi's Proposal to Reduce Number of Abortions Might Establish Middle Ground." *Washington Post,* February 14.

Doan, Alesha E. 2000. "Expanding the Scope of Conflict over Abortion Policy: Congress, Interest Groups, and Venue Shopping." Presented at the annual meeting of the Midwest Political Science Association, Chicago, April.

Doan, Alesha E., and Jean Williams. 2003. "Good Girls or Dirty Ho's? The Social Construction of Sex Education Policy." Presented at the annual meetings of the Midwest Political Science Association, April.

Donovan, Patricia. 1995. *The Politics of Blame: Family Planning, Abortion, and the Poor.* New York: Alan Guttmacher Institute.

Douglas, Emily Taft. 1970. *Margaret Sanger: Pioneer of the Future.* New York: Holt, Rinehart, and Winston.

Dudley, Ryan, and Ross A. Miller. 1998. "Group Rebellion in the 1980s." *Journal of Conflict Resolution* 42:77–96.

Earth First. 1990. "Tree Spiking Renunciation and Mississippi Summer in the California Redwoods." www.things.org. June.

Economist. 1995. "Vengeance." *Economist,* January 7.

Edwards, S. 1997. "Abortion Study Finds No Long-Term Ill Effects on Emotional Well-Being." *Family Planning Perspectives* 29, no. 4: 193–94.

Encyclopedia Britannica, 14th ed., s.v. "Medicine, Custom of (Ancient Medicine)," 197.

Epstein, Lee, and Joseph F. Kobylka. 1992. *The Supreme Court and Legal Change: Abortion and the Death Penalty.* Chapel Hill: University of North Carolina Press.

Evans, John H. 2002. "Polarization in Abortion Attitudes in U.S. Religious Traditions, 1972–1998." *Sociological Forum* 17, no. 3: 397–422.

Falik, Marilyn. 1983. *Ideology and Abortion Policy Politics.* New York: Praeger.

Faux, Marian. 1990. *Crusaders: Voices from the Abortion Front.* New York: Carol Publishing Group.

Feierabend, Ivo K., and Rosalind L. Feierabend. 1966. "Aggressive Behavior within Polities." *Journal of Conflict Resolution* 10:249–71.

Finch, B. E., and H. Green. 1963. *Contraception through the Ages.* London: Peter Owen.

Fine, G. A. 1985. "Can the Circle Be Unbroken? Small Groups and Social Movements." In *Advances in Group Processes,* ed. E. Lawler. Greenwich: JAI Press.

Finer, Lawrence, and Stanley K. Henshaw. 2003. "Abortion Incidence and Services in the United States in 2000." *Perspectives on Sexual and Reproductive Health* 35, no. 1.

Finkbine, Sherri. 1967. "The Lesser of Two Evils." In *The Case for Legalized Abortion Now,* ed. Alan F. Guttmacher. Berkeley, CA: Diablo Press.

Finkel, Steven E., and Edward N. Muller. 1998. "Rational Choice and the Dynamics of Collective Political Action: Evaluating Alternative Models with Panel Data." *American Political Science Review* 92, no. 1: 37–49.

Finkel, Steven E., Edward N. Muller, and Karl-Dieter Opp. 1989. "Personal Influence, Collective Rationality, and Mass Political Action." *American Political Science Review* 83, no. 3: 885–903.

Fireman, Bruce, and William A. Gamson. 1979. "Utilitarian Logic in the Resource Mobilization Perspective." In *The Dynamics of Social Movements: Resource Mobilization, Social Control, and Tactics,* ed. Mayer N. Zald and John D. McCarthy. Cambridge: Winthrop.

Forrest, Jacqueline D., and Stanley K. Henshaw. 1987. "The Harassment of U.S. Abortion Providers." *Family Planning Perspectives* 19 (January/February): 9–13.

Fournier, Keith A. 2002. "Persons Not Property—Begotten Not Made." Common Good. www.nprcouncil.org.

Francisco, Ronald A. 2004a. "After the Massacre: Mobilization in the Wake of Harsh Repression." *Mobilization* 9, no. 2: 107–26.

Francisco, Ronald A. 2004b. "The Dictator's Dilemma." In *Repression and Mobilization,* ed. Christian Davenport and Carol Mueller. Minneapolis: University of Minnesota Press.

Fredrix, Emily. 2005. "Obama: American Girl Threats 'Silly.'" Associated Press, October 25.

Freedman, Estelle B. 1982. "Sexuality in Nineteenth-Century America: Behavior, Ideology, and Politics." *Reviews in American History* 10, no. 4 (December): 196–215.

Freeman, Jo. 1975. *The Politics of Women's Liberation.* New York: David McKay.

Freeman, Jo. 1979. "Resource Mobilization and Strategy." In *The Dynamics of Social Movements,* ed. Mayer N. Zald and John D. McCarthy, 167–89. Cambridge: Winthrop.

Freeman, Jo. 1999. "On the Origins of Social Movements." In *Waves of Protest: Social Movements since the Sixties,* ed. Jo Freeman and Victoria Johnson. New York: Rowman and Littlefield.

Frey, Scott R., Thomas Dietz, and Linda Kalof. 1992. "Characteristics of Successful American Protest Groups: Another Look at Gamson's Strategy of Social Protest." *American Journal of Sociology* 98, no. 2: 368–87.

Frost, Jennifer J. 1996. "Family Planning Clinic Services in the United States, 1994." *Family Planning Perspectives* 3 (May/June): 92–100.

Gamson, William A. 1968. *Power and Discontent.* Homewood, IL: Dorsey.

Gamson, William A. 1975. *The Strategy of Social Protest.* Homewood, IL: Dorsey.

Gamson, William A. 1990. *The Strategy of Social Protest.* Belmont, CA: Wadsworth.

Gamson, William A. 1992. "The Social Psychology of Collective Action." In *Frontiers in Social Movement Theory,* ed. Aldon Morris and Carol M. Mueller. New Haven: Yale University Press.

Garrow, David J. 1994. *Liberty and Sexuality.* New York: Macmillan.

Garrow, David J. 1999. "Abortion Before and After Roe v. Wade: An Historical Perspective." *Albany Law Review* 62, no. 3: 833–43.

Geller, Daniel S. 1987. "The Impact of Political System Structure on Probability Patterns of Internal Disorder." *American Journal of Political Science* 31:217–35.

Ginsburg, Faye D. 1989. *Contested Lives: The Abortion Debate in an American Community.* Berkeley: University of California Press.

Ginsburg, Faye D. 1998. "Rescuing the Nation: Operation Rescue and the Rise of Anti-Abortion Militance." In *Abortion Wars: A Half Century of Struggle, 1950–2000,* ed. Rickie Solinger. Los Angeles: University of California Press.

Goldwater, Barry. 1960. *Conscience of a Conservative.* Shepherdsville, KY: Victor Publishing.

Goodwin, Jeff, James M. Jasper, and Francesca Polletta. 2000. "The Return of the Repressed: The Fall and Rise of Emotions in Social Movement Theory." *Mobilization: An International Journal* 5, no. 1: 65–84.

Gordon, Linda. 1976. *Woman's Body, Woman's Right: A Social History of Birth Control in America.* New York: Viking.

Gordon, Linda. 2002. *The Moral Property of Women: A History of Birth Control Politics in America.* Champagne: University of Illinois Press.

Gould, Roger V. 1995. *Insurgent Identities: Class Community and Protest in Paris from 1848 to the Commune.* Chicago: University of Chicago Press.

Gould, Roger V. 1998. "Political Networks and the Local/National Boundary in the Whiskey Rebellion." In *Challenging Authority,* ed. M. Hanagan, L. P. Moch, and W. Brake. Minneapolis: University of Minnesota Press.

Gould, Roger V. 1999. "Collective Violence and Group Solidarity: Evidence from a Feuding Society." *American Sociological Review* 64:356–80.

Graber, Mark A. 1996. *Rethinking Abortion: Equal Choice, the Constitution, and Reproductive Politics.* Princeton: Princeton University Press.

Grant, George. 1991. *Third Time Around: A History of the Pro-Life Movement from the First Century to the Present.* Brentwood, TN: Wolgemuth and Hyatt.

Green, John C. 1999. "The Spirit Willing: Collective Identity and the Development of the Christian Right." In *Waves of Protest: Social Movements since the Sixties,* ed. Jo Freeman and Victoria Johnson. New York: Rowman and Littlefield.

Grimes, David A., Jacqueline D. Forrest, Alice L. Kirkman, and Barbara Radford. 1991. "An Epidemic of Antiabortion Violence in the United States." *American Journal of Obstetrics and Gynecology* 165:1263–68.

Griswold, Robert. 1986. "Law, Sex, Cruelty, and Divorce in Victorian America, 1840–1900." *American Quarterly* 38, no. 5: 721–45.

Gujarati, Damodar N. 1995. *Basic Econometrics.* New York: McGraw-Hill.

Gurr, Ted Robert. 1968. "A Causal Model of Civil Strife: A Comparative Analysis Using New Indices." *American Political Science Review* 62:1104–24.

Gurr, Ted Robert. 1970. *Why Men Rebel.* Princeton: Princeton University Press.

Gurr, Ted Robert. 1989. "Political Terrorism: Historical Antecedents and Contemporary Trends." In *Violence in America,* ed. Ted Robert Gurr. Newbury Park, CA: Sage.

Haider-Markel, Donald P., and Kenneth J. Meier. 1996. "The Politics of Gay and Lesbian Rights: Expanding the Scope of Conflict." *Journal of Politics* 58 (May): 332–49.

Halva-Neubauer, Glen A. 1993. "The States after *Roe:* 'No Paper Tigers.'" In *Understanding the New Politics of Abortion,* ed. Malcolm L. Goggin. Newbury Park, CA: Sage.

Hartshorn, Margaret. 2003. "Putting It All Together." In *Back to the Drawing Board: The Future of the Pro-Life Movement,* ed. Teresa R. Wagner. South Bend, IN: St. Augustine's Press.

Henshaw, Stanley K. 1995a. "Factors Hindering Access to Abortion Services." *Family Planning Perspectives* 2 (March/April): 54–59, 87.

Henshaw, Stanley K. 1995b. "The Impact of Requirements for Parental Consent on Minors' Abortions in Mississippi." *Family Planning Perspectives* 3 (May/June): 120–22.

Henshaw, Stanley K. 1998a. "Abortion Incidence and Services in the United States, 1995–1996." *Family Planning Perspectives* 6 (November): 263–70, 287.

Henshaw, Stanley K. 1998b. "Barriers to Access to Abortion Services." In *The New Civil War: The Psychology, Culture, and Politics of Abortion*, ed. Linda J. Beckman and S. Marie Harvey. Washington, DC: American Psychological Association.

Henshaw, Stanley K., and Lawrence B. Finer. 2003. "The Accessibility of Abortion Services in the United States, 2001." *Perspectives on Sexual and Reproductive Health* 35, no. 1.

Henshaw, Stanley K., Lisa Konan, and Jack C. Smith. 1991. "Characteristics of U.S. Women Having Abortions, 1987." *Family Planning Perspectives* 23 (March/April): 75–82.

Henshaw, Stanley K., and Kathryn Kost. 1996. "Abortion Patients in 1994–1995: Characteristics and Contraceptive Use." *Family Planning Perspectives* 28, no. 4: 140–47, 158.

Henshaw, Stanley K., and Jennifer Van Vort. 1994. "Abortion Services in the United States, 1991 and 1992." *Family Planning Perspectives* 3 (May/June): 100–106, 112.

Hern, Warren M. 1991. "Proxemics: The Application of Theory to Conflict Arising from Antiabortion Demonstrations." *Population and Environment: A Journal of Interdisciplinary Studies* 12:379–88.

Hern, Warren M. 1994. "Life on the Front Lines." *Women's Health Issues* 4 (January/February): 48–54.

Hill, Stuart, and Donald Rothchild. 1992. "The Impact of Regime on the Diffusion of Political Conflict." In *The Internationalization of Communal Strife*, ed. M. Midlarsky. New York: Routledge.

Hoover, Dean, and David Kowalewski. 1992. "Dynamic Models of Dissent and Repression." *Journal of Conflict Resolution* 36:150–82.

Hopfensperger, Jean. 2005. "Doctors Ask Questions about Fetal-Pain Bill; State Will Be Second to Require Doctors to Offer Anesthesia for Late-Term Fetuses." *Minneapolis Star Tribune*, July 16.

Houston, Paul. 1985. "White House Showcases Abortion Film." *Los Angeles Times*, February 13.

Hout, Michael. 1999. "Abortion Politics in the United States, 1972–1994: From Single Issue to Ideology." *Gender Issues* (Spring).

Human Life International. 1999. HLI, 4 Family Life, Front Royal, VA. 22630. E-mail: brianc@hli.org.

Hunter, James Davidson. 1991. *Culture Wars: The Struggle to Define America.* New York: Basic Books.

Hunter, James Davidson. 1994. *Before the Shooting Begins: Searching for Democracy in America's Culture War.* New York: Free Press.

Inglehart, Ronald. 1977. *The Silent Revolution: Changing Values and Political Styles.* Princeton: Princeton University Press.

Jacoby, Kerry N. 1998. *Souls, Bodies, Spirits: The Drive to Abolish Abortion since 1973.* Westport, CT: Praeger.

Jadhav, Adam. 2006. "Both Sides Believe They Save Lives." *St. Louis Post-Dispatch*, February 10.

Jasper, James M. 1997. *The Art of Moral Protest.* Chicago: University of Chicago Press.

Jelen, Ted G., and Clyde Wilcox. 2003. "Causes and Consequences of Public Attitudes toward Abortion: A Review and Research Agenda." *Political Research Quarterly* 56, no. 4: 489–500.

Jelen, Ted G., and Clyde Wilcox. 2005. "Continuity and Change in Attitudes toward Abortion: Poland and the United States." *Politics and Gender* 1, no. 2: 297–317.

Jenkins, J. Craig. 1987. "Nonprofit Organizations and Policy Advocacy." In *The Nonprofit Sector: A Research Handbook*, ed. Walter W. Powell, 296–318. New Haven: Yale University Press.

Jenkins, J. Craig, and Charles Perrow. 1977. "Insurgency of the Powerless: Farm Worker Movements (1946–1972)." *American Sociological Review* 42:249–68.

Joffe, C. 1995. *Doctors of Conscience: The Struggle to Provide Abortion Before and After Roe v. Wade.* Boston: Beacon Press.

Johnson, Douglas. 2003. "Partial Birth Abortion Used on Healthy Mothers." *Wall Street Journal*, November 10.

Johnson, Victoria. 1999. "The Strategic Determinants of a Countermovement: The Emergence and Impact of Operation Rescue Blockades." In *Waves of Protest: Social Movements since the Sixties*, ed. Jo Freeman and Victoria Johnson. New York: Rowman and Littlefield.

Kaiser Foundation. 2006. www.kff.org.

Kaiser Network. 2006. www.kaisernetwork.org/daily_reports.

Kaplan, Jeffrey. 1995. "Absolute Rescue: Absolutism, Defensive Action, and the Resort to Violence." *Terrorism and Political Violence* 7, no. 3: 128–63.

Kaplan, Laura. 1998. "Beyond Safe and Legal: The Lessons of Jane." In *Abortion Wars: A Half Century of Struggle, 1950–2000*, ed. Rickie Solinger. Los Angeles: University of California Press.

Karnein, Anja. 2005. "Liberty vs. Progress? The Ethical Implications of Contemporary Biomedicine in Germany and the United States." Dissertation, Brandeis University.

Katz, Nikki. 2004. "Partial Birth Abortion—Abortion Ban Issue." *Women's Issues* www.womensissues.about.com.

Kennedy, David M. 1970. *Birth Control in America: The Career of Margaret Sanger.* New Haven: Yale University Press.

KGET News. 2006. "Intelligent Design Lawsuit in Kern County." January 11. www.kget.com.

Kingdon, John W. 1995 [1984]. *Agendas, Alternatives, and Public Policies.* New York: HarperCollins.

Korosec, Thomas. 2004. "Roe No More, But Still a Voice on Abortion: Norma McCorvey Resurfaces on Other Side of Issue That Has Defined Her Life." *Houston Chronicle*, February 29.

Krakauer, Jon. 2004. *Under the Banner of Heaven.* New York: Anchor Books.

Landry, David, Lisa Kaeser, and Cory L. Richards. 1999. "Abstinence Promotion and the Provision of Information about Contraception in Public School District Sexuality Education Policies." *Family Planning Perspectives* 31, no. 6: 280–86.

Langer, William. 1963. "Europe's Initial Population Explosion." *American Historical Review* 69:7–9.

Lichbach, Mark Irving. 1990. "Will Rational People Rebel against Inequality? Samson's Choice." *American Journal of Political Science* 34:1049–76.

Lichbach, Mark Irving. 1994a. "Rethinking Rationality and Rebellion: Theories of Collective Action and Problems of Collective Dissent." *Rationality and Society* 6:8–39.

Lichbach, Mark Irving. 1994b. "What Makes Rational Peasants Revolutionary?" *World Politics* 46:383–418.

Lichbach, Mark Irving. 1995. *The Rebel's Dilemma*. Ann Arbor: University of Michigan Press.

Life Dynamics. 2006. "Death Camps." www.lifedynamics.com.

Lonsway, Kimberly A., Tracy Sefl, Jennifer Jackman, Michel Cicero, Michelle Wood, Elizabeth Koenig, and Sandi Aguilar. 2001. "2000 National Clinic Violence Survey Report." Feminist Majority Foundation. www.feminist.org.

Luker, Kristin. 1984. *Abortion and the Politics of Motherhood*. Los Angeles: University of California Press.

Luker, Kristin. 1996. *Dubious Conceptions: The Politics of Teenage Pregnancy*. Cambridge: Harvard University Press.

Major, B., J. M. Zubek, M. L. Cooper, C. Cozzarelli, and C. Richards. 1998. "Personal Resilience, Cognitive Appraisals, and Coping: An Integrative Model of Adjustment to Abortion. *Journal of Personality and Social Psychology* 74:735–52.

Mansbridge, Jane J. 1986. *Why We Lost the ERA*. Chicago: University of Chicago Press.

Markels, Alex. 2005. "Supreme Court's Evolving Rulings on Abortion." National Public Radio, November 30.

Mason, Carol. 2002a. *Killing for Life: The Apocalyptic Narrative of Pro-Life Rhetoric*. Ithaca: Cornell University Press.

Mason, Carol. 2002b. "From Protest to Retribution: The Guerrilla Politics of Pro-Life Violence." In *Violence and Politics: Globalization's Paradox*, ed. Kenton Worcester, Sally Avery Bermanzohn, and Mark Ungar. New York: Routledge.

May, Larry. 1998. *Masculinity and Morality*. Ithaca: Cornell University Press.

Mazzuca, Josephine. 2003. "Current Teen Views on Abortion." Gallup Organization. www.gallup.com. March 11.

McAdam, Doug. 1982. *Political Process and the Development of Black Insurgency, 1930–1970*. Chicago: University of Chicago Press.

McAdam, Doug, John D. McCarthy, and Mayer N. Zald, eds. 1996 [1997]. "Introduction: Opportunities, Mobilizing Structures, and Framing Processes—Toward a Synthetic, Comparative Perspective on Social Movements." In *Comparative Perspectives on Social Movements: Political Opportunities, Mobilizing Structures, and Cultural Framing*, ed. Doug McAdam, John D. McCarthy, and Mayer N. Zald, 1–20. Cambridge: Cambridge University Press.

McAdam, Doug, Sidney Tarrow, and Charles Tilly. 2001. *Dynamics of Contention*. Cambridge: Cambridge University Press.

McCann, Carole R. 1994. *Birth Control Politics in the United States, 1916–1945*. Ithaca: Cornell University Press.

McCarthy, John D. 1987. "Pro-Life and Pro-Choice Mobilization: Infrastructure Deficits and New Technologies." In *Social Movements in an Organizational Society*, ed. John McCarthy and Mayer N. Zald. New Brunswick, NJ: Transaction Books.

McCarthy, John D. 1997. "Constraints and Opportunities in Adopting, Adapting, and Inventing." In *Comparative Perspectives on Social Movements: Political Opportunities, Mobilizing Structures, and Cultural Framings*, ed. Doug McAdam, John D. McCarthy, and Mayer N. Zald. Cambridge: Cambridge University Press.

McCool, Grant. 2004. "Huge Anti-Bush March Hits New York on Eve of Convention." Reuters. August 29.

McFarlane, Deborah R., and Kenneth J. Meier. 2000. *The Politics of Fertility Control Policy*. New York: Chatham House.

McKeegan, Michele. 1992. *Abortion Politics: Mutiny in the Ranks of the Right*. New York: Free Press.

McVeigh, Rory, and David Sikkink. 2001. "God, Politics, and Protest: Religious Beliefs and the Legitimation of Contentious Tactics." *Social Forces* 79, no. 4: 1425–58.

Meehan, Mary. 1998. "How Eugenics Birthed Population Control." *Human Life Review* 24, no. 4 (Fall): 1–9.

Meier, Kenneth J. 1994. *The Politics of Sin: Drugs, Alcohol, and Public Policy*. New York: M. E. Sharpe.

Meier, Kenneth J. 1999. "Symposium: The Politics of Morality Policy—Drugs, Sex, Rock and Roll: A Theory of Morality Politics." *Journal of Policy Studies* 27, no. 4: 681–95.

Meier, Kenneth J., and Deborah McFarlane. 1994. "State Family Planning and Abortion Expenditures: Their Effect on Public Health." *American Journal of Public Health* 84 (September): 1468–72.

Meyer, David S. 1993. "Protest Cycles and Political Process: American Peace Movements in the Nuclear Age." *Political Research Quarterly* 46:451–79.

Meyer, David S., and Suzanne Staggenborg. 1996. "Movements, Countermovements, and the Structure of Political Opportunity." *American Journal of Sociology* 101, no. 6: 1628–60.

Michels, Robert. 1962. *Political Parties: A Sociological Study of the Oligarchical Tendencies of Modern Democracy*. New York: Free Press.

Midlarsky, Manus I. 1988. "Rulers and the Ruled: Patterned Inequality and the Onset of Mass Political Violence." *American Political Science Review* 82:491–509.

Mische, A. 1996. "Projecting Democracy: The Construction of Citizenship across Youth Networks in Brazil." In *Citizenship, Identity, and Social History*, ed. Charles Tilly. Cambridge: Cambridge University Press.

Mooney, Christopher. 1999. "The Politics of Morality Policy: Symposium Editor's Introduction." *Policy Studies Journal* 27, no. 4: 675–80.

Mooney, Christopher. 2001. *The Public Clash of Private Values: The Politics of Morality Policy.* New York: Chatham House.

Mooney, Christopher, and Mei-Hsien Lee. 1995. "Legislating Morality in the American States: The Case of Pre-*Roe* Abortion Regulation Reform." *American Journal of Political Science* 39:599–627.

Mooney, Christopher, and Mei-Hsien Lee. 2000. "The Influence of Values on Consensus and Contentious Morality Policy: U.S. Death Penalty Reform, 1965–82." *Journal of Politics* 62, no. 1: 223–39.

Moore, Will H. 1995. "Rational Rebels: Overcoming the Free-Rider Problem." *Political Research Quarterly* 48:403–16.

Morone, James A. 2003. *Hellfire Nation: The Politics of Sin in American History.* New Haven: Yale University Press.

Morris, A. 1984. *The Origins of the Civil Rights Movement.* New York: Free Press.

Muller, Edward. 1979. *Aggressive Political Participation.* Princeton: Princeton University Press.

Muller, Edward. 1985. "Income Inequality, Regime Repressiveness, and Political Violence." *American Sociological Review* 50:47–61.

Muller, Edward N., Henry A. Dietz, and Steven E. Finkel. 1991. "Discontent and the Expected Utility of Rebellion: The Case of Peru." *American Political Science Review* 85, no. 4: 1261–82.

Muller, Edward N., and Karl-Dieter Opp. 1986. "Rational Choice and Rebellious Collective Action." *American Political Science Review* 80, no. 2: 471–88.

Munson, Ziad. 2002. "Becoming an Activist: Believers, Sympathizers, and Mobilization in the American Pro-Life Movement." Dissertation, Harvard University.

Munson, Ziad. 2005. "God, Abortion and Democracy in the Pro-Life Movement." In *Taking Faith Seriously,* ed. Mary Jo Bane, Brent Coffin, and Richard Higgins. Cambridge: Harvard University Press.

Munt, Sally R. 1998. *Butch/Femme: Inside Lesbian Gender.* London: Cassell.

Nasman, V. T. 1992. ". . . And Then the Decision Was Mine." Manuscript, Dayton, Ohio. Cited in Catherine Cozzarelli and Brenda Major, "The Impact of Antiabortion Activities on Women." In *The New Civil War: The Psychology, and Politics of Abortion,* ed. Linda J. Beckman and S. Marie Harvey. Washington, DC: American Psychological Association, 1998.

National Abortion Federation. 2006. "Incidents of Violence and Disruption Against Abortion Providers." www.prochoice.org/violence.

National Abortion and Reproductive Rights Action League (NARAL) Pro-Choice America. 2006. www.prochoiceamerica.org.

National Right to Life Committee (NRLC). 2004. www.nrlc.org.

National Right to Life Committee. (NRLC). 2006. www.nrcl.org.

Neumeister, Larry. 2006. "Appeals Courts: Partial Birth Abortion Ban Act Unconstitutional." Associated Press, February 1.

News Media and the Law. 2001. "'Hit List' Kept by Anti-abortionists Deemed Protected Speech." *News Media and the Law* (Spring).

Nice, David. 1988. "Abortion Clinic Bombings as Political Violence." *American Journal of Political Science* 21 (February): 178–95.

Nieburg, H. L. 1969. *Political Violence: The Behavioral Process.* New York: St. Martin's Press.

Nossiff, Rosemary. 2001. *Before Roe: Abortion Policy in the States.* Philadelphia: Temple University Press.

Oberschall, Anthony. 1973. *Social Conflict and Social Movements.* Englewood Cliffs, NJ: Prentice-Hall.

Offe, Claus. 1990. "Reflections on the Institutional Self-Transformation of Movement Politics: A Tentative Stage Model." In *Challenging the Political Order,* ed. Russell J. Dalton and Manford Kuechler. Cambridge, UK: Polity Press.

Olasky, Marvin. 1988. *The Press and Abortion, 1838–1988.* Hillsdale, NJ: Lawrence Erlbaum Associates.

Oliver, Pamela E., and Kelley D. Strawn. 2003. "Emerging Trends in the Study of Protest and Social Movements." *Political Sociology for the Twenty-first Century* 12:213–44.

Opp, Karl-Dieter. 1986. "Soft Incentives and Collective Action: Participation in the Anti-Nuclear Movement." *British Journal of Political Science* 16:87–112.

Paige, Connie. 1983. *The Right to Lifers: Who They Are, How They Operate, Where They Get Their Money.* New York: Summit Books.

Petchesky, Rosalind Pollack. 1984. *Abortion and Woman's Choice: The State, Sexuality, and Reproductive Freedom.* New York: Longman.

Petchesky, Rosalind Pollack. 1997. "The Role of Popular Organizing: Feminists and Libertarians." In *Controlling Reproduction: An American History,* ed. Andrea Tone. Wilmington, DE: Scholarly Resources.

Piven, Frances Fox, and Richard A. Cloward. 1977. *Poor People's Movements.* New York: Vintage Books.

Pizzorno, A. 1978. "Political Exchange and Collective Identity in Industrial Conflict." In *The Resurgence of Class Conflict in Western Europe since 1968,* ed. C. Crouch and A. Pizzorno, 277–98. London: Macmillan.

Polletta, Francesca. 1999. "Free Spaces in Collective Action." *Theory and Society* 28:1–38.

Polletta, Francesca, and James M. Jasper. 2001. "Collective Identity and Social Movements." *Annual Review of Sociology* 27:283–305.

Posner, Richard A. 1992. *Sex and Reason.* Cambridge: Harvard University Press.

Prescott, James W. 1989. "The Abortion of *The Silent Scream.*" In *Abortion Rights and Fetal "Personhood,"* ed. Edd Doerr and James W. Prescott. Long Beach, CA: Centerline Press.

Press, Andrea L., and Elizabeth R. Cole. 1995. "Reconciling Faith and Fact: Pro-Life Women Discuss Media, Science, and the Abortion Debate." *Critical Studies in Mass Communication* 12:380–402.

Pro-Life Action League. 2006. "About the Pro-Life Action League: Confronting the Abortionists." www.prolifeaction.org/about.

Pro-Life Infonet. 2000. www.roevwade.org. January 16.

Pro-Life Rally for Life. 2003. Held in College Station, TX, December 5.

Quotations Page. 2006. "Quotations by Author." www.quotationspage.com.

Reagan, Leslie J. 1997 [1991]. "About to Meet Her Maker: Women, Doctors, Dying Declarations, and the State's Investigation of Abortion, Chicago, 1867–1940." *Journal of American History* 78:1240–64.

Reed, James. 1978. *From Private Vice to Public Virtue: The Birth Control Movement and American Society since 1830.* New York: Basic Books.

Reger, Jo, and Verta Taylor. 2002. "Women's Movement Research and Social Movement Theory: A Symbiotic Relationship." *Sociological Views on Political Participation in the Twenty-first Century* 10:85–121.

Risen, James, and Judy L. Thomas. 1998. *Wrath of Angels: The American Abortion War.* New York: Basic Books.

Roberts, Dorothy. 1999. *Killing the Black Body: Race, Reproduction, and the Meaning of Liberty.* New York: Vintage Books.

Rozell, Mark J., and Clyde Wilcox. 1996. "Second Coming: The Strategies of the New Christian Right." *Political Science Quarterly* 111, no. 2: 271–94.

Rubin, Eva. 1994. *The Abortion Controversy: A Documentary History.* Westport, CT: Greenwood.

Rubin, J. 1998. "Ambiguity and Contradiction in a Radical Popular Movement." In *Cultures of Politics—Politics of Culture,* ed. S. E. Alvarez, E. Dagnino, and A. Escobar. Boulder: Westview.

Russo, Nancy Felipe, and Jean E. Denious. 1998. "Why Is Abortion Such a Controversial Issue in the United States?" In *The New Civil War: The Psychology, and Politics of Abortion,* ed. Linda J. Beckman and S. Marie Harvey. Washington, DC: American Psychological Association.

Saad, Lydia. 2004. "The Cultural Landscape: What's Morally Acceptable? Divorce and Premarital Sex Are OK, but Polygamy and Extramarital Affairs Still Frowned On." Gallup Organization. www.gallup.com. June 22.

Sanger, Margaret. 1923. "Prevention or Abortion—Which? Letters Showing the Dilemma Faced by Many Mothers." *Birth Control Review* 7, no. 7: 181–82.

Sanger, Margaret. 1970. *Margaret Sanger: An Autobiography.* New York: Dover.

Schabner, Dean. 2004. "Christian Terrorists: Anti-Abortion Calls for Violence, Says It Is Religious Duty." January 22. www.ABCNEWS.com.

Schnucker, Robert V. 1975. "Elizabethan Birth Control and Puritan Attitudes." *Journal of Interdisciplinary History* 4:655–67.

Schuster, Henry. 2003. "FBI: Olympic Bombing Suspect Arrested." www.CNN.com. May 31.

Scott, J. C. 1990. *Domination and the Arts of Resistance.* New Haven: Yale University Press.

Sharp, Elaine B. 1994. "The Dynamics of Issue Expansion: Cases from Disability Rights and Fetal Research Controversy." *Journal of Politics* 56, no. 4: 919–39.

Sharp, Elaine B. 1999. *Culture Wars and Local Politics.* Lawrence: University Press of Kansas.

Sharp, Elaine B. 2002. "Culture, Institutions, and Urban Officials' Responses to Morality Issues." *Political Research Quarterly* 55, no. 4: 861–83.

Sharp, Elaine B. 2005. *Morality Politics in American Cities*. Lawrence: University of Kansas Press.

Simon, Stephanie. 2005. "Offering Abortion, Rebirth." *Los Angeles Times*. November 29.

Singh, Susheela, Akinrinola Bankole, and Taylor Haas. 1998. "Reasons Why Women Have Induced Abortions: Evidence from 27 Countries." *International Family Planning Perspectives* 24, no. 3 (September).

Smith, Daniel Scott. 1997. "Family Limitation, Sexual Control, and Domestic Feminism in Victorian America." In *Controlling Reproduction: An American History*, ed. Andrea Tone. Wilmington, DE: Scholarly Resources.

Smith, Kevin B. 1999. "Clean Thoughts and Dirty Minds: The Politics of Porn." *Policy Studies Journal* 27, no. 4: 723–34.

Snow, David, and Robert D. Benford. 1988. "Ideology, Frame Resonance, and Participant Mobilization." In *From Structure to Action: Social Movement Participation across Culture*, ed. Bert Klandermans, Hanspeter Kriesi, and Sidney Tarrow. Greenwich, CT: JAI Press.

Snow, David, and Robert D. Benford. 1992. "Master Frames and Cycles of Protest." In *Frontiers in Social Movement Theories*, ed. Aldon Morris and Carol McClurg Mueller. New Haven: Yale University Press.

Snow, David A., E. Burke Rochford Jr., Steven K. Worden, and Robert D. Benford. 1986. "Frame Alignment Processes, Micromobilization, and Movement Participation." *American Sociological Review* 51:464–81.

Snyder, David, and Charles Tilly. 1972. "Hardship and Collective Violence in France, 1830 to 1960." *American Sociological Review* 37:520–32.

Solinger, Rickie. 1998. "Pregnancy and Power before *Roe* v. *Wade*, 1950–1970." In *Abortion Wars: A Half a Century of Struggle, 1950–2000*, ed. Rickie Solinger. Los Angeles: University of California Press.

Solinger, Rickie. 2000. *Wake Up Little Susie: Single Pregnancy and Race Before Roe v. Wade*. New York: Routledge.

Songer, Donald R., and Susan J. Tabrizi. 1999. "The Religious Right in Court: The Decision Making of Christian Evangelicals in State Supreme Courts." *Journal of Politics* 61, no. 2: 507–26.

Southern Poverty Law Center. 2004. "A Hundred Years of Terror." Southern Poverty Law Center. www.iupui.edu/~aao/kkk.html.

Staggenborg, Suzanne. 1988. "The Consequences of Professionalization and Formalization in the Pro-Choice Movement." *American Sociological Review* 53:585–605.

Staggenborg, Suzanne. 1989. "Organizational and Environmental Influences on the Development of the Pro-Choice Movement." *Social Forces* 68, no. 1: 204–40.

Staggenborg, Suzanne. 1991. *The Pro-Choice Movement: Organization and Activism in the Abortion Conflict*. New York: Oxford University Press.

Staggenborg, Suzanne. 1999. "The Consequences of Professionalization and Formalization in the Pro-Choice Movement." In *Waves of Protest: Social Movements since the Sixties*, ed. Jo Freeman and Victoria Johnson. Lanham, MD: Rowman and Littlefield.

Stearns, Peter N. 1990. *Be a Man! Males in Modern Society*. New York: Holmes and Meier.

Stimson, James A. 1991. *Public Opinion in America: Moods, Cycles, and Swings.* Boulder: Westview.

Stolley, Anna, and Ellen Uchimiya. 2004. "Judge Blocks Partial-Birth Abortion Ban." Fox News, www.foxnews.com. June 2.

Tabachnick, Barbara G., and Linda S. Fidell. 2001. *Using Multivariate Statistics.* 4th ed. Boston: Allyn and Bacon.

Tarrow, Sidney. 1994. *Power in Movement: Social Movements, Collective Action, and Politics.* Cambridge: Cambridge University Press.

Tarrow, Sidney. 1998. *Power in Movement: Social Movements and Contentious Politics.* Cambridge: Cambridge University Press.

Tatalovich, Raymond, and Byron W. Daynes. 1988. "Conclusion: Social Regulatory Policymaking." In *Social Regulatory Policy,* ed. Raymond Tatalovich and Byron W. Daynes. Boulder: Westview.

Tatalovich, Raymond, and Byron W. Daynes. 1989. "The Geographic Distribution of U.S. Hospitals with Abortion Facilities." *Family Planning Perspectives* 21 (March/April): 81–85.

Texas Abortion and Reproductive Rights Action League. 2000. TARAL, PO Box 684602, Austin, Texas 78768.

Tilly, Charles. 1975. "Food Supply and Public Order in Modern Europe." In *The Formation of National States in Western Europe,* ed. Charles Tilly. Princeton: Princeton University Press.

Tilly, Charles. 1978. *From Mobilization to Revolution.* Reading, MA: Addison-Wesley.

Tilly, Charles. 1992. "How to Detect, Describe, and Explain Repertoires of Contention." Working Paper No. 150. Center for Studies of Social Change, New School for Social Research, New York.

Tilly, Charles. 1998. "Political Identities." In *Challenging Authority,* ed. M. Hanagan, L. P. Moch, and W. Brake. Minneapolis: University of Minnesota Press.

Tilly, Charles. 2002. "Violent and Nonviolent Trajectories in Contentious Politics." In *Violence and Politics: Globalization's Paradox,* ed. Kenton Worcester, Sally Avery Bermanzohn, and Mark Ungar. New York: Routledge.

Timeline of Women's Suffrage in the United States. 2005. http://dpsinfo.com/women/history/timeline.html.

Tone, Andrea. 1997. *Controlling Reproduction: An American History.* Wilmington, DE: Scholarly Resources.

Tone, Andrea. 2001. *Devices and Desires: A History of Contraception in America.* New York: Hill and Wang.

Torres, A., and J. D. Forrest. 1988. "Why Do Women Have Abortions?" *Family Planning Perspectives* 20, no. 4: 169–76.

Tribe, Lawrence H. 1992. *Abortion: The Clash of Absolutes.* New York: W. W. Norton.

United for Peace and Justice. 2004. "Iraq Campaign." www.unitedforpeace.org. January 18.

United States Conference of Catholic Bishops. 2006. Office of Media Relations. www.usccb.org.

United States House of Representatives. 2004. "The Content of Federally Funded Abstinence-Only Education Programs." Committee on Government Reform, Minority Staff. Prepared for Rep. Henry A. Waxman.

Viguerie, Richard A. 1981. *The New Right: We're Ready to Lead.* Falls Church, VA: Viguerie.

Vogel, David. 1974. "The Politicization of the Corporation." *Social Policy* (May/June).

Vogel, David. 1975. "The Corporation as Government: Challenges and Dilemmas." *Polity* 87:5–37.

Vogel, David. 1978. *Lobbying the Corporation: Citizen Challenges to Business Authority.* New York: Basic Books.

Vogel, David. 1981. "The Public-Interest Movement and the American Reform Tradition." *Political Science Quarterly* 95, no. 4: 607–27.

Voice. 2000. "Supreme Court to Consider Partial-Birth Abortion Case." *Voice,* February.

Wallace, Michael. 1991. "Why Do Strikes Turn Violent?" *American Journal of Sociology* 96:1117–50.

Walsh, Edward J. 1981. "Resource Mobilization and Citizen Protest in Communities around Three Mile Island." *Social Problems* 29:1–21.

Walsh, Edward J. 1986. "The Role of Target Vulnerabilities in High Technology Protest Movements: The Nuclear Establishment at Three Mile Island." *Sociological Forum* 1:199–218.

Watson, Justin. 1997. *The Christian Coalition: Dreams of Restoration, Demands for Recognition.* New York: St. Martin's Press.

Weisbord, Robert G. 1973. "Birth Control and the Black American: A Matter of Genocide?" *Demography* 10, no. 4 (November): 571–90.

Whittier, N. 1995. *Feminist Generations.* Philadelphia: Temple University Press.

Whittier, N. 1997. "Political Generations, Micro-Cohorts, and the Transformation of Social Movements." *American Sociological Review* 67:760–78.

Wilcox, Clyde. 1996. *Onward Christian Soldiers? The Religious Right in American Politics.* Boulder: Westview.

Wilkinson, Paul. 1971. *Social Movements.* London: Pall Mall.

Williams, Robin M., Jr. 2003. *The Wars Within: Peoples and States in Conflict.* Ithaca: Cornell University Press.

Wood, B. Dan, and Alesha E. Doan. 2003. "The Politics of Problem Definition: A Theory and Application to Sexual Harassment." *American Journal of Political Science* 47, no. 4: 640–53.

Young, Michael P. 2002. "Confessional Protest: The Religious Birth of U.S. National Social Movements." *American Sociological Review* 67:660–88.

Zald, Mayer N. 1997. "Culture, Ideology, and Strategic Framing." In *Comparative Perspectives on Social Movements: Political Opportunities, Mobilizing Structures, and Cultural Framing,* ed. Doug McAdam, John D. McCarthy, and Mayer N. Zald. Cambridge: Cambridge University Press.

Zald, Mayer N., and Roberta Ash. 1966. "Social Movement Organizations: Growth, Decay, and Change." *Social Forces* 44:327–40.

Zald, Mayer N., and Bert Useem. 1987. "Movement and Countermovement Interaction: Mobilization, Tactics, and State Involvement." In *Social Movements in an Organizational Society,* ed. Mayer N. Zald and John D. McCarthy, 241–71. New Brunswick, NJ: Transaction.

INDEX